I0764490

THE BEAUTIES OF SHAKSPEARE,

REGULARLY SELECTED FROM EACH PLAY.

WITH A

GENERAL INDEX,

DIGESTING THEM UNDER PROPER HEADS.

THE

Beauties

OF

SHAKSPEARE.

William Shakespeare

BY THE LATE

REV. WILLIAM DODD, LL.D.

From the Chiswick Press,

BY C. WHITTINGHAM.

SOLD BY R. JENNINGS, POULTRY; T. TEGG, CHEAPSIDE;
A. K. NEWMAN AND CO. LEADENHALL STREET; LONDON.
J. SUTHERLAND, EDINBURGH;
AND RICHARD GRIFFIN AND CO. GLASGOW.

1821.

PREFACE.

I SHALL not attempt any laboured encomiums on Shakspeare, or endeavour to set forth his perfections, at a time when such universal and just applause is paid him, and when every tongue is big with his boundless fame. He himself tells us,

> To gild refined gold, to paint the lily,
> To throw a perfume on the violet,
> To smooth the ice, or add another hue
> Unto the rainbow, or with taper-light
> To seek the beauteous eye of heav'n to garnish,
> Is wasteful and ridiculous excess.

And wasteful and ridiculous indeed it would be, to say any thing in his praise, when presenting the world with such a collection of BEAUTIES as perhaps is no where to be met with, and, I may very safely affirm, cannot be paralleled from the productions of any other single author, ancient or modern. There is scarcely a topic, common with other writers, on which he has not excelled them all; there are many nobly peculiar to himself, where he shines unrivaled, and, like the eagle, properest emblem of his daring genius, soars beyond the common reach, and gazes undazzled on the sun. His flights are sometimes so bold, frigid criticism almost dares to disapprove them; and those narrow minds, which are incapable of elevating their ideas to the sublimity of their author's, are willing to bring them down to a level with their own. Hence many fine passages have been condemned in Shakspeare, as rant, and fustian, intolerable bombast,

and turgid nonsense, which, if read with the least glow of the same imagination that warmed the writer's bosom, would blaze in the robes of sublimity, and obtain the commendations of a Longinus. And, unless some of the same spirit that elevated the poet, elevate the reader too, he must not presume to talk of taste and elegance; he will prove a languid reader, an indifferent judge, and a far more indifferent critic and commentator.

It is some time since I first proposed publishing this collection; for Shakspeare was ever, of all modern authors, my chief favourite; and during my relaxations from my more severe and necessary studies at college, I never omitted to read and indulge myself in the rapturous flights of this delightful and sweetest child of fancy: and when my imagination has been heated by the glowing ardour of his uncommon fire, have never failed to lament, that his BEAUTIES should be so obscured, and that he himself should be made a kind of stage, for bungling critics to show their clumsy activity upon.

It was my first intention to have considered each play critically and regularly through all its parts; but as this would have swelled the work beyond proper bounds, I was obliged to confine myself solely to a collection of his Poetical Beauties: and I doubt not, every reader will find so large a fund for observation, so much excellent and refined morality, that he will prize the work as it deserves, and pay, with me, all due adoration to the manes of Shakspeare.

Longinus* tells us, that the most infallible test of the true sublime is the impression a performance makes upon our minds, when read or recited. "If," says he, "a person finds, that a performance trans-

* See Longinus on the Sublime, Sect. 7. The translation in the text is from the learned Mr. Smith.

ports *not* his soul, nor exalts his thoughts; that it calls not up into his mind ideas more enlarged than the mere sounds of the words convey, but on attentive examination its dignity lessens and declines, he may conclude, that whatever pierces no deeper than the ears can never be the true sublime. That, on the contrary, is grand and lofty, which the more we consider, the greater ideas we conceive of it: whose force we cannot possibly withstand; which immediately sinks deep, and makes such impression on the mind as cannot easily be worn out or effaced: in a word, you may pronounce that sublime, beautiful, and genuine, which always pleases and takes equally with all sorts of men. For when persons of different humours, ages, professions, and inclinations, agree in the same joint approbation of any performance, then this union of assent, this combination of so many different judgments, stamps a *high* and indisputable value on that performance which meets with such general applause." This fine observation of Longinus is most remarkably verified in Shakspeare; for all humours, ages, and inclinations, jointly proclaim their approbation and esteem of him; and will, I hope, be found true in most of the passages which are here collected from him: I say, most, because there are some which I am convinced will not stand this test: the old, the grave, and the severe, will disapprove, perhaps, the more soft (and as they may call them) trifling love-tales, so elegantly breathed forth, and so emphatically extolled by the young, the gay, and the passionate; while these will esteem as dull and languid the sober saws of morality, and the home-felt observations of experience. However, as it was my business to collect for readers of all tastes, and all complexions, let me desire none to disapprove what hits not with their own humour, but to turn over the page, and they will surely find something acceptable and engaging. But I have yet another apology to make, for some passages introduced merely on account of their peculiarity, which to some, possibly, will appear neither sublime nor beautiful, and yet deserve attention, as indicating the vast stretch, and sometimes particular turn of the poet's imagination.

There are many passages in Shakspeare so closely connected with the plot and characters, and on which their beauties so wholly depend, that it would have been absurd and idle to have produced them here: hence the reader will find little of the inimitable Falstaff in this work, and not one line extracted from the Merry Wives of Windsor, one of Shakspeare's best, and most justly admired comedies: whoever reads that play, will immediately see, there was nothing either proper or possible for this work: which, such as it is, I most sincerely and cordially recommend to the candour and benevolence of the world: and wish every one that peruses it may feel the satisfaction I have frequently felt in composing it, and receive such instructions and advantages from it as it is well calculated and well able to bestow. For my own part, better and more important things henceforth demand my attention, and I here, with no small pleasure, take leave of Shakspeare and the critics; as this work was begun and finished before I entered upon the sacred function, in which I am now happily employed, let me trust, this juvenile performance will prove no objection, since graver, and some very eminent members of the church, have thought it no improper employ, to comment, explain, and publish the works of their own country poets.

W. DODD.

CONTENTS.

COMEDIES.

HISTORICAL PLAYS.

TRAGEDIES.

THE

Beauties of Shakspeare.

PART I.

COMEDIES.

THE

BEAUTIES OF SHAKSPEARE.

ALL'S WELL THAT ENDS WELL.

ACT I.

ADVICE.

Be thou blest, Bertram! and succeed thy father
In manners, as in shape! Thy blood, and virtue,
Contend for empire in thee; and thy goodness
Share with thy birthright! Love all, trust a few,
Do wrong to none: be able for thine enemy
Rather in power, than use; and keep thy friend
Under thy own life's key: be check'd for silence,
But never tax'd for speech.

TOO AMBITIOUS LOVE.

I am undone; there is no living, none,
If Bertram be away. It were all one,
That I should love a bright particular star,
And think to wed it, he is so above me:
In his bright radiance and collateral light
Must I be comforted, not in his sphere.
The ambition in my love thus plagues itself:
The hind that would be mated by the lion,
Must die for love. 'Twas pretty, though a plague,
To see him every hour; to sit and draw
His arched brows, his hawking eye, his curls,
In our heart's table*; heart, too capable

* Helena considers her heart as the tablet on which his resemblance was portrayed.

Of every line and trick * of his sweet favour † :
But now he's gone, and my idolatrous fancy
Must sanctify his relics.

COWARDICE.

I know him a notorious liar,
Think him a great way fool, solely a coward ;
Yet these fix'd evils sit so fit in him,
That they take place, when virtue's steely bones
Look bleak in the cold wind.

THE REMEDY OF EVILS GENERALLY IN OURSELVES.

Our remedies oft in ourselves do lie,
Which we ascribe to heaven : the fated sky
Gives us free scope ; only, doth backward pull
Our slow designs, when we ourselves are dull.

CHARACTER OF A NOBLE COURTIER.

In his youth
He had the wit, which I can well observe
To-day in our young lords ; but they may jest
Till their own scorn return to them unnoted,
Ere they can hide their levity in honour.
So like a courtier, contempt nor bitterness
Were in his pride or sharpness ; if they were,
His equal had awak'd them ; and his honour,
Clock to itself, knew the true minute when
Exception bid him speak, and, at this time,
His tongue obey'd his hand ‡ : who were below him
He us'd as creatures of another place :
And bow'd his eminent top to their low ranks,
Making them proud of his humility.
Such a man
Might be a copy to these younger times.

* Peculiarity of feature. † Countenance.
‡ *His* is put for *its*.

ACT II.

HONOUR DUE TO PERSONAL VIRTUE ONLY, NOT TO BIRTH.

From lowest place when virtuous things proceed,
The place is dignified by the doer's deed:
Where great additions * swell, and virtue none,
It is a dropsied honour: good alone
Is good, without a name; vileness is so †:
The property by what it is should go,
Not by the title. She is young, wise, fair;
In these to nature she's immediate heir;
And these breed honour: that is honour's scorn,
Which challenges itself as honour's born,
And is not like the sire: Honours best thrive,
When rather from our acts we them derive
Than our foregoers: the mere word's a slave
Debauch'd on every tomb; on every grave,
A lying trophy, and as oft is dumb,
Where dust, and damn'd oblivion, is the tomb
Of honour'd bones indeed.

ACT III.

SELF-ACCUSATION OF TOO GREAT LOVE.

Poor lord! is't I
That chase thee from thy country, and expose
Those tender limbs of thine to the event
Of the none-sparing war? and is it I
That drive thee from the sportive court, where thou
Wast shot at with fair eyes, to be the mark
Of smoky muskets? O you leaden messengers,
That ride upon the violent speed of fire,
Fly with false aim; move the still-piecing air,
That sings with piercing, do not touch my lord!

* Titles.

† Good is good independent of any worldly distinction, and so is vileness vile.

Whoever shoots at him, I set him there;
Whoever charges on his forward breast,
I am the caitiff that do hold him to it;
And, though I kill him not, I am the cause
His death was so effected: better 'twere,
I met the ravin* lion when he roar'd
With sharp constraint of hunger; better 'twere
That all the miseries, which nature owes,
Were mine at once: No, come thou home, Roussillon,
Whence honour but of danger wins a scar,
As oft it loses all; I will be gone:
My being here it is that holds thee hence:
Shall I stay here to do't? no, no, although
The air of paradise did fan the house,
And angels offic'd all: I will be gone;
That pitiful rumour may report my flight,
To consolate thine ear.

A MAID'S HONOUR.

The honour of a maid is her name; and no legacy is so rich as honesty.

ADVICE TO YOUNG WOMEN.

Beware of them, Diana; their promises, enticements, oaths, tokens, and all these engines of lust, are not the things they go under†: many a maid hath been seduced by them; and the misery is, example, that so terrible shows in the wreck of maidenhood, cannot for all that dissuade succession, but that they are limed with the twigs that threaten them. I hope, I need not to advise you further; but, I hope, your own grace will keep you where you are, though there were no further danger known, but the modesty which is so lost.

* Ravenous.

† They are not the things for which their names would make them pass.

ACT IV.

CUSTOM OF SEDUCERS.

Ay, so you serve us,
Till we serve you: but when you have our roses,
You barely leave our thorns to prick ourselves,
And mock us with our bareness.

CHASTITY.

Mine honour's such a ring:
My chastity's the jewel of our house,
Bequeathed down from many ancestors;
Which were the greatest obloquy i' the world
In me to lose.

LIFE CHEQUERED.

The web of our life is of a mingled yarn, good and ill together: our virtues would be proud, if our faults whipped them not; and our crimes would despair, if they were not cherished by our virtues.

A COWARDLY BRAGGART.

Yet am I thankful: if my heart were great,
'Twould burst at this: Captain, I'll be no more;
But I will eat and drink, and sleep as soft
As captain shall: simply the thing I am
Shall make me live. Who knows himself a braggart,
Let him fear this; for it will come to pass,
That every braggart shall be found an ass.
Rust, sword! cool, blushes! and, Parolles, live,
Safest in shame! being fool'd, by foolery thrive!
There's place, and means, for every man alive.

ACT V.

AGAINST DELAY.

Let's take the instant by the forward top;
For we are old, and on our quick'st decrees
The inaudible and noiseless foot of time
Steals ere we can effect them.

EXCUSE FOR UNSEASONABLE DISLIKE.

At first
I stuck my choice upon her, ere my heart
Durst make too bold a herald of my tongue:
Where the impression of mine eye infixing,
Contempt his scornful perspective did lend me,
Which warp'd the line of every other favour;
Scorn'd a fair colour, or express'd it stol'n;
Extended or contracted all proportions,
To a most hideous object: Thence it came,
That she, whom all men prais'd, and whom myself,
Since I have lost, have lov'd, was in mine eye
The dust that did offend it.

AS YOU LIKE IT.

ACT I.

MODESTY AND COURAGE IN YOUTH.

I BESEECH you, punish me not with your hard thoughts; wherein I confess me much guilty, to deny so fair and excellent ladies any thing. But let your fair eyes, and gentle wishes, go with me to my trial: wherein if I be foiled, there is but one shamed that was never gracious; if killed, but one dead that is willing to be so: I shall do my friends no wrong, for I have none to lament me; the world no injury, for in it I have nothing; only in the world I fill up a place, which may be better supplied when I have made it empty.

PLAY-FELLOWS.

We still have slept together,
Rose at an instant, learn'd, play'd, eat together;
And wheresoe'er we went, like Juno's swans,
Still we went coupled, and inseparable.

BEAUTY.

Beauty provoketh thieves sooner than gold.

ROSALIND PROPOSING TO WEAR MEN'S CLOTHES.

Were it not better,
Because that I am more than common tall,
That I did suit me all points like a man?
A gallant curtle-ax * upon my thigh,
A boar-spear in my hand; and (in my heart
Lie there what hidden woman's fear there will),
We'll have a swashing † and a martial outside;
As many other mannish cowards have,
That do outface it with their semblances.

ACT II.

SOLITUDE PREFERRED TO A COURT LIFE, AND THE ADVANTAGES OF ADVERSITY.

Now, my co-mates, and brothers in exile,
Hath not old custom made this life more sweet
Than that of painted pomp? Are not these woods
More free from peril than the envious court?
Here feel we but the penalty of Adam,
The seasons' difference; as the icy fang,
And churlish chiding of the winter's wind;
Which when it bites and blows upon my body,
Even till I shrink with cold, I smile, and say,
This is no flattery: these are counsellors
That feelingly persuade me what I am.
Sweet are the uses of adversity;
Which, like the toad, ugly and venomous,
Wears yet a precious jewel in his head;
And this our life, exempt from public haunt,
Finds tongues in trees, books in the running brooks,
Sermons in stones, and good in every thing.

* Cutlass. † Swaggering.

REFLECTIONS ON THE WOUNDED STAG.

Duke S. Come, shall we go and kill us venison?
And yet it irks me, the poor dappled fools,—
Being native burghers of this desert city,—
Should, in their own confines, with forked heads*,
Have their round haunches gor'd.
1 *Lord.* Indeed, my lord,
The melancholy Jaques grieves at that;
And, in that kind, swears you do more usurp
Than doth your brother that hath banish'd you.
To-day, my lord of Amiens, and myself,
Did steal behind him, as he lay along
Under an oak, whose antique root peeps out
Upon the brook that brawls along this wood:
To the which place a poor sequester'd stag,
That from the hunters' aim had ta'en a hurt,
Did come to languish: and, indeed, my lord,
The wretched animal heav'd forth such groans,
That their discharge did stretch his leathern coat
Almost to bursting; and the big round tears
Cours'd one another down his innocent nose
In piteous chase: and thus the hairy fool,
Much marked of the melancholy Jaques,
Stood on the extremest verge of the swift brook,
Augmenting it with tears.
Duke S. But what said Jaques?
Did he not moralize this spectacle?
1 *Lord.* O, yes, into a thousand similes.
First, for his weeping in the needless stream;
Poor deer; quoth he, *thou mak'st a testament*
As worldlings do, *giving thy sum of more*
To that which had too much: Then, being alone,
Left and abandon'd of his velvet friends;
'Tis right, quoth he; *this misery doth part*
The flux of company: Anon, a careless herd,
Full of the pasture, jumps along by him,
And never stays to greet him; *Ay,* quoth Jaques,
Sweep on, you fat and greasy citizens;
'Tis just the fashion: Wherefore do you look
Upon that poor and broken bankrupt there?

* Barbed arrows.

GRATITUDE IN AN OLD SERVANT.

But do not so: I have five hundred crowns,
The thrifty hire I sav'd under your father,
Which I did store, to be my foster nurse,
When service should in my old limbs lie lame,
And unregarded age in corners thrown;
Take that: and He that doth the ravens feed,
Yea, providently caters for the sparrow,
Be comfort to my age! Here is the gold;
All this I give you: Let me be your servant;
Though I look old, yet I am strong and lusty:
For in my youth I never did apply
Hot and rebellious liquors in my blood;
Nor did not with unbashful forehead woo
The means of weakness and debility;
Therefore my age is as a lusty winter,
Frosty, but kindly: let me go with you;
I'll do the service of a younger man
In all your business and necessities.

DESCRIPTION OF A LOVER.

O, thou didst then ne'er love so heartily:
If thou remember'st not the slightest folly
That ever love did make thee run into,
Thou hast not lov'd:
Or if thou hast not sat as I do now,
Wearying thy hearer in thy mistress' praise,
Thou hast not lov'd:
Or if thou hast not broke from company,
Abruptly, as my passion now makes me,
Thou hast not lov'd.

DESCRIPTION OF A FOOL, AND HIS MORALIZING ON TIME.

Good-morrow, fool, quoth I: *No, sir*, quoth he,
Call me not fool, till heaven hath sent me fortune:
And then he drew a dial from his poke;
And, looking on it with lack-lustre eye,
Says, very wisely, *It is ten o'clock:*
Thus may we see, quoth he, *how the world wags:*
'Tis but an hour ago, since it was nine;

And after an hour more, 'twill be eleven:
And so, from hour to hour, we ripe, and ripe,
And then, from hour to hour, we rot, and rot,
And thereby hangs a tale. When I did hear
The motley fool thus moral on the time,
My lungs began to crow like chanticleer,
That fools should be so deep-contemplative;
And I did laugh, sans intermission,
An hour by his dial.—O noble fool!
A worthy fool! Motley's the only wear*.
Duke S. What fool is this?
Jaq. O worthy fool!—One that hath been a courtier;
And says, if ladies be but young, and fair,
They have the gift to know it: and in his brain,—
Which is as dry as the remainder biscuit
After a voyage,—he hath strange places cramm'd
With observation, the which he vents
In mangled forms.

A FOOL'S LIBERTY OF SPEECH.

I must have liberty
Withal, as large a charter as the wind,
To blow on whom I please; for so fools have:
And they that are most galled with my folly,
They most must laugh: And why, sir, must they so?
The *why* is plain as way to parish church:
He, that a fool doth very wisely hit,
Doth very foolishly, although he smart,
Not to seem senseless of the bob; if not,
The wise man's folly is anatomiz'd
Even by the squand'ring glances of the fool.

APOLOGY FOR SATIRE.

Why, who cries out on pride,
That can therein tax any private party?
Doth it not flow as hugely as the sea,
Till that the very very means do ebb?
What woman in the city do I name,
When that I say, The city-woman bears

* The fool was anciently dressed in a party-coloured coat.

The cost of princes on unworthy shoulders?
Who can come in, and say, that I mean her,
When such a one is she, such is her neighbour?
Or what is he of basest function,
That says, his bravery * is not on my cost,
(Thinking that I mean him), but therein suits
His folly to the mettle of my speech?
There then; How, what then? Let me see wherein
My tongue hath wrong'd him: if it do him right,
Then he hath wrong'd himself: if he be free,
Why then, my taxing like a wild goose flies,
Unclaim'd of any man.

A TENDER PETITION.

But whate'er you are,
That in this desert inaccessible,
Under the shade of melancholy boughs,
Lose and neglect the creeping hours of time;
If ever you have looked on better days,
If ever been where bells have knoll'd to church;
If ever sat at any good man's feast;
If ever from your eyelids wip'd a tear,
And know what 'tis to pity and be pitied,
Let gentleness my strong enforcement be.

THE SEVEN AGES.

All the world's a stage,
And all the men and women merely players!
They have their exits, and their entrances;
And one man in his time plays many parts,
His acts being seven ages. At first, the infant,
Mewling and puking in the nurse's arms;
And then, the whining school-boy, with his satchel,
And shining morning face, creeping like snail
Unwillingly to school; And then, the lover;
Sighing like furnace, with a woful ballad
Made to his mistress' eyebrow. Then, a soldier;
Full of strange oaths, and bearded like the pard,
Jealous in honour, sudden † and quick in quarrel,
Seeking the bubble reputation

* Finery. † Violent.

Even in the cannon's mouth. And then, the justice;
In fair round belly, with good capon lin'd,
With eyes severe, and beard of formal cut,
Full of wise saws and modern* instances,
And so he plays his part: The sixth age shifts
Into the lean and slipper'd pantaloon;
With spectacles on nose, and pouch on side;
His youthful hose well sav'd, a world too wide
For his shrunk shank; and his big manly voice,
Turning again toward childish treble, pipes
And whistles in his sound: Last scene of all
That ends this strange eventful history,
Is second childishness, and mere oblivion;
Sans teeth, sans eyes, sans taste, sans every thing.

INGRATITUDE. A SONG.

Blow, blow, thou winter wind,
Thou art not so unkind†
As man's ingratitude;
Thy tooth is not so keen,
Because thou art not seen,
Although thy breath be rude.
Heigh, ho! sing, heigh, ho! unto the green holly:
Most friendship is feigning, most loving mere folly:
Then, heigh, ho, the holly!
This life is most jolly.

Freeze, freeze, thou bitter sky,
That dost not bite so nigh
As benefits forgot:
Though thou the waters warp,
Thy sting is not so sharp
As friend remember'd‡ not.
Heigh, ho! sing, heigh, ho! &c.

* Trite, common. † Unnatural. ‡ Remembering.

ACT III.

A SHEPHERD'S PHILOSOPHY.

I know, the more one sickens, the worse at ease he is; and that he that wants money, means, and content, is without three good friends:—That the property of rain is to wet, and fire to burn: That good pasture makes fat sheep: and that a great cause of the night, is lack of the sun: That he, that hath learned no wit by nature or art, may complain of good breeding, or comes of a very dull kindred.

CHARACTER OF AN HONEST AND SIMPLE SHEPHERD.

Sir, I am a true labourer; I earn that I eat, get that I wear; owe no man hate, envy no man's happiness; glad of other men's good, content with my harm: and the greatest of my pride is, to see my ewes graze, and my lambs suck.

DESCRIPTION OF A LOVER.

A lean cheek; which you have not: a blue eye, and sunken; which you have not: an unquestionable spirit *; which you have not: a beard neglected; which you have not:—but I pardon you for that; for, simply, your having † in beard is a younger brother's revenue: Then your hose should be ungartered, your bonnet unbanded, your sleeve unbuttoned, your shoe untied, and every thing about you demonstrating a careless desolation. But you are no such man: you are rather point-device ‡ in your accoutrements; as loving yourself, than seeming the lover of any other.

REAL PASSION DISSEMBLED.

Think not I love him, though I ask for him;
'Tis but a peevish § boy:—yet he talks well;—
But what care I for words? yet words do well,
When he that speaks them pleases those that hear.
It is a pretty youth:—not very pretty:—

* A spirit averse to conversation. † Estate.
‡ Over-exact. § Silly.

But, sure, he's proud; and yet his pride becomes him:
He'll make a proper man: The best thing in him
Is his complexion; and faster than his tongue
Did make offence, his eye did heal it up.
He is not tall; yet for his years he's tall;
His leg is but so, so; and yet 'tis well:
There was a pretty redness in his lip;
A little riper and more lusty red
Than that mix'd in his cheek; 'twas just the difference
Betwixt the constant red, and mingled damask.
There be some women, Silvius, had they mark'd him
In parcels as I did, would have gone near
To fall in love with him: but, for my part,
I love him not, nor hate him not; and yet
I have more cause to hate him than to love him:
For what had he to do to chide at me?
He said, mine eyes were black, and my hair black;
And, now I am remember'd, scorn'd at me:
I marvel, why I answer'd not again:
But that's all one; omittance is no quittance.

ACT IV.

THE VARIETIES OF MELANCHOLY.

I have neither the scholar's melancholy, which is emulation; nor the musician's, which is fantastical; nor the courtier's, which is proud; nor the soldier's, which is ambitious; nor the lawyer's, which is politic; nor the lady's, which is nice*; nor the lover's, which is all these.

MARRIAGE ALTERS THE TEMPER OF BOTH SEXES.

Say a day, without the ever: No, no, Orlando, men are April when they woo, December when they wed: maids are May when they are maids, but the sky changes when they are wives. I will be more jealous of thee than a Barbary cock-pigeon over his hen; more clamorous than a parrot against rain; more new-fangled than an ape; more giddy in my desires than a monkey; I will weep for nothing, like Diana in the fountain, and

* Trifling.

I will do that when you are disposed to be merry; I will laugh like a hyen, and that when thou art inclined to sleep.

CUPID'S PARENTAGE.

No, that same wicked bastard of Venus, that was begot of thought*, conceived of spleen, and born of madness; that blind rascally boy, that abuses every one's eyes, because his own are out, let him be judge, how deep I am in love.

OLIVER'S DESCRIPTION OF HIS DANGER WHEN SLEEPING.

Under an oak, whose boughs were moss'd with age,
And high top bald with dry antiquity,
A wretched ragged man, o'ergrown with hair,
Lay sleeping on his back: about his neck
A green and gilded snake had wreath'd itself,
Who with her head, nimble in threats, approach'd
The opening of his mouth; but suddenly
Seeing Orlando, it unlink'd itself,
And with indented glides did slip away
Into a bush: under which bush's shade
A lioness, with udders all drawn dry,
Lay couching, head on ground, with catlike watch,
When that the sleeping man should stir; for 'tis
The royal disposition of that beast,
To prey on nothing that doth seem as dead.

ACT V.

LOVE.

Good shepherd, tell this youth what 'tis to love.
It is to be all made of sighs and tears;
It is to be all made of faith and service;—
It is to be all made of fantasy,
All made of passion, and all made of wishes;
All adoration, duty, and observance,
All humbleness, all patience, and impatience,
All purity, all trial, all observance.

* Melancholy.

COMEDY OF ERRORS.

ACT II.

MAN'S PREEMINENCE.

There's nothing, situate under heaven's eye,
But hath his bound, in earth, in sea, in sky:
The beasts, the fishes, and the winged fowls,
Are their males' subject, and at their controls:
Men, more divine, the masters of all these,
Lords of the wide world, and wild watery seas,
Endued with intellectual sense or souls,
Of more preeminence than fish and fowls,
Are masters to their females, and their lords:
Then let your will attend on their accords.

PATIENCE EASIER TAUGHT THAN PRACTISED.

Patience, unmov'd, no marvel though she pause;
They can be meek, that have no other cause.
A wretched soul, bruis'd with adversity,
We bid be quiet, when we hear it cry;
But were we burden'd with like weight of pain,
As much, or more, we should ourselves complain.

DEFAMATION.

I see, the jewel, best enameled,
Will lose his beauty; and though gold 'bides still,
That others touch, yet often touching will
Wear gold: and so no man, that hath a name,
But falsehood and corruption doth it shame.

JEALOUSY.

Ay, ay, Antipholus, look strange, and frown;
Some other mistress hath thy sweet aspects,
I am not Adriana, nor thy wife.
The time was once, when thou unurg'd wouldst vow
That never words were music to thine ear,
That never object pleasing in thine eye,
That never touch well-welcome to thy hand,

That never meat sweet-savour'd in thy taste,
Unless I spake, look'd, touch'd, or carv'd to thee.

SLANDER.

For slander lives upon succession;
For ever hous'd, where it once gets possession.

ACT V.

A WOMAN'S JEALOUSY MORE DEADLY THAN POISON.

The venom clamours of a jealous woman
Poison more deadly than a mad dog's tooth.
It seems his sleeps were hinder'd by thy railing:
And thereof comes it that his head is light.
Thou say'st, his meat was sauc'd with thy upbraidings;
Unquiet meals make ill digestions,
Thereof the raging fire of fever bred;
And what's a fever but a fit of madness?
Thou say'st, his sports were hinder'd by thy brawls;
Sweet recreation barr'd, what doth ensue,
But moody and dull melancholy
(Kinsman to grim and comfortless despair);
And, at her heels, a huge infectious troop
Of pale distemperatures, and foes to life?

DESCRIPTION OF A BEGGARLY FORTUNETELLER.

A hungry lean-fac'd villain,
A mere anatomy, a mountebank,
A threadbare juggler, and a fortuneteller;
A needy, hollow-ey'd, sharp-looking wretch,
A living dead man: this pernicious slave,
Forsooth, took on him as a conjurer;
And, gazing in mine eyes, feeling my pulse,
And with no face, as 'twere outfacing me,
Cries out, I was possess'd.

OLD AGE.

Though now this grained * face of mine be hid
In sap-consuming winter's drizzled snow,
And all the conduits of my blood froze up;
Yet hath my night of life some memory,

* Furrowed, lined.

My wasting lamp some fading glimmer left,
My dull deaf ears a little use to hear:
All these old witnesses (I cannot err),
Tell me, thou art my son Antipholus.

LOVE'S LABOUR'S LOST.

ACT I.

SELF-DENIAL.

BRAVE conquerors!—for so you are,
That war against your own affections,
And the huge army of the world's desires.

VANITY OF PLEASURE.

Why, all delights are vain; but that most vain,
Which, with pain purchas'd, doth inherit pain.

ON STUDY.

Study is like the heaven's glorious sun,
That will not be deep search'd with saucy looks;
Small have continual plodders ever won,
Save base authority from others' books.
These earthly godfathers of heaven's lights,
That give a name to every fixed star,
Have no more profit of their shining nights,
Than those that walk, and wot not what they are.
Too much to know, is, to know nought but fame;
And every godfather can give a name.

FROST.

An envious sneaping* frost,
That bites the first-born infants of the spring.

A CONCEITED COURTIER.

A man in all the world's new fashion planted,
That hath a mint of phrases in his brain:

* Nipping.

One, whom the music of his own vain tongue
Doth ravish, like enchanting harmony;
A man of compliments, whom right and wrong
Have chose as umpire of their mutiny:
This child of fancy, that Armado hight *,
For interim to our studies, shall relate,
In high-born words, the worth of many a knight
From tawny Spain, lost in the world's debate.

ACT II.

BEAUTY.

My beauty, though but mean,
Needs not the painted flourish of your praise;
Beauty is bought by judgment of the eye,
Not utter'd by base sale of chapmen's tongues.

A MERRY MAN.

A merrier man,
Within the limit of becoming mirth,
I never spent an hour's talk withal:
His eye begets occasion for his wit;
For every object that the one doth catch,
The other turns to a mirth-moving jest;
Which his fair tongue (conceit's expositor),
Delivers in such apt and gracious words,
That aged years play truant at his tales,
And younger hearings are quite ravished;
So sweet and voluble is his discourse.

ACT III.

HUMOROUS DESCRIPTION OF LOVE.

O!—And I, forsooth, in love! I, that have been
love's whip;
A very beadle to a humorous sigh:
A critic; nay, a night-watch constable;
A domineering pedant o'er the boy,
Than whom no mortal so magnificent!

* Called.

This wimpled *, wining, purblind, wayward boy;
This senior-junior, giant-dwarf, Dan Cupid;
Regent of love-rhymes, lord of folded arms,.
The anointed sovereign of sighs and groans,
Liege of all loiterers and malcontents,
Dread prince of plackets †, king of codpieces,
Sole imperator and great general
Of trotting paritors ‡.—O my little heart!—
And I to be a corporal of his field,
And wear his colours like a tumbler's hoop!
What? I! I love! I sue! I seek a wife!
A woman, that is like a German clock,
Still a repairing: ever out of frame;
And never going aright, being a watch,
But being watch'd that it may still go right?

ACT IV.

SONNET.

Did not the heavenly rhetoric of thine eye
  ('Gainst whom the world cannot hold argument),
Persuade my heart to this false perjury?
  Vows, for thee broke, deserve not punishment.
A woman I forswore; but, I will prove,
  Thou being a goddess, I forswore not thee:
My vow was earthly, thou a heavenly love;
  Thy grace being gain'd, cures all disgrace in me.
Vows are but breath, and breath a vapour is:
  Then thou, fair sun, which on my earth dost shine,
Exhal'st this vapour vow; in thee it is:
  If broken then, it is no fault of mine;
If by me broke, What fool is not so wise,
To lose an oath to win a paradise?

SONG.

On a day, (alack the day!)
Love, whose month is ever May,

* Hooded, veiled. † Petticoats.
‡ The officers of the spiritual courts who serve citations

Spied a blossom, passing fair,
Playing in the wanton air:
Through the velvet leaves the wind,
All unseen, 'gan passage find;
That the lover, sick to death,
Wish'd himself the heaven's breath.
Air, *quoth he*, thy cheeks may blow;
Air, would I might triumph so!
But, alack, my hand is sworn,
Ne'er to pluck thee from thy thorn:
Vow, alack, for youth unmeet;
Youth so apt to pluck a sweet.
Do not call it sin in me,
That I am forsworn for thee:
Thou for whom even Jove would swear,
Juno but an Ethiop were;
And deny himself for Jove,
Turning mortal for thy love.

THE POWER OF LOVE.

But love, first learned in a lady's eyes,
Lives not alone immured in the brain;
But with the motion of all elements,
Courses as swift as thought in every power;
And gives to every power a double power,
Above their functions and their offices.
It adds a precious seeing to the eye;
A lover's eyes will gaze an eagle blind;
A lover's ear will hear the lowest sound,
When the suspicious head of theft is stopp'd;
Love's feeling is more soft, and sensible,
Than are the tender horns of cockled snails:
Love's tongue proves dainty Bacchus gross in taste:
For valour, is not love a Hercules,
Still climbing trees in the Hesperides?
Subtle as sphinx, as sweet and musical
As bright Apollo's lute, strung with his hair;
And, when love speaks, the voice of all the gods
Makes heaven drowsy with the harmony.
Never durst poet touch a pen to write,
Until his ink were temper'd with love's sighs;

O, then his lines would ravish savage ears,
And plant in tyrants mild humility.

WOMEN'S EYES.

From women's eyes this doctrine I derive:
They sparkle still the right Promethean fire;
They are the books, the arts, the academies,
That show, contain, and nourish all the world;
Else, none at all in aught proves excellent.

ACT V.

JEST AND JESTER.

Your task shall be
With all the fierce* endeavour of your wit
To enforce the pained impotent to smile.
Biron. To move wild laughter in the throat of death?
It cannot be; it is impossible:
Mirth cannot move a soul in agony.
Ros. Why, that's the way to choke a gibing spirit,
Whose influence is begot of that loose grace,
Which shallow laughing hearers give to fools:
A jest's prosperity lies in the ear
Of him that hears it, never in the tongue
Of him that makes it.

SONG.

Spring. When daisies pied, and violets blue,
And lady-smocks all silver-white,
And cuckoo-buds of yellow hue,
Do paint the meadows with delight,
The cuckoo then, on every tree,
Mocks married men, for thus sings he,
Cuckoo;
Cuckoo, cuckoo,—O word of fear,
Unpleasing to a married ear!

When shepherds pipe on oaten straws,
And merry larks are ploughmen's clocks,
When turtles tread, and rooks, and daws,
And maidens bleach their summer smocks,

* Vehement.

The cuckoo then, on every tree,
Mocks married men, for thus sings he,
Cuckoo;
Cuckoo, cuckoo,—O word of fear,
Unpleasing to a married ear!

Winter. When icicles hang by the wall,
And Dick the shepherd blows his nail,
And Tom bears logs into the hall,
And milk comes frozen home in pail,
When blood is nipp'd, and ways be foul,
Then nightly sings the staring owl,
To-who;
Tu-whit, to-who, a merry note,
While greasy Joan doth keel* the pot.

When all aloud the wind doth blow,
And coughing drowns the parson's saw,
And birds sit brooding in the snow,
And Marian's nose looks red and raw,
When roasted crabs † hiss in the bowl,
Then nightly sings the staring owl,
To-who;
Tu-whit, to-who, a merry note,
While greasy Joan doth keel the pot.

MEASURE FOR MEASURE.

ACT I.

VIRTUE GIVEN TO BE EXERTED.

HEAVEN doth with us, as we with torches do;
Not light them for themselves: for if our virtues
Did not go forth of us, 'twere all alike
As if we had them not. Spirits are not finely touch'd,
But to fine issues ‡: nor nature never lends
The smallest scruple of her excellence,
But, like a thrifty goddess, she determines

* Cool. † Wild apples. ‡ For high purposes.

Herself the glory of a creditor,
Both thanks and use *.

THE CONSEQUENCE OF LIBERTY INDULGED.

As surfeit is the father of much fast,
So every scope by the immoderate use
Turns to restraint: Our natures do pursue,
(Like rats that ravin † down their proper bane),
A thirsty evil; and when we drink, we die.

ELOQUENCE AND BEAUTY.

In her youth
There is a prone ‡ and speechless dialect,
Such as moves men; beside, she hath prosperous art
When she will play with reason and discourse,
And well she can persuade.

PARDON THE SANCTION OF WICKEDNESS.

For we bid this be done,
When evil deeds have their permissive pass,
And not the punishment.

A SEVERE GOVERNOR.

Lord Angelo is precise;
Stands at a guard § with envy; scarce confesses
That his blood flows, or that his appetite
Is more to bread than stone: Hence shall we see,
If power change purpose, what our seemers be.

RESOLUTION.

Our doubts are traitors,
And make us lose the good we oft might win,
By fearing to attempt.

THE PRAYERS OF MAIDENS EFFECTUAL.

Go to lord Angelo,
And let him learn to know, when maidens sue,
Men give like gods; but when they weep and kneel,
All their petitions are as freely theirs
As they themselves would owe ‖ them.

* Interest. † Voraciously devour. ‡ Prompt.
§ On his defence. ‖ Have.

ACT II.

ALL MEN FRAIL.

Let but your honour know*
(Whom I believe to be most straight in virtue),
That, in the working of your own affections,
Had time coherd† with place, or place with wishing,
Or that the resolute acting of your blood
Could have attain'd the effect of your own purpose,
Whether you had not sometime in your life
Err'd in this point which now you censure him,
And pull'd the law upon you.

THE FAULTS OF OTHERS NO JUSTIFICATION OF OUR OWN.

'Tis one thing to be tempted, Escalus,
Another thing to fall. I not deny,
The jury, passing on the prisoner's life,
May, in the sworn twelve, have a thief or two
Guiltier than him they try: What's open made to justice,
That justice seizes. What know the laws,
That thieves do pass‡ on thieves? 'Tis very pregnant§,
The jewel that we find, we stoop and take it,
Because we see it; but what we do not see,
We tread upon, and never think of it.
You may not so extenuate his offence,
For‖ I have had such faults; but rather tell me,
When I, that censure¶ him, do so offend,
Let mine own judgment pattern out my death,
And nothing come in partial.

MERCY FREQUENTLY MISTAKEN.

Mercy is not itself, that oft looks so;
Pardon is still the nurse of second woe.

* Examine. † Suited. ‡ Pass judgment.
§ Plain. ‖ Because. ¶ Sentence.

MERCY IN GOVERNORS COMMENDED.

No ceremony that to great ones 'longs,
Not the king's crown, nor the deputed sword,
The marshal's truncheon, nor the judge's robe,
Become them with one half so good a grace,
As mercy does.

THE DUTY OF MUTUAL FORGIVENESS.

Alas! alas!
Why, all the souls that were, were forfeit once;
And He that might the vantage best have took,
Found out the remedy: How would you be,
If he, which is the top of judgment, should
But judge you as you are? O think on that;
And mercy then will breathe within your lips,
Like man new made.

JUSTICE.

Yet show some pity.
Ang. I show it most of all, when I show justice;
For then I pity those I do not know,
Which a dismiss'd offence would after gall;
And do him right, that, answering one foul wrong,
Lives not to act another.

THE ABUSE OF AUTHORITY.

O, it is excellent
To have a giant's strength; but it is tyrannous
To use it like a giant.
Could great men thunder,
As Jove himself does, Jove would ne'er be quiet,
For every pelting * petty officer
Would use his heaven for thunder; nothing but thunder.——
Merciful heaven!
Thou rather, with thy sharp and sulphurous bolt,
Split'st the unwedgeable and gnarled † oak,
Than the soft myrtle——O, but man, proud man!
Drest in a little brief authority;

* Paltry. † Knotted.

Most ignorant of what he's most assur'd,
His glassy essence,—like an angry ape,
Plays such fantastic tricks before high heaven,
As make the angels weep: who, with our spleens,
Would all themselves laugh mortal.

THE PRIVILEGE OF AUTHORITY.

Great men may jest with saints: 'tis wit in them;
But, in the less, foul profanation.
That in the captain's but a choleric word,
Which in the soldier is flat blasphemy.

HONEST BRIBERY.

Hark, how I'll bribe you.
Ang. How! bribe me?
Isab. Ay, with such gifts, that heaven shall share with you.
Lucio. You had marr'd all else.
Isab. Not with fond shekels of the tested* gold,
Or stones, whose rates are either rich, or poor,
As fancy values them: but with true prayers,
That shall be up at heaven, and enter there,
Ere sunrise; prayers from preserved † souls,
From fasting maids, whose minds are dedicate
To nothing temporal.

THE POWER OF VIRTUOUS DUTY.

Is this her fault, or mine?
The tempter, or the tempted, who sins most? Ha!
Not she; nor doth she tempt: but it is I,
That lying by the violet, in the sun,
Do, as the carrion does, not as the flower,
Corrupt with virtuous season. Can it be,
That modesty may more betray our sense
Than woman's lightness? Having waste ground enough,
Shall we desire to raze the sanctuary,
And pitch our evils there ‡? O, fy, fy, fy!
What dost thou? or what art thou, Angelo?

* Attested, stamped.
† Preserved from the corruption of the world.
‡ See 2 Kings, x. 27.

Dost thou desire her foully, for those things
That make her good? O, let her brother live:
Thieves for their robbery have authority,
When judges steal themselves. What? do I love her,
That I desire to hear her speak again,
And feast upon her eyes? What is't I dream on?
O cunning enemy, that, to catch a saint,
With saints dost bait thy hook! Most dangerous
Is that temptation, that doth goad us on,
To sin in loving virtue: never could the strumpet,
With all her double vigour, art, and nature,
Once stir my temper; but this virtuous maid
Subdues me quite.

LOVE IN A GRAVE SEVERE GOVERNOR.

When I would pray and think, I think and pray
To several subjects: heaven hath my empty words;
Whilst my invention, hearing not my tongue,
Anchors on Isabel: Heaven in my mouth,
As if I did but only chew his name;
And in my heart the strong and swelling evil
Of my conception: The state, whereon I studied,
Is like a good thing, being often read,
Grown fear'd and tedious; yea, my gravity,
Wherein (let no man hear me) I take pride,
Could I, with boot*, change for an idle plume,
Which the air beats for vain. O place! O form!
How often dost thou with thy case†, thy habit,
Wrench awe from fools, and tie the wiser souls
To thy false seeming?

FORNICATION AND MURDER EQUALED.

It were as good
To pardon him, that hath from nature stolen
A man already made, as to remit
Their saucy sweetness, that do coin heaven's image,
In stamps that are forbid: 'tis all as easy
Falsely to take away a life true made,
As to put mettle in restrained means,
To make a false one.

* Profit. † Outside.

LOWLINESS OF MIND.

Let me be ignorant, and in nothing good,
But graciously to know I am no better.
Ang. Thus wisdom wishes to appear most bright,
When it doth tax itself.

TEMPORAL FAR BETTER THAN ETERNAL DEATH.

Better it were, a brother died at once,
Than that a sister by redeeming him,
Should die for ever.

WOMEN'S FRAILTY.

Nay, women are frail too.
Isab. Ay, as the glasses where they view themselves;
Which are as easy broke as they make forms.
Women!—Help, heaven! men their creation mar
In profiting by them. Nay, call us ten times frail;
For we are soft as our complexions are,
And credulous to false prints*.

ACT III.

HOPE.

The miserable have no other medicine,
But only hope.

REFLECTIONS ON THE VANITY OF LIFE.

Reason thus with life,—
If I do lose thee, I do lose a thing
That none but fools would keep; a breath thou art
(Servile to all the skiey influences),
That dost this habitation, where thou keep'st,
Hourly afflict: merely, thou art death's fool;
For him thou labour'st by thy flight to shun,
And yet runn'st toward him still: Thou art not noble;
For all the accommodations that thou bear'st,

* Impressions.

Are nursed by baseness: Thou art by no means valiant;
For thou dost fear the soft and tender fork
Of a poor worm: Thy best of rest is sleep,
And that thou oft provok'st: yet grossly fear'st
Thy death, which is no more. Thou art not thyself;
For thou exist'st on many a thousand grains
That issue out of dust: Happy thou art not:
For what thou hast not, still thou striv'st to get;
And what thou hast, forget'st: Thou art not certain;
For thy complexion shifts to strange effects *,
After the moon: If thou art rich, thou art poor;
For, like an ass, whose back with ingots bows,
Thou bear'st thy heavy riches but a journey,
And death unloads thee: Friend hast thou none;
For thine own bowels, which do call thee sire,
The mere effusion of thy proper loins,
Do curse the gout, serpigo †, and the rheum,
For ending thee no sooner: Thou hast nor youth, nor age;
But, as it were, an after-dinner's sleep,
Dreaming on both: for all thy blessed youth
Becomes as aged, and doth beg the alms
Of palsied eld ‡; and when thou art old, and rich,
Thou hast neither heat, affection, limb, nor beauty,
To make thy riches pleasant. What's yet in this,
That bears the name of life? Yet in this life
Lie hid more thousand deaths: yet death we fear,
That makes these odds all even.

THE TERRORS OF DEATH MOST IN APPREHENSION.

O, I do fear thee, Claudio; and I quake,
Lest thou a feverish life shouldst entertain,
And six or seven winters more respect
Than a perpetual honour. Dar'st thou die?
The sense of death is most in apprehension;
And the poor beetle, that we tread upon,
In corporal sufferance finds a pang as great
As when a giant dies.

* Affects, affections. † Leprous eruptions.
‡ Old age.

RESOLUTION FROM A SENSE OF HONOUR.

Why give you me this shame?
Think you I can a resolution fetch
From flowery tenderness? If I must die,
I will encounter darkness as a bride,
And hug it in mine arms.

THE HYPOCRISY OF ANGELO.

There my father's grave
Did utter forth a voice! Yes, thou must die:
Thou art too noble to conserve a life
In base appliances. This outward-sainted deputy,—
Whose settled visage and deliberate word
Nips youth i'the head, and follies doth enmew *,
As falcon doth the fowl,—is yet a devil;
His filth within being cast, he would appear
A pond as deep as hell.

THE TERRORS OF DEATH.

Death is a fearful thing.
Isab. And shamed life a hateful.
Claud. Ay, but to die, and go we know not where;
To lie in cold obstruction, and to rot:
This sensible warm motion to become
A kneaded clod; and the delighted spirit
To bathe in fiery floods, or to reside
In thrilling regions of thick-ribbed ice;
To be imprison'd in the viewless † winds,
And blown with restless violence about
The pendent world; or to be worse than worst
Of those, that lawless and incertain thoughts
Imagine howling!—'tis too horrible!
The weariest and most loathed worldly life,
That age, ach, penury, and imprisonment
Can lay on nature, is a paradise
To what we fear of death.

VIRTUE AND GOODNESS.

Virtue is bold, and goodness never fearful.

* Shut up. † Invisible.

A BAWD.

The evil that thou causest to be done,
That is thy means to live: Do thou but think
What 'tis to cram a maw, or clothe a back,
From such a filthy vice: say to thyself,—
From their abominable and beastly touches
I drink, I eat, array myself, and live.
Canst thou believe thy living is a life,
So stinkingly depending? Go, mend, go, mend.

ACT IV.

SONG.

Take, oh take, those lips away,
  That so sweetly were forsworn;
And those eyes, the break of day,
  Lights that do mislead the morn:
But my kisses bring again,
Seals of love, but seal'd in vain.

Hide, oh hide, those hills of snow,
  Which thy frozen bosom bears,
On whose tops the pinks that grow
  Are of those that April wears:
But my poor heart first set free,
Bound in those icy chains by thee.

GREATNESS SUBJECT TO CENSURE.

O place and greatness, millions of false eyes,
Are stuck upon thee! volumes of report
Run with these false and most contrarious quests
Upon thy doings! thousand scapes * of wit
Make thee the father of their idle dream,
And rack thee in their fancies.

SOUND SLEEP.

As fast lock'd up in sleep, as guiltless labour
When it lies starkly † in the traveller's bones.

* Sallies. † Stiffly.

ACT V.

CHARACTER OF AN ARCH HYPOCRITE.

O prince, I conjure thee, as thou believ'st
There is another comfort than this world,
That thou neglect me not, with that opinion
That I am touch'd with madness: make not impossible
That which but seems unlike: 'tis not impossible,
But one, the wicked'st caitiff on the ground,
May seem as shy, as grave, as just, as absolute,
As Angelo; even so may Angelo,
In all his dressings *, characts, titles, forms,
Be an arch-villain: believe it, royal prince,
If he be less, he's nothing; but he's more,
Had I more name for badness.

MERCHANT OF VENICE.

ACT I.

MIRTH AND MELANCHOLY.

Now, by two-headed Janus,
Nature hath fram'd strange fellows in her time:
Some that will evermore peep through their eyes,
And laugh, like parrots, at a bagpiper;
And other of such vinegar aspect,
That they'll not show their teeth in way of smile,
Though Nestor swear the jest be laughable.

WORLDLINESS.

You have too much respect upon the world:
They lose it, that do buy it with much care.

* Habits and characters of office.

THE WORLD'S TRUE VALUE.

I hold the world but as the world, Gratiano;
A stage, where every man must play a part.

CHEERFULNESS.

Let me play the Fool:
With mirth and laughter let old wrinkles come;
And let my liver rather heat with wine,
Than my heart cool with mortifying groans.
Why should a man, whose blood is warm within,
Sit like his grandsire cut in alabaster?
Sleep when he wakes? and creep into the jaundice
By being peevish?

AFFECTED GRAVITY.

I tell thee what, Antonio,—
I love thee, and it is my love that speaks;—
There are a sort of men, whose visages
Do cream and mantle, like a standing pond;
And do a wilful stillness* entertain,
With purpose to be dress'd in an opinion
Of wisdom, gravity, profound conceit;
As who should say, *I am Sir Oracle,*
And, when I ope my lips, let no dog bark!
O, my Antonio, I do know of these,
That therefore only are reputed wise,
For saying nothing.

LOQUACITY.

Gratiano speaks an infinite deal of nothing, more than any man in all Venice: His reasons are as two grains of wheat hid in two bushels of chaff; you shall seek all day ere you find them: and when you have them, they are not worth the search.

MEDIOCRITY.

For aught I see, they are as sick, that surfeit with too much, as they that starve with nothing: It is no mean happiness, therefore, to be seated in the mean; super-

* Obstinate silence

finity comes sooner by white hairs, but competency lives longer.

SPECULATION MORE EASY THAN PRACTICE.

If to do were as easy as to know what were good to do, chapels had been churches, and poor men's cottages, princes' palaces. It is a good divine that follows his own instructions: I can easier teach twenty what were good to be done, than be one of the twenty to follow mine own teaching. The brain may devise laws for the blood; but a hot temper leaps over a cold decree; such a hare is madness the youth, to skip o'er the meshes of good counsel the cripple.

THE JEW'S MALICE.

Bass. This is signior Antonio.
Shy. [*Aside.*] How like a fawning publican he looks!
I hate him, for he is a Christian:
But more, for that, in low simplicity,
He lends out money gratis, and brings down
The rate of usance here with us in Venice.
If I can catch him once upon the hip,
I will feed fat the ancient grudge I bear him.
He hates our sacred nation; and he rails,
Even there where merchants most do congregate,
On me, my bargains, and my well won thrift,
Which he calls interest: Cursed be my tribe,
If I forgive him!

HYPOCRISY.

Mark you this, Bassanio,
The devil can cite scripture for his purpose.
An evil soul, producing holy witness,
Is like a villain with a smiling cheek;
A goodly apple rotten at the heart;
O, what a goodly outside falsehood hath!

THE JEW'S EXPOSTULATION.

Signior Antonio, many a time and oft,
In the Rialto you have rated me

About my monies, and my usances*:
Still have I borne it with a patient shrug;
For sufferance is the badge of all our tribe:
You call me—misbeliever, cut-throat dog,
And spit upon my Jewish gaberdine,
And all for use of that which is mine own.
Well then, it now appears, you need my help:
Go to then; you come to me, and you say,
Shylock, we would have monies: You say so;
You, that did void your rheum upon my beard,
And foot me, as you spurn a stranger cur
Over your threshold: Monies is your suit.
What should I say to you? Should I not say,
Hath a dog money? is it possible,
A cur can lend three thousand ducats? or
Shall I bend low, and, in a bondman's key,
With 'bated breath, and whispering humbleness,
Say this,——
Fair sir, you spit on me on Wednesday last;
You spurn'd me such a day; another time
You call'd me—dog; and for these courtesies
I'll lend you thus much monies.

ACT II.

GRAVITY ASSUMED.

Signior Bassanio, hear me:
If I do not put on a sober habit,
Talk with respect, and swear but now and then,
Wear prayer books in my pocket, look demurely;
Nay more, while grace is saying, hood mine eyes
Thus with my hat, and sigh, and say, amen;
Use all the observance of civility,
Like one well studied in a sad ostent†
To please his grandam, never trust me more.

* Interest. † Show of staid and serious demeanour.

THE JEW'S COMMANDS TO HIS DAUGHTER.

Lock up my doors; and when you hear the drum,
And the vile squeaking of the wry-neck'd fife,
Clamber not you up to the casements then,
Nor thrust your head into the public street,
To gaze on Christian fools with varnish'd faces:
But stop my house's ears, I mean my casements;
Let not the sound of shallow foppery enter
My sober house.

POSSESSION MORE LANGUID THAN EXPECTATION.

O, ten times faster Venus' pigeons fly
To seal love's bonds new made, than they are wont,
To keep obliged faith unforfeited!
Who riseth from a feast,
With that keen appetite that he sits down?
Where is the horse that doth untread again
His tedious measures with the unbated fire
That he did pace them first? All things that are,
Are with more spirit chased than enjoy'd.
How like a younker, or a prodigal,
The scarfed* bark puts from her native bay,
Hugg'd and embraced by the strumpet wind!
How like the prodigal doth she return,
With overweather'd ribs, and ragged sails,
Lean, rent, and beggar'd by the strumpet wind!

PORTIA'S SUITORS.

From the four corners of the earth they come,
To kiss this shrine, this mortal breathing saint.
The Hyrcanian deserts, and the vasty wilds
Of wide Arabia, are as through-fares now,
For princes to come view fair Portia:
The watery kingdom, whose ambitious head
Spits in the face of heaven, is no bar
To stop the foreign spirits; but they come,
As o'er a brook, to see fair Portia.

* Decorated with flags.

THE PARTING OF FRIENDS.

I saw Bassanio and Antonio part:
Bassanio told him, he would make some speed
Of his return; he answered—*Do not so,*
Slubber not business for my sake, Bassanio,*
But stay the very riping of the time;
And for the Jew's bond, which he hath of me,
Let it not enter in your mind of love:
Be merry; and employ your chiefest thoughts
To courtship, and such fair ostents† of love
As shall conveniently become you there:
And even there, his eye being big with tears,
Turning his face, he put his hand behind him,
And with affection wondrous sensible
He wrung Bassanio's hand, and so they parted.

HONOUR TO BE CONFERRED ON MERIT ONLY.

For who shall go about
To cozen fortune, and be honourable
Without the stamp of merit! Let none presume
To wear an undeserved dignity.
O, that estates, degrees, and offices,
Were not deriv'd corruptly! and that clear honour
Were purchased by the merit of the wearer!
How many then should cover, that stand bare?
How many be commanded, that command?
How much low peasantry would then be glean'd
From the true seed of honour? and how much honour
Pick'd from the chaff and ruin of the times,
To be new varnish'd?

LOVE MESSENGER COMPARED TO AN APRIL DAY.

I have not seen
So likely an embassador of love:
A day in April never came so sweet,
To show how costly summer was at hand,
As this fore-spurrer comes before his lord.

* To slubber is to do a thing carelessly. † Shows, tokens.

ACT III.

THE JEW'S REVENGE.

If it will feed nothing else, it will feed my revenge. He hath disgraced me, and hindered me of half a million; laughed at my losses, mocked at my gains, scorned my nation, thwarted my bargains, cooled my friends, heated mine enemies; and what's his reason? I am a Jew. Hath not a Jew eyes? hath not a Jew hands, organs, dimensions, senses, affections, passions? fed with the same food, hurt with the same weapons, subject to the same diseases, healed by the same means, warmed and cooled by the same winter and summer, as a Christian is? if you prick us, do we not bleed? if you tickle us, do we not laugh? if you poison us, do we not die? and if you wrong us, shall we not revenge? If we are like you in the rest, we will resemble you in that. If a Jew wrong a Christian, what is his humility? revenge: if a Christian wrong a Jew, what should his sufferance be by Christian example? why, revenge. The villany, you teach me, I will execute: and it shall go hard, but I will better the instruction.

MUSIC.

Let music sound, while he doth make his choice;
Then, if he lose, he makes a swanlike end,
Fading in music: that the comparison
May stand more proper, my eye shall be the stream,
And wat'ry deathbed for him: He may win;
And what is music then? then music is
Even as the flourish when true subjects bow
To a new-crowned monarch: such it is,
As are those dulcet sounds in break of day,
That creep into the dreaming bridegroom's ear,
And summon him to marriage. Now he goes,
With no less presence *, but with much more love.

* Dignity of mien.

Than young Alcides, when he did redeem
The virgin tribute paid by howling Troy
To the seamonster: I stand for sacrifice,
The rest aloof are the Dardanian wives,
With bleared visages, come forth to view
The issue of the exploit.

THE DECEIT OF ORNAMENT OR APPEARANCES.

The world is still deceiv'd with ornament.
In law, what plea so tainted and corrupt,
But, being season'd with a gracious* voice,
Obscures the show of evil? In religion,
What damned error, but some sober brow
Will bless it, and approve it with a text,
Hiding the grossness with fair ornament?
There is no vice so simple, but assumes
Some mark of virtue on his outward parts.
How many cowards, whose hearts are all as false
As stairs of sand, wear yet upon their chins
The beards of Hercules, and frowning Mars;
Who, inward search'd, have livers white as milk?
And these assume but valour's excrement,
To render them redoubted. Look on beauty,
And you shall see 'tis purchas'd by the weight;
Which therein works a miracle in nature,
Making them lightest that wear most of it:
So are those crisped†, snaky, golden locks,
Which make such wanton gambols with the wind,
Upon supposed fairness, often known
To be the dowry of a second head,
The skull that bred them, in the sepulchre.
Thus ornament is but the guiled‡ shore
To a most dangerous sea; the beauteous scarf
Veiling an Indian beauty; in a word,
The seeming truth which cunning times put on
To entrap the wisest.

* Winning favour. † Curled.
‡ Treacherous.

PORTIA'S PICTURE.

What find I here? [*Opening the leaden casket.*
Fair Portia's counterfeit*? What demigod
Hath come so near creation? Move these eyes!
Or whether, riding on the balls of mine,
Seem they in motion? Here are sever'd lips,
Parted with sugar breath; so sweet a bar
Should sunder such sweet friends: Here in her hairs
The painter plays the spider; and hath woven
A golden mesh to entrap the hearts of men,
Faster than gnats in cobwebs: But her eyes,—
How could he see to do them? having made one,
Methinks, it should have power to steal both his,
And leave itself unfurnish'd.

SUCCESSFUL LOVER COMPARED TO A CONQUEROR.

Like one of two contending in a prize,
That thinks he hath done well in people's eyes,
Hearing applause, and universal shout,
Giddy in spirit, still gazing, in a doubt
Whether those peals of praise be his or no;
So, thrice fair lady, stand I.

HIS THOUGHTS TO THE INARTICULATE JOYS OF A CROWD.

There is such confusion in my powers,
As, after some oration fairly spoke
By a beloved prince, there doth appear
Among the buzzing pleased multitude:
Where every something, being blent† together,
Turns to a wild of nothing save of joy,
Express'd and not express'd.

IMPLACABLE REVENGE.

Shy. I'll have my bond; I will not hear thee speak:
I'll have my bond: and therefore speak no more,
I'll not be made a soft and dull-ey'd fool.

* Likeness, portrait. † Blended.

To shake the head, relent, and sigh, and yield
To Christian intercessors.

THE BOASTING OF YOUTH.

I'll hold thee any wager,
When we are both accoutred like young men,
I'll prove the prettier fellow of the two,
And wear my dagger with the braver grace;
And speak, between the change of man and boy,
With a reed voice; and turn two mincing steps
Into a manly stride; and speak of frays,
Like a fine bragging youth: and tell quaint lies,
How honourable ladies sought my love,
Which I denying, they fell sick and died;
I could not do with all;—then I'll repent,
And wish, for all that, that I had not kill'd them:
And twenty of these puny lies I'll tell,
That men shall swear, I have discontinued school
Above a twelvemonth.

AFFECTATION IN WORDS.

O dear discretion, how his words are suited!
The fool hath planted in his memory
An army of good words: And I do know
A many fools, that stand in better place,
Garnish'd like him, that for a tricksy word
Defy the matter.

THE JEW'S REASON FOR REVENGE.

You'll ask me why I rather chose to have
A weight of carrion flesh, than to receive
Three thousand ducats: I'll not answer that:
But, say, it is my humour*: Is it answer'd?
What if my house be troubled with a rat,
And I be pleased to give ten thousand ducats
To have it baned? What, are you answer'd yet?
Some men there are, love not a gaping pig;
Some, that are mad, if they behold a cat;
And others, when the bagpipe sings i'the nose,

* Particular fancy.

Cannot contain their urine: For affection *,
Mistress of passion, sways it to the mood
Of what it likes, or loathes: Now, for your answer;
As there is no firm reason to be render'd,
Why he cannot abide a gaping † pig;
Why he, a harmless necessary cat;
Why he, a swollen bagpipe; but of force
Must yield to such inevitable shame,
As to offend, himself being offended;
So can I give no reason, nor I will not,
More than a lodg'd hate, and a certain loathing,
I bear Antonio, that I follow thus
A losing suit against him. Are you answer'd?

MERCY.

The quality of mercy is not strain'd;
It droppeth, as the gentle rain from heaven
Upon the place beneath: it is twice bless'd;
It blesseth him that gives, and him that takes:
'Tis mightiest in the mightiest; it becomes
The throned monarch better than his crown:
His sceptre shows the force of temporal power,
The attribute to awe and majesty,
Wherein doth sit the dread and fear of kings;
But mercy is above the sceptred sway,
It is enthroned in the hearts of kings,
It is an attribute to God himself;
And earthly power doth then show likest God's,
When mercy seasons justice.

FORTUNE.

For herein fortune shows herself more kind
Than is her custom: it is still her use,
To let the wretched man outlive his wealth,
To view with hollow eye, and wrinkled brow,
An age of poverty.

* Prejudice. † Crying.

ACT V.

MOONLIGHT.

How sweet the moonlight sleeps upon this bank!
Here will we sit, and let the sounds of music
Creep in our ears; soft stillness, and the night,
Become the touches of sweet harmony.
Sit, Jessica: Look, how the floor of heaven
Is thick inlaid with patines * of bright gold;
There's not the smallest orb, which thou behold'st,
But in his motion like an angel sings,
Still quiring to the young eyed cherubim:
Such harmony is in immortal souls;
But, whilst this muddy vesture of decay
Doth grossly close it in, we cannot hear it.

MUSIC.

I am never merry when I hear sweet music.
Lor. The reason is, your spirits are attentive:
For do but note a wild and wanton herd,
Or race of youthful and unhandled colts,
Fetching mad bounds, bellowing, and neighing loud,
Which is the hot condition of their blood;
If they but hear perchance a trumpet sound,
Or any air of music touch their ears,
You shall perceive them make a mutual stand,
Their savage eyes turn'd to a modest gaze,
By the sweet power of music: Therefore the poet
Did feign that Orpheus drew trees, stones, and floods,
Since nought so stockish, hard, and full of rage,
But music for the time doth change his nature:
The man that hath no music in himself,
Nor is not mov'd by concord of sweet sounds,
Is fit for treasons, stratagems, and spoils;
The motions of his spirit are dull as night,
And his affections dark as Erebus:
Let no such man be trusted.

* A small flat dish, used in the administration of the Eucharist.

A GOOD DEED COMPARED.

How far that little candle throws his beams!
So shines a good deed in a naughty world.

NOTHING GOOD OUT OF SEASON.

The crow doth sing as sweetly as the lark,
When neither is attended; and, I think,
The nightingale, if she should sing by day,
When every goose is cackling, would be thought
No better a musician than the wren.
How many things by season season'd are
To their right praise, and true perfection!—
Peace, hoa! the moon sleeps with Endymion,
And would not be awak'd!

MOONLIGHT NIGHT.

This night, methinks, is but the daylight sick,
It looks a little paler; 'tis a day,
Such as the day is when the sun is hid.

A MIDSUMMER NIGHT'S DREAM.

ACT I.

A FATHER'S AUTHORITY.

To you your father should be as a god;
One that compos'd your beauties; yea, and one
To whom you are but as a form in wax,
By him imprinted, and within his power
To leave the figure, or disfigure it.

A RECLUSE LIFE.

Therefore, fair Hermia, question your desires,
Know of your youth, examine well your blood,
Whether, if you yield not to your father's choice,

You can endure the livery of a nun;
For aye * to be in shady cloister mew'd,
To live a barren sister all your life,
Chanting faint hymns to the cold fruitless moon.
Thrice blessed they, that master so their blood,
To undergo such maiden pilgrimage:
But earthlier happy is the rose distill'd,
Than that, which, withering on the virgin thorn,
Grows, lives, and dies, in single blessedness.

TRUE LOVE EVER CROSSED.

For aught that ever I could read,
Could ever hear by tale or history,
The course of true love never did run smooth:
But, either it was different in blood:
Or else misgraffed, in respect of years;
Or else it stood upon the choice of friends:
Or, if there were a sympathy in choice,
War, death, or sickness did lay siege to it;
Making it momentany † as a sound,
Swift as a shadow, short as any dream;
Brief as the lightning in the collied ‡ night,
That, in a spleen, unfolds both heaven and earth,
And ere a man hath power to say,—Behold!
The jaws of darkness do devour it up:
So quick bright things come to confusion.

ASSIGNATION.

I swear to thee, by Cupid's strongest bow;
By his best arrow with the golden head;
By the simplicity of Venus' doves;
By that which knitteth souls, and prospers loves;
And by that fire which burn'd the Carthage queen,
When the false Trojan under sail was seen;
By all the vows that ever men have broke,
In number more than ever women spoke;—
In that same place thou hast appointed me,
To-morrow truly will I meet with thee.

* Ever. † Momentary. ‡ Black.

THE MOON.

When Phœbe doth behold
Her silver visage in the wat'ry glass,
Decking with liquid pearl the bladed grass.

LOVE.

Things base and vile, holding no quantity,
Love can transpose to form and dignity.
Love looks not with the eyes, but with the mind;
And therefore is winged Cupid painted blind;
Nor hath love's mind of any judgment taste;
Wings, and no eyes, figure unheedy haste:
And therefore is love said to be a child,
Because in choice he is so oft beguil'd.
As waggish boys in game * themselves forswear,
So the boy love is perjur'd every where.

PUCK.

I am that merry wanderer of the night,
I jest to Oberon, and make him smile,
When I a fat and bean-fed horse beguile,
Neighing in likeness of a silly foal:
And sometime lurk I in the gossip's bowl,
In very likeness of a roasted crab †;
And, when she drink, against her lips I bob,
And on her wither'd dew-lap pour the ale.
The wisest aunt telling the saddest tale,
Sometime for three-foot stool mistaketh me;
Then slip I from her bum, down topples she,
And *tailor* cries, and falls into a cough;
And then the whole quire hold their hips and loffe;
And waxen in their mirth, and neeze, and swear
A merrier hour was never wasted there.

FAIRY JEALOUSY, AND THE EFFECTS OF IT.

These are the forgeries of jealousy:
And never, since the middle summer's spring,
Met we on hill, in dale, forest, or mead,
By paved fountain, or by rushy brook,

* Sport. † Wild apple.

Or on the beachy margent of the sea,
To dance our ringlets to the whistling wind,
But with thy brawls thou hast disturb'd our sport.
Therefore the winds, piping to us in vain,
As in revenge, have suck'd up from the sea
Contagious fogs; which falling in the land,
Have every pelting * river made so proud,
That they have overborne their continents †;
The ox hath therefore stretch'd his yoke in vain,
The ploughman lost his sweat; and the green corn
Hath rotted, ere his youth attain'd a beard:
The fold stands empty in the drowned field,
And crows are fatted with the murrain flock;
The nine men's morris ‡ is fill'd up with mud;
And the quaint mazes in the wanton green,
For lack of tread, are undistinguishable;
The human mortals want their winter here;
No night is now with hymn or carol bless'd:—
Therefore the moon, the governess of floods,
Pale in her anger, washes all the air,
That rheumatic diseases do abound:
And thorough this distemperature, we see
The seasons alter: hoary-headed frosts
Fall in the fresh lap of the crimson rose;
And on old Hyems' chin, and icy crown,
An odorous chaplet of sweet summer buds
Is, as in mockery, set: The spring, the summer,
The childing § autumn, angry winter, change
Their wonted liveries; and the 'mazed world,
By their increase ||, now knows not which is which.

LOVE IN IDLENESS.

Thou remember'st
Since once I sat upon a promontory,
And heard a mermaid, on a dolphin's back,
Uttering such dulcet and harmonious breath,
That the rude sea grew civil at her song;
And certain stars shot madly from their spheres,

* Petty. † Banks which contain them.
‡ A game played by boys.
§ Autumn producing flowers unseasonably. || Produce.

To hear the seamaid's music.
That very time I saw (but thou couldst not),
Flying between the cold moon and the earth,
Cupid all arm'd: a certain aim he took
At a fair vestal, throned by the west;
And loosed his love-shaft smartly from his bow,
As it should pierce a hundred thousand hearts:
But I might see young Cupid's fiery shaft
Quench'd in the chaste beams of the wat'ry moon;
And the imperial vot'ress passed on,
In maiden meditation, fancy-free *.
Yet mark'd I where the bolt of Cupid fell:
It fell upon a little western flower,—
Before, milk-white; now purple with love's wound,—
And maidens call it, love-in-idleness.

A FAIRY BANK.

I know a bank whereon the wild thyme blows,
Where ox-lips † and the nodding violet grows;
Quite over-canopied with lush ‡ woodbine,
With sweet musk-roses, and with eglantine:
There sleeps Titania, some time of the night,
Lull'd in these flowers with dances and delight.

ACT III.

FAIRY COURTESIES.

Be kind and courteous to this gentleman;
Hop in his walks, and gambol in his eyes;
Feed him with apricocks and dewberries §,
With purple grapes, green figs, and mulberries;
The honey bags steal from the humble-bees,
And, for night tapers, crop their waxen thighs,
And light them at the fiery glowworm's eyes,
To have my love to bed, and to arise;
And pluck the wings from painted butterflies,
To fan the moonbeams from his sleeping eyes:
Nod to him, elves, and do him courtesies.

* Exempt from love. † The greater cowslip.
‡ Vigorous. § Gooseberries.

FEMALE FRIENDSHIP.

Is all the counsel that we two have shar'd,
The sisters' vows, the hours that we have spent,
When we have chid the hasty-footed time
For parting us,—O, and is all forgot?
All school-days' friendship, childhood innocence?
We, Hermia, like two artificial* gods,
Have with our neelds † created both one flower,
Both on one sampler, sitting on one cushion,
Both warbling of one song, both in one key;
As if our hands, our sides, voices, and minds,
Had been incorporate. So we grew together,
Like to a double cherry, seeming parted;
But yet a union in partition,
Two lovely berries moulded on one stem:
So, with two seeming bodies, but one heart;
Two of the first, like coats in heraldry,
Due but to one, and crowned with one crest.
And will you rent our ancient love asunder,
To join with men in scorning your poor friend?
It is not friendly, 'tis not maidenly:
Our sex, as well as I, may chide you for it,
Though I alone do feel the injury.

DAYBREAK.

Night's swift dragons cut the clouds full fast,
And yonder shines Aurora's harbinger;
At whose approach, ghosts, wandering here and there,
Troop home to church-yards.

ACT IV.

DEW IN FLOWERS.

And that same dew, which sometime on the buds
Was wont to swell, like round and orient pearls,
Stood now within the pretty flow'rets' eyes,
Like tears, that did their own disgrace bewail.

* Ingenious. † Needles.

HUNTING.

We will, fair queen, up to the mountain's top,
And mark the musical confusion
Of hounds and echo in conjunction.
Hip. I was with Hercules, and Cadmus, once,
When in a wood of Crete they bay'd the bear
With hounds of Sparta: never did I hear
Such gallant chiding *; for, besides the groves,
The skies, the fountains, every region near
Seem'd all one mutual cry: I never heard
So musical a discord, such sweet thunder.

HOUNDS.

My hounds are bred out of the Spartan kind,
So flew'd †, so sanded; and their heads are hung
With ears that sweep away the morning dew;
Crook-kneed, and dew-lapp'd like Thessalian bulls,
Slow in pursuit, but match'd in mouth like bells,
Each under each. A cry more tuneable
Was never holla'd to, nor cheer'd with horn.

ACT V.

THE POWER OF IMAGINATION.

The lunatic, the lover, and the poet,
Are of imagination all compact ‡:
One sees more devils than vast hell can hold;
That is, the madman: the lover, all as frantic,
Sees Helen's beauty in a brow of Egypt:
The poet's eye, in a fine frenzy rolling,
Doth glance from heaven to earth, from earth to heaven;
And, as imagination bodies forth
The forms of things unknown, the poet's pen
Turns them to shapes, and gives to airy nothing
A local habitation, and a name.

* Sound. † The flews are the large chaps of a hound.
‡ Are made of mere imagination.

SIMPLICITY AND DUTY.

For never any thing can be amiss,
When simpleness and duty tender it.
Hip. I love not to see wretchedness o'ercharg'd,
And duty in his service perishing.

MODEST DUTY ALWAYS ACCEPTABLE.

Where I have come, great clerks have purposed
To greet me with premeditated welcomes;
Where I have seen them shiver and look pale,
Make periods in the midst of sentences,
Throttle their practis'd accents in their fears,
And, in conclusion, dumbly have broke off,
Not paying me a welcome: Trust me, sweet,
Out of this silence, yet, I pick'd a welcome;
And in the modesty of fearful duty
I read as much, as from the rattling tongue
Of saucy and audacious eloquence.

TIME.

The iron tongue of midnight hath told twelve.

NIGHT.

Now the hungry lion roars,
And the wolf behowls the moon;
Whilst the heavy ploughman snores,
All with weary task fordone *.
Now the wasted brands do glow,
Whilst the scritch-owl, scritching loud,
Puts the wretch that lies in woe,
In remembrance of a shroud.
Now it is the time of night,
That the graves, all gaping wide,
Every one lets forth his sprite,
In the church-way paths to glide.

* Overcome.

MUCH ADO ABOUT NOTHING.

ACT I.

PEACE INSPIRES LOVE.

But now I am return'd, and that war-thoughts
Have left their places vacant, in their rooms
Come thronging soft and delicate desires,
All prompting me how fair young Hero is.
D. Pedro. Thou wilt be like a lover presently,
And tire the hearer with a book of words:
If thou dost love fair Hero, cherish it;
And I will break with her, and with her father,
And thou shalt have her: Was't not to this end,
That thou began'st to twist so fine a story?
Claud. How sweetly do you minister to love,
That know love's grief by his complexion!
But lest my liking might too sudden seem,
I would have salv'd it with a longer treatise.
D. Pedro. What need the bridge much broader than the flood?
The fairest grant is the necessity:
Look, what will serve, is fit: 'tis once*, thou lov'st;
And I will fit thee with the remedy.
I know we shall have reveling to-night;
I will assume thy part in some disguise,
And tell fair Hero I am Claudio;
And in her bosom I'll unclasp my heart.

ACT II.

FRIENDSHIP IN LOVE.

Friendship is constant in all other things,
Save in the office and affairs of love:

* Once for all.

Therefore, all hearts in love use their own tongues;
Let every eye negotiate for itself,
And trust no agent: for beauty is a witch,
Against whose charms faith melteth into blood *.

MERIT ALWAYS MODEST.

It is the witness still of excellency,
To put a strange face on his own perfection.

BENEDICT THE BACHELOR'S RECANTATION.

This can be no trick: The conference was sadly borne †.—They have the truth of this from Hero. They seem to pity the lady; it seems, her affections have their full bent. Love me! why it must be requited. I hear how I am censured: they say, I will bear myself proudly, if I perceive the love come from her; they say too, that she will rather die than give any sign of affection.—I did never think to marry:—I must not seem proud: Happy are they that hear their detractions, and can put them to mending. They say, the lady is fair; 'tis a truth, I can bear them witness: and virtuous;—'tis so, I cannot reprove it; and wise, but for loving me:—By my troth, it is no addition to her wit;—nor no great argument of her folly, for I will be horribly in love with her.—I may chance have some odd quirks and remnants of wit broken on me, because I have railed so long against marriage:—But doth not the appetite alter? A man loves the meat in his youth, that he cannot endure in his age: Shall quips, and sentences, and these paper bullets of the brain, awe a man from the career of his humour? No: The world *must* be peopled. When I said, I would die a bachelor, I did not think I should live till I were married.—Here comes Beatrice: By this day, she's a fair lady: I do spy some marks of love in her.

* Passion. † Seriously carried on.

ACT III.

FAVOURITES COMPARED TO HONEYSUCKLES.

Bid her steal into the pleached bower,
Where honeysuckles, ripen'd by the sun,
Forbid the sun to enter;—like favourites,
Made proud by princes, that advance their pride
Against that power that bred it.

A SCORNFUL AND SATYRICAL BEAUTY.

Disdain and scorn ride sparkling in her eyes,
Misprising * what they look on; and her wit
Values itself so highly, that to her
All matter else seems weak: she cannot love,
Nor take no shape nor project of affection,
She is so self-endeared.
I never yet saw man,
How wise, how noble, young, how rarely featur'd,
But she would spell him backward: if fair-faced,
She'd swear, the gentleman should be her sister;
If black, why, nature, drawing of an antic,
Made a foul blot: if tall, a lance ill headed:
If low, an agate very vilely cut:
If speaking, why, a vane blown with all wind;
If silent, why a block moved with none.
So turns she every man the wrong side out;
And never gives to truth and virtue, that
Which simpleness and merit purchaseth.

ACT IV.

DISSIMULATION.

O, what authority and show of truth
Can cunning sin cover itself withal!
Comes not that blood as modest evidence,
To witness simple virtue? Would you not swear,

* Undervaluing.

All you that see her, that she were a maid,
By these exterior shows? But she is none:
She knows the heat of a luxurious * bed:
Her blush is guiltiness, not modesty.

A FATHER LAMENTING HIS DAUGHTER'S INFAMY.

Griev'd I, I had but one?
Chid I for that at frugal nature's frame †?
O, one too much by thee! Why had I one?
Why ever wast thou lovely in my eyes?
Why had I not, with charitable hand,
Took up a beggar's issue at my gates;
Who smirched ‡ thus, and mired with infamy,
I might have said, *No part of it is mine,*
This shame derives itself from unknown loins?
But mine, and mine I lov'd, and mine I prais'd,
And mine that I was proud on; mine so much,
That I myself was to myself not mine,
Valuing of her; why, she—O, she is fallen
Into a pit of ink! that the wide sea
Hath drops too few to wash her clean again.

INNOCENCE DISCOVERED BY THE COUNTENANCE.

I have mark'd
A thousand blushing apparitions start
Into her face; a thousand innocent shames
In angel whiteness bear away those blushes;
And in her eye there hath appear'd a fire,
To burn the errors that these princes hold
Against her maiden truth.

RESOLUTION.

I know not: If they speak but truth of her,
These hands shall tear her; if they wrong her honour,
The proudest of them shall well hear of it.
Time hath not yet so dried this blood of mine,
Nor age so eat up my invention,
Nor fortune made such havoc of my means,
Nor my bad life reft me so much of friends,

* Lascivious. † Disposition of things. ‡ Sullied.

But they shall find, awak'd in such a kind,
Both strength of limb and policy of mind,
Ability in means, and choice of friends,
To quit me of them throughly.

THE DESIRE OF BELOVED OBJECTS HEIGHTENED BY THEIR LOSS.

For it so falls out,
That what we have we prize not to the worth,
Whiles * we enjoy it; but being lack'd and lost,
Why, then we rack † the value; then we find
The virtue, that possession would not show us
Whiles it was ours:—So will it fare with Claudio:
When he shall hear she died upon ‡ his words,
The idea of her life shall sweetly creep
Into his study of imagination;
And every lovely organ of her life
Shall come apparel'd in more precious habit,
More moving delicate, and full of life,
Into the eye and prospect of his soul,
Than when she liv'd indeed.

TALKING BRAGGARTS.

But manhood is melted into courtesies §, valour into compliment, and men are only turned into tongue, and trim ones too: he is now as valiant as Hercules, that only tells a lie, and swears it.

ACT V.

COUNSEL OF NO WEIGHT IN MISERY.

I pray thee, cease thy counsel,
Which falls into mine ears as profitless
As water in a sieve; give not me counsel;
Nor let no comforter delight mine ear,
But such a one whose wrongs do suit with mine.

* While. † Overrate. ‡ By. § Ceremony.

Bring me a father, that so lov'd his child,
Whose joy of her is overwhelm'd like mine,
And bid him speak of patience;.
Measure his woe the length and breadth of mine,
And let it answer every strain for strain;
As thus for thus, and such a grief for such,
In every lineament, branch, shape and form:
If such a one will smile, and stroke his beard;
Cry—sorrow, wag! and hem, when he should groan;
Patch grief with proverbs; make misfortune drunk
With candle-wasters; bring him yet to me,
And I of him will gather patience.
But there is no such man: For, brother, men
Can counsel, and speak comfort to that grief
Which they themselves not feel; but, tasting it,
Their counsel turns to passion, which before
Would give preceptial medicine to rage,
Fetter strong madness in a silken thread,
Charm ach with air, and agony with words:
No, no; 'tis all men's office to speak patience
To those that wring under the load of sorrow:
But no man's virtue, nor sufficiency,
To be so moral, when he shall endure
The like himself: therefore give me no counsel,
My griefs cry louder than advertisement.

SATIRE ON THE STOIC PHILOSOPHERS.

I pray thee, peace: I will be flesh and blood;
For there was never yet philosopher,
That could endure the tooth-ach patiently;
However they have writ the style of gods,
And made a pish at chance and sufferance.

TALKING BRAGGARTS.

Hold you content: What man! I know them, yea,
And what they weigh, even to the utmost scruple;
Scambling, out-facing, fashion-mong'ring boys,
That lie and cog, and flout, deprave and slander,
Go anticly, and show outward hideousness,
And speak off half a dozen dangerous words,

How they might hurt their enemies, if they durst,
And this is all.

VILLAIN TO BE NOTED.

Which is the villain? Let me see his eyes;
That when I note another man like him,
I may avoid him.

DAYBREAK.

The wolves have prey'd; and look, the gentle day,
Before the wheels of Phœbus, round about
Dapples the drowsy east with spots of gray.

TAMING OF THE SHREW.

INDUCTION.

HOUNDS.

Thy hounds shall make the welkin answer them,
And fetch shrill echoes from the hollow earth.

PAINTING.

Dost thou love pictures? we will fetch thee straight
Adonis painted by a running brook:
And Cytherea all in sedges hid;
Which seem to move and wanton with her breath,
Even as the waving sedges play with wind.

ACT I.

WOMAN'S TONGUE.

Think you, a little din can daunt mine ears?
Have I not in my time heard lions roar?
Have I not heard the sea, puff'd up with winds,
Rage like an angry boar, chafed with sweat?
Have I not heard great ordnance in the field?
And heaven's artillery thunder in the skies?

Have I not in a pitched battle heard
Loud 'larums, neighing steeds, and trumpets' clang?
And do you tell me of a woman's tongue;
That gives not half so great a blow to the ear,
As will a chesnut in a farmer's fire?

ACT III.

A MAD WEDDING.

When the priest
Should ask—if Katherine should be his wife,
Ay, by gogs-wouns, quoth he; and swore so loud,
That, all amaz'd, the priest let fall the book:
And, as he stoop'd again to take it up,
The mad-brain'd bridegroom took him such a cuff,
That down fell priest and book, and book and priest;
Now take them up, quoth he, *if any list*.
Tra. What said the wench, when he arose again?
Gre. Trembled and shook; for why, he stamp'd, and swore,
As if the vicar meant to cozen him.
But after many ceremonies done,
He calls for wine:—*A health*, quoth he; as if
He had been aboard carousing to his mates
After a storm:—Quaff'd off the muscadel*,
And threw the sops all in the sexton's face!
Having no other reason,—
But that his beard grew thin and hungerly,
And seem'd to ask him sops as he was drinking.
This done, he took the bride about the neck;
And kiss'd her lips with such a clamorous smack,
That, at the parting, all the church did echo.

* It was the custom for the company present to drink wine immediately after the marriage ceremony.

ACT IV.

THE MIND ALONE VALUABLE.

For tis the mind that makes the body rich;
And as the sun breaks through the darkest clouds,
So honour peereth * in the meanest habit.
What, is the jay more precious than the lark,
Because his feathers are more beautiful?
Or is the adder better than the eel,
Because his painted skin contents the eye?
O, no, good Kate; neither art thou the worse
For this poor furniture and mean array.

ACT V.

THE WIFE'S DUTY TO HER HUSBAND.

Fie, fie! unknit that threat'ning unkind brow;
And dart not scornful glances from those eyes,
To wound thy lord, thy king, thy governor:
It blots thy beauty, as frosts bite the meads;
Confounds thy fame, as whirlwinds shake fair buds;
And in no sense is meet or amiable.
A woman mov'd, is like a fountain troubled,
Muddy, ill-seeming, thick, bereft of beauty;
And while it is so, none so dry or thirsty
Will deign to sip, or touch one drop of it.
Thy husband is thy lord, thy life, thy keeper,
Thy head, thy sovereign; one that cares for thee,
And for thy maintenance: commits his body
To painful labour, both by sea and land;
To watch the night in storms, the day in cold,
While thou liest warm at home, secure and safe,
And craves no other tribute at thy hands,
But love, fair looks, and true obedience;
Too little payment for so great a debt.
Such duty as the subject owes the prince,
Even such, a woman oweth to her husband:

* Appeareth.

And, when she's froward, peevish, sullen, sour,
And not obedient to his honest will,
What is she, but a foul contending rebel,
And graceless traitor to her loving lord?—
I am asham'd, that women are so simple
To offer war, where they should kneel for peace;
Or seek for rule, supremacy, and sway,
When they are bound to serve, love, and obey.
Why are our bodies soft, and weak, and smooth,
Unapt to toil and trouble in the world;
But that our soft conditions * and our hearts,
Should well agree with our external parts?

TEMPEST.

ACT I.

AN USURPING SUBSTITUTE COMPARED TO IVY.

THAT now he was
The ivy, which had hid my princely trunk,
And suck'd my verdure out on't.

ARIEL'S DESCRIPTION OF MANAGING THE STORM.

I boarded the king's ship; now on the beak,
Now in the waist, the deck, in every cabin,
I flam'd amazement: Sometimes, I'd divide,
And burn in many places; on the topmast,
The yards, and bowsprit, would I flame distinctly,
Then meet, and join: Jove's lightnings, the precursors
O' the dreadful thunder-claps, more momentary
And sight-outrunning were not: The fire and cracks
Of sulphurous roaring, the most mighty Neptune

* Gentle tempers.

Seem'd to besiege, and make his bold waves tremble,
Yea, his dread trident shake.——
——Not a soul,
But felt a fever of the mad, and play'd
Some tricks of desperation: All, but mariners,
Plung'd in the foaming brine, and quit the vessel,
Then all a-fire with me: the king's son, Ferdinand,
With hair up-staring (then like reeds, not hair),
Was the first man that leap'd; cried, *Hell is empty,*
And all the devils are here.

PROSPERO REPROVING ARIEL.

Thou dost; and think'st
It much, to tread the ooze of the salt deep;
To run upon the sharp wind of the north;
To do me business in the veins o'the earth,
When it is bak'd with frost.

CALIBAN'S CURSES.

Cal. As wicked dew as e'er my mother brush'd
With raven's feather from unwholesome fen,
Drop on you both! a south-west blow on ye,
And blister you all o'er!
Pro. For this, be sure, to-night thou shalt have cramps,
Side-stiches that shall pen thy breath up; urchins*
Shall, for that vast of night that they may work,
All exercise on thee: thou shalt be pinch'd
As thick as honeycombs, each pinch more stinging
Than bees that made them.
Cal. I must eat my dinner.
This island's mine, by Sycorax my mother,
Which thou tak'st from me. When thou camest first,
Thou strok'dst me, and mad'st much of me; would'st give me
Water with berries in't; and teach me how
To name the bigger light, and how the less,
That burn by day and night: and then I lov'd thee,
And show'd thee all the qualities o'the isle,

* Fairies.

The fresh springs, brine pits, barren place, and fertile;
Cursed be I that did so!—All the charms
Of Sycorax, toads, beetles, bats, light on you!
For I am all the subjects that you have,
Which first was mine own king: and here you sty me
In this hard rock, whiles you do keep from me
The rest of the island.

CALIBAN'S EXULTATION AFTER PROSPERO TELLS HIM HE SOUGHT TO VIOLATE THE HONOUR OF HIS CHILD.

O ho, O ho!—would it had been done!
Thou didst prevent me; I had peopled else
This isle with Calibans.

MUSIC.

Where should this music be? i'the air, or the earth,
It sounds no more:—and sure it waits upon
Some god of the island. Sitting on a bank,
Weeping again the king my father's wreck,
This music crept by me upon the waters;
Allaying both their fury and my passion,
With its sweet air.

ARIEL'S SONG.

Full fathom five thy father lies;
Of his bones are coral made;
Those are pearls, that were his eyes:
Nothing of him that doth fade,
But doth suffer a sea-change
Into something rich and strange.
Seanymphs hourly wring his knell:
Hark! now I hear them,—ding-dong bell.

A LOVER'S SPEECH.

My spirits, as in a dream, are all bound up.
My father's loss, the weakness which I feel,
The wreck of all my friends, or this man's threats,
To whom I am subdued, are but light to me,
Might I but through my prison once a day

Behold this maid: all corners else o' the earth
Let liberty make use of; space enough
Have I in such a prison.

ACT II.

DESCRIPTION OF FERDINAND'S SWIMMING ASHORE.

I saw him beat the surges under him,
And ride upon their backs; he trod the water,
Whose enmity he flung aside, and breasted
The surge most swoln that met him: his bold head
'Bove the contentious wave he kept, and oar'd
Himself with his good arms in lusty stroke
To the shore, that o'er his wave-worn basis bow'd,
As stooping to relieve him: I not doubt
He came alive to land.

SLEEP.

Do not omit the heavy offer of it:
It seldom visits sorrow; when it doth,
It is a comforter.

A FINE APOSIOPESIS.

They fell together all, as by consent;
They dropp'd, as by a thunder-stroke. What might
Worthy Sebastian?—O, what might?—No more:—
And yet, methinks, I see it in thy face,
What thou should'st be: the occasion speaks thee: and
My strong imagination sees a crown
Dropping upon thy head.

CALIBAN'S CURSES.

All the infections that the sun sucks up
From bogs, fens, flats, on Prosper fall, and make him
By inch-meal a disease! His spirits hear me,
And yet I needs must curse. But they'll nor pinch,
Fright me with urchin shows, pitch me i' the mire,
Nor lead me, like a firebrand, in the dark
Out of my way, unless he bid them; but
For every trifle are they set upon me:

Sometime like apes that moe* and chatter at me,
And after, bite me; then like hedgehogs, which
Lie tumbling in my barefoot way, and mount
Their pricks at my footfall; sometime am I
All wound with adders, who, with cloven tongues,
Do hiss me into madness: Lo! now! lo!
Here comes a spirit of his; and to torment me,
For bringing wood in slowly: I'll fall flat:
Perchance he will not mind me.

SATIRE ON ENGLISH CURIOSITY.

Were I in England now (as once I was), and had but this fish painted, not a holiday fool there but would give a piece of silver: there would this monster make a man; any strange beast there makes a man: when they will not give a doit to relieve a lame beggar, they will lay out ten to see a dead Indian.

CALIBAN'S PROMISES.

I'll show thee the best springs; I'll pluck thee berries;
I'll fish for thee, and get thee wood enough.
A plague upon the tyrant that I serve!
I'll bear him no more sticks, but follow thee,
Thou wondrous man.
I pr'ythee let me bring thee where crabs grow;
And I with my long nails will dig thee pig-nuts;
Show thee a jay's nest, and instruct thee how
To snare the nimble marmozet; I'll bring thee
To clust'ring filberds, and sometimes I'll get thee
Young sea-mells† from the rock.

ACT III.

FERDINAND.

There be some sports are painful; but their labour
Delight in them sets off: some kinds of baseness

* Make mouths. † Seagulls.

Are nobly undergone; and most poor matters
Point to rich ends. This my mean task would be
As heavy to me as tis odious; but
The mistress, which I serve, quickens what's dead,
And makes my labours pleasures: O, she is
Ten times more gentle than her father's crabbed;
And he's composed of harshness. I must remove
Some thousands of these logs, and pile them up,
Upon a sore injunction: My sweet mistress
Weeps when she sees me work: and says, such baseness
Had ne'er like executor. I forget:
But these sweet thoughts do even refresh my labours;
Most busyless, when I do it.

Enter MIRANDA; *and* PROSPERO *at a distance.*

Mira. Alas, now! pray you,
Work not so hard: I would, the lightning had
Burnt up those logs, that you are enjoin'd to pile!
Pray, set it down, and rest you: when this burns,
'Twill weep for having wearied you: My father
Is hard at study; pray now, rest yourself;
He's safe for these three hours.

Fer. O most dear mistress,
The sun will set, before I shall discharge
What I must strive to do.

Mira. If you'll sit down,
I'll bear your logs the while; Pray give me that;
I'll carry it to the pile.

Fer. No, precious creature:
I had rather crack my sinews, break my back,
Than you should such dishonour undergo,
While I sit lazy by.

Mira. It would become me
As well as it does you: and I should do it
With much more ease; for my good will is to it,
And yours against.

Pro. Poor worm! thou art infected;
This visitation shows it.

Mira. You look wearily.

Fer. No, noble mistress; 'tis fresh morning with me,
When you are by at night. I do beseech you,
(Chiefly that I might set it in prayers),
What is your name?

Mira. Miranda:—O my father,
I have broke your best* to say so!

Fer. Admir'd Miranda!
Indeed the top of admiration; worth
What's dearest to the world! Full many a lady
I have ey'd with best regard; and many a time
The harmony of their tongues hath into bondage
Brought my too diligent ear; for several virtues
Have I lik'd several women; never any
With so full soul, but some defect in her
Did quarrel with the noblest grace she ow'd†,
And put it to the foil: But you, O you,
So perfect and so peerless, are created
Of every creature's best.

Mira. I do not know
One of my sex; no woman's face remember,
Save, from my glass, mine own; nor have I seen
More that I may call men, than you, good friend,
And my dear father; how features are abroad,
I am skill-less of; but, by my modesty
(The jewel in my dower), I would not wish
Any companion in the world but you;
Nor can imagination form a shape,
Besides yourself, to like of: but I prattle
Something too wildly, and my father's precepts
Therein forget.

Fer. I am, in my condition,
A prince, Miranda; I do think, a king:
(I would, not so!) and would no more endure
This wooden slavery, than I would suffer
The flesh-fly blow my mouth,—Hear my soul speak;—
The very instant that I saw you, did
My heart fly to your service; there resides,
To make me slave to it; and, for your sake,
Am I this patient log-man.

* Command. † Own'd.

Mira. Do you love me?

Fer. O heaven, O earth, bear witness to this sound,
And crown what I profess with kind event,
If I speak true; if hollowly, invert
What best is boded me, to mischief! I,
Beyond all limit of what else* i' the world,
Do love, prize, honour you.

Mira. I am a fool,
To weep at what I am glad of.

Pro. Fair encounter
Of two most rare affections! Heavens rain grace
On that which breeds between them!

Fer. Wherefore weep you?

Mira. At mine unworthiness, that dare not offer
What I desire to give; and much less take,
What I shall die to want: But this is trifling;
And all the more it seeks to hide itself,
The bigger bulk it shows. Hence, bashful cunning,
And prompt me, plain and holy innocence!
I am your wife, if you will marry me;
If not, I'll die your maid: to be your fellow
You may deny me: but I'll be your servant,
Whether you will or no.

Fer. My mistress, dearest,
And I thus humble ever.

Mira. My husband then?

Fer. Ay, with a heart as willing
As bondage e'er of freedom: here's my hand.

Mira. And mine, with my heart in't; And now farewell,
Till half an hour hence.

Fer. A thousand! thousand!

A GUILTY CONSCIENCE.

O, it is monstrous! monstrous!
Methought, the billows spoke and told me of it;
The winds did sing it to me; and the thunder,
That deep and dreadful organ-pipe, pronounc'd
The name of Prosper.

* Whatsoever.

ACT IV.

CONTINENCE BEFORE MARRIAGE.

If thou dost break her virgin knot before
All sanctimonious ceremonies may
With full and holy rite be minister'd,
No sweet aspersion * shall the heavens let fall
To make this contract grow; but barren hate,
Sour-ey'd disdain, and discord, shall bestrew
The union of your bed with weeds so loathly,
That you shall hate it both.

A LOVER'S PROTESTATION.

As I hope
For quiet days, fair issue, and long life,
With such love as 'tis now; the murkiest den,
The most opportune place, the strong'st suggestion,
Our worser genius can, shall never melt
Mine honour into lust; to take away
The edge of that day's celebration,
When I shall think, or Phœbus' steeds are founder'd,
Or night kept chain'd below.

PASSION TOO STRONG FOR VOWS.

Look thou be true; do not give dalliance
Too much the rein; the strongest oaths are straw
To the fire i' the blood: be more abstemious,
Or else, good night, your vow!

VANITY OF HUMAN NATURE.

These our actors,
As I foretold you, were all spirits, and
Are melted into air, into thin air:
And, like the baseless fabric of this vision,
The cloud-capp'd towers, the gorgeous palaces,
The solemn temples, the great globe itself,
Yea, all which it inherit shall dissolve;
And, like this insubstantial pageant faded †,

* Sprinkling. † Vanished.

Leave not a rack * behind: We are such stuff
As dreams are made of, and our little life
Is rounded with a sleep.

DRUNKARDS ENCHANTED BY ARIEL.

I told you, sir, they were red-hot with drinking;
So full of valour, that they smote the air
For breathing in their faces; beat the ground
For kissing of their feet; yet always bending
Towards their project; Then I beat my tabor,
At which, like unback'd colts, they prick'd their ears,
Advanc'd their eyelids, lifted up their noses,
As they smelt music; so I charm'd their ears,
That, calf-like, they my lowing follow'd, through
Tooth'd briers, sharp furzes, pricking goss, and thorns,
Which enter'd their frail shins: at last I left them
I' the filthy mantled pool beyond your cell,
There dancing up to the chins.

LIGHTNESS OF FOOT.

Pray you, tread softly, that the blind mole may not
Hear a foot fall.

ACT V.

TEARS.

His tears run down his beard, like winter's drops
From eaves † of reeds.

COMPASSION AND CLEMENCY SUPERIOR TO REVENGE.

Hast thou, which art but air, a touch, a feeling
Of their afflictions? and shall not myself,
One of their kind, that relish all as sharply,
Passion as they, be kindlier mov'd than thou art?
Though with their high wrongs I am struck to the quick,

* A body of clouds in motion; but it is most probable that the author wrote *track*.

† Thatch.

Yet, with my nobler reason, 'gainst my fury
Do I take part: the rarer action is
In virtue than in vengeance: they being penitent,
The sole drift of my purpose doth extend
Not a frown further.

FAIRIES AND MAGIC.

Ye elves of hills, brooks, standing lakes, and groves;
And ye, that on the sands, with printless foot
Do chase the ebbing Neptune, and do fly him,
When he comes back; you demi-puppets, that
By moonshine do the green-sour ringlets make,
Whereof the ewe not bites; and you, whose pastime
Is to make midnight mushrooms; that rejoice
To hear the solemn curfew; by whose aid
(Weak masters though you be) I have be-dimm'd
The noontide sun, call'd forth the mutinous winds,
And 'twixt the green sea and the azur'd vault
Set roaring war: to the dread rattling thunder
Have I given fire, and rifted Jove's stout oak
With his own bolt: the strong-bas'd promontory
Have I made shake; and by the spurs pluck'd up
The pine, and cedar: graves, at my command,
Have wak'd their sleepers; op'd, and let them forth
By my so potent art.

SENSES RETURNING.

The charm dissolves apace,
And as the morning steals upon the night,
Melting the darkness, so their rising senses
Begin to chase the ignorant fumes that mantle
Their clearer reason.—O my good Gonzalo,
My true preserver, and a loyal sir
To him thou follow'st; I will pay thy graces
Home, both in word and deed.—Most cruelly
Didst thou, Alonzo, use me and my daughter:
Thy brother was a furtherer in the act:—
Thou'rt pinch'd for't now, Sebastian.—Flesh and blood,
You brother mine, that entertain'd ambition,

Expell'd remorse* and nature; who with Sebastian
(Whose inward pinches therefore are most strong),
Would here have kill'd our king; I do forgive thee,
Unnatural though thou art!—Their understanding
Begins to swell; and the approaching tide
Will shortly fill the reasonable shores,
That now lie foul and muddy. Not one of them,
That yet looks on me, or would know me.

ARIEL'S SONG.

Where the bee sucks, there suck I;
In a cowslip's bell I lie:
There I couch when owls do cry.
On the bat's back, I do fly,
After summer, merrily:
Merrily, merrily, shall I live now,
Under the blossom that hangs on the bough.

TWELFTH NIGHT.

ACT I.

MUSIC.

If music be the food of love, play on,
Give me excess of it; that, surfeiting,
The appetite may sicken, and so die.——
That strain again; it had a dying fall:
O, it came o'er my ear like the sweet south,
That breathes upon a bank of violets,
Stealing and giving odour.

NATURAL AFFECTION ALLIED TO LOVE.

O, she, that hath a heart of that fine frame,
To pay this debt of love but to a brother,

* Pity, or tenderness of heart.

How will she love, when the rich golden shaft,
Hath kill'd the flock of all affections else
That live in her! when liver, brain, and heart,
These sovereign thrones, are all supplied, and fill'd,
(Her sweet perfections) with one self king!

ESCAPE FROM DANGER.

I saw your brother,
Most provident in peril, bind himself
(Courage and hope both teaching him the practice)
To a strong mast, that lived upon the sea;
Where, like Arion on the dolphin's back,
I saw him hold acquaintance with the wave,
So long as I could see.

A BEAUTIFUL BOY.

Dear lad, believe it;
For they shall yet belie thy happy years
That say, thou art a man: Diana's lip
Is not more smooth, and rubious; thy small pipe
Is as the maiden's organ, shrill, and sound,
And all is semblative a woman's part.

DETERMINED LOVE.

Oli. Why, what would you?
Vio. Make me a willow cabin at your gate,
And call upon my soul within the house;
Write loyal cantons * of contemned love,
And sing them loud even in the dead of night:
Holla your name to the reverberate † hills,
And make the babbling gossip of the air
Cry out, Olivia! O, you should not rest
Between the elements of air and earth,
But you should pity me.

* Cantos, verses. † Echoing.

ACT II.

DISGUISE.

Disguise, I see thou art a wickedness,
Wherein the pregnant* enemy does much.
How easy is it, for the proper-false†
In women's waxen hearts to set their forms!
Alas, our frailty is the cause, not we;
For such as we are made of, such we be.

TRUE LOVE.

Come hither, boy: If ever thou shalt love,
In the sweet pangs of it, remember me:
For, such as I am, all true lovers are;
Unstaid and skittish in all motions else,
Save, in the constant image of the creature
That is belov'd.

THE WOMAN SHOULD BE YOUNGEST IN LOVE.

Too old, by heaven; Let still the woman take
An elder than herself; so wears she to him,
So sways she level in her husband's heart.
For, boy, however we do praise ourselves,
Our fancies are more giddy and unfirm,
More longing, wavering, sooner lost and worn,
Than women's are.

CHARACTER OF AN OLD SONG.

Mark it, Cesario; it is old and plain:
The spinsters and the knitters in the sun,
And the free maids, that weave their thread with bones‡,
Do use to chant it; it is silly sooth§,
And dallies with the innocence of love,
Like the old age||.

* Dexterous, ready fiend.
† Fair deceiver.
‡ Lace-makers.
§ Simple truth.
|| Times of simplicity.

SONG.

Come away, come away, death,
And in sad cypress let me be laid;
Fly away, fly away, breath:
I am slain by a fair cruel maid.
My shroud of white, stuck all with yew,
O, prepare it;
My part of death no one so true
Did share it.

Not a flower, not a flower sweet,
On my black coffin let there be strown;
Not a friend, not a friend greet
My poor corpse where my bones shall be thrown;
A thousand thousand sighs to save,
Lay me, O, where
Sad true lover ne'er find my grave,
To weep there.

CONCEALED LOVE.

She never told her love,
But let concealment, like a worm i' the bud,
Feed on her damask cheek: she pin'd in thought;
And, with a green and yellow melancholy,
She sat like patience on a monument,
Smiling at grief.

ACT III.

JESTER.

This fellow's wise enough to play the fool;
And, to do that well, craves a kind of wit:
He must observe their mood on whom he jests,
The quality of persons, and the time;
And, like the haggard*, check at every feather
That comes before his eye. This is a practice,

* A hawk not well trained.

As full of labour as a wise man's art:
For folly, that he wisely shows, is fit;
But wise men, folly-fallen, quite taint their wit.

UNSOUGHT LOVE.

Cesario, by the roses of the spring,
By maidhood, honour, truth, and every thing,
I love thee so, that, maugre * all thy pride,
Nor wit, nor reason, can my passion hide.
Do not extort thy reasons from this clause,
For, that I woo, thou therefore hast no cause:
But, rather, reason thus with reason fetter:
Love sought is good, but given unsought is better.

TWO GENTLEMEN OF VERONA.

ACT I.

LOVE COMMENDED AND CENSURED.

Yet writers say, As in the sweetest bud,
The eating canker dwells, so eating love
Inhabits in the finest wits of all.
And writers say, As the most forward bud
Is eaten by the canker ere it blow,
Even so by love the young and tender wit
Is turn'd to folly; blasting in the bud,
Losing his verdure even in the prime,
And all the fair effects of future hopes.

LOVE FROWARD AND DISSEMBLING.

Maids, in modesty, say *No*, to that
Which they would have the profferer construe, *Ay*.
Fie, fie, how wayward is this foolish love,
That, like a testy babe, will scratch the nurse,
And presently, all humbled, kiss the rod!

* In spite of.

ADVANTAGE OF TRAVELLING.

He cannot be a perfect man,
Not being tried and tutor'd in the world:
Experience is by industry achiev'd,
And perfected by the swift course of time.

LOVE COMPARED TO AN APRIL DAY.

O, how this spring of love resembleth
The uncertain glory of an April day;
Which now shows all the beauty of the sun,
And by a by a cloud takes all away!

ACT II.

HUMOROUS DESCRIPTION OF A MAN IN LOVE.

Marry, by these special marks: First, you have learned, like sir Proteus, to wreath your arms like a male-content: to relish a lovesong, like a robin-redbreast; to walk alone, like one that had the pestilence; to sigh, like a school-boy that had lost his A, B, C; to weep, like a young wench that had buried her grandam; to fast, like one that takes diet*; to watch, like one that fears robbing; to speak puling, like a beggar at Hallowmas†. You were wont, when you laughed, to crow like a cock; when you walked, to walk like one of the lions; when you fasted, it was presently after dinner; when you looked sadly, it was for want of money: and now you are metamorphosed with a mistress, that, when I look on you, I can hardly think you my master.

AN ACCOMPLISHED YOUNG GENTLEMAN.

His years but young, but his experience old;
His head unmellow'd, but his judgment ripe;
And, in a word (for far behind his worth
Come all the praises that I now bestow),

* Under a regimen. † Allhallowmas

He is complete in feature, and in mind,
With all good grace to grace a gentleman.

CONTEMPT OF LOVE PUNISHED.

I have done penance for contemning love;
Whose high imperious thoughts have punished me
With bitter fasts, with penitential groans,
With nightly tears, and daily heartsore sighs;
For, in revenge of my contempt of love,
Love hath chas'd sleep from my enthralled eyes,
And made them watchers of mine own heart's sorrow.
O, gentle Proteus, love's a mighty lord;
And hath so humbled me, as I confess,
There is no woe to his correction,
Nor, to his service, no such joy on earth!
Now, no discourse, except it be of love;
Now can I break my fast, dine, sup, and sleep,
Upon the very naked name of love.

LOVE COMPARED TO A WAXEN IMAGE.

For now my love is thaw'd;
Which, like a waxen image 'gainst a fire,
Bears no impression of the thing it was.

LOVE INCREASED BY ATTEMPTS TO SUPPRESS IT.

Didst thou but know the inly touch of love,
Thou wouldst as soon go kindle fire with snow,
As seek to quench the fire of love with words.
Luc. I do not seek to quench your love's hot fire;
But qualify the fire's extreme rage,
Lest it should burn above the bounds of reason.
Jul. The more thou dam'st* it up, the more it burns;
The current, that with gentle murmur glides,
Thou know'st, being stopp'd, impatiently doth rage;
But, when his fair course is not hindered,
He makes sweet music with the enamel'd stones,
Giving a gentle kiss to every sedge

* Closest.

He overtaketh in his pilgrimage;
And so by many winding nooks he strays,
With willing sport to the wild ocean.
Then let me go, and hinder not my course:
I'll be as patient as a gentle stream,
And make a pastime of each weary step,
Till the last step have brought me to my love;
And, there I'll rest, as, after much turmoil*,
A blessed soul doth in Elysium.

A FAITHFUL AND CONSTANT LOVER.

His words are bonds, his oaths are oracles;
His love sincere, his thoughts immaculate;
His tears, pure messengers sent from his heart;
His heart as far from fraud as heaven from earth.

ACT III.

PRESENTS PREVAIL WITH WOMAN.

Win her with gifts, if she respect not words;
Dumb jewels often, in their silent kind,
More than quick words do move a woman's mind.

A LOVER'S BANISHMENT.

And why not death, rather than living torment?
To die, is to be banish'd from myself;
And Silvia is myself: banish'd from her,
Is self from self; a deadly banishment!
What light is light, if Silvia be not seen?
What joy is joy, if Silvia be not by?
Unless it be to think that she is by,
And feed upon the shadow of perfection.
Except I be by Silvia in the night,
There is no music in the nightingale;
Unless I look on Silvia in the day,
There is no day for me to look upon.

* Trouble.

BEAUTY PETITIONING IN VAIN.

Ay, ay; and she hath offer'd to the doom
(Which, unreserv'd, stands in effectual force),
A sea of melting pearl, which some call tears:
Those at her father's churlish feet she tender'd;
With them, upon her knees, her humble self;
Wringing her hands, whose whiteness so became them,
As if but now they waxed pale for woe:
But neither bended knees, pure hands held up,
Sad sighs, deep groans, nor silver-shedding tears,
Could penetrate her uncompassionate sire.

HOPE.

Hope is a lover's staff; walk hence with that,
And manage it against despairing thoughts.

LOVE COMPARED TO A FIGURE ON ICE.

This weak impress of love is as a figure
Trenched * in ice; which with an hour's heat
Dissolves to water, and doth lose his form.

THREE THINGS IN MAN DISLIKED BY FEMALES.

The best way is to slander Valentine
With falsehood, cowardice, and poor descent;
Three things that women highly hold in hate.

THE POWER OF POETRY WITH FEMALES.

Say, that upon the altar of her beauty
You sacrifice your tears, your sighs, your heart:
Write till your ink be dry; and with your tears
Moist it again; and frame some feeling line,
That may discover such integrity:—
For Orpheus' lute was strung with poets' sinews;
Whose golden touch could soften steel and stones,
Make tigers tame, and huge leviathans
Forsake unsounded deeps to dance on sands.

* Cut.

ACT IV.

THE POWER OF ACTION.

At that time I made her weep a-good *,
For I did play a lamentable part:
Madam, 'twas Ariadne, passioning
For Theseus perjury, and unjust flight;
Which I so lively acted with my tears,
That my poor mistress, moved therewithal,
Wept bitterly; and, would I might be dead,
If I in thought felt not her very sorrow!

ACT V.

A LOVER IN SOLITUDE.

How use doth breed a habit in a man!
This shadowy desert, unfrequented woods,
I better brook than flourishing peopled towns:
Here can I sit alone, unseen of any,
And, to the nightingale's complaining notes,
Tune my distresses, and record † my woes.
O thou that dost inhabit in my breast,
Leave not the mansion so long tenantless;
Lest, growing ruinous, the building fall,
And leave no memory of what it was!
Repair me with thy presence, Silvia;
Thou gentle nymph, cherish thy forlorn swain!

LOVE UNRETURNED.

What dangerous action, stood it next to death,
Would I not undergo for one calm look?
O, 'tis the curse in love, and still approv'd ‡,
When women cannot love where they're belov'd.

* In good earnest. † Sing.
‡ Felt, experienced.

INFIDELITY IN A FRIEND.

Who should be trusted now, when one's right hand
Is perjur'd to the bosom? Proteus,
I am sorry, I must never trust thee more,
But count the world a stranger for thy sake.
The private wound is deepest.

REPENTANCE.

Who by repentance is not satisfied,
Is nor of heaven, nor earth.

INCONSTANCY IN MAN.

O heaven! were man
But constant, he were perfect: that one error
Fills him with faults.

WINTER'S TALE.

ACT I.

YOUTHFUL INNOCENCE.

We were, fair queen,
Two lads, that thought there was no more behind,
But such a day to-morrow as to-day,
And to be boy eternal.
We were as twinn'd lambs, that did frisk i' the sun,
And bleat the one at the other: what we chang'd,
Was innocence for innocence; we knew not
The doctrine of ill-doing, no, nor dream'd
That any did: Had we pursued that life,
And our weak spirits ne'er been higher rear'd
With stronger blood, we should have answer'd heaven

Boldly, *Not guilty*; the imposition clear'd,
Hereditary ours *.

FONDNESS OF A FATHER FOR HIS CHILD.

Leon. Are you so fond of your young prince as we
Do seem to be of ours?
Pol. If at home, sir,
He's all my exercise, my mirth, my matter:
Now my sworn friend, and then mine enemy:
My parasite, my soldier, statesman, all:
He makes a July's day short as December;
And, with his varying childness cures in me
Thoughts that would thick my blood.

JEALOUSY.

Is whispering nothing?
Is leaning cheek to cheek? is meeting noses?
Kissing with inside lip? stopping the career
Of laughter with a sigh? (a note infallible
Of breaking honesty:) horsing foot on foot?
Skulking in corners? wishing clocks more swift?
Hours, minutes? noon, midnight? and all eyes blind
With the pin and web †, but theirs, theirs only,
That would unseen be wicked? is this nothing?
Why, then the world, and all that's in't, is nothing;
The covering sky is nothing; Bohemia nothing;
My wife is nothing; nor nothing have these nothings,
If this be nothing.

REGICIDES DETESTABLE.

To do this deed,
Promotion follows: If I could find example
Of thousands that had struck anointed kings,
And flourish'd after, I'd not do't: but since
Nor brass nor stone, nor parchment, bears not one,
Let villany itself forswear't.

* Setting aside original sin. † Disorders of the eye.

ACT II.

KNOWLEDGE SOMETIMES HURTFUL.

There may be in the cup
A spider* steep'd, and one may drink; depart,
And yet partake no venom; for his knowledge
Is not infected: but if one present
The abhorr'd ingredient to his eye, make known
How he hath drank, he cracks his gorge, his sides,
With violent hefts †.

ELOQUENCE OF SILENT INNOCENCE.

The silence often of pure innocence
Persuades, when speaking fails.

EXPOSING AN INFANT.

Come on, poor babe:
Some powerful spirit instruct the kites and ravens,
To be thy nurses! Wolves, and bears, they say,
Casting their savageness aside, have done
Like offices of pity.

ACT III.

INNOCENCE.

Innocence shall make
False accusation blush, and tyranny
Tremble at patience.

DESPAIR OF PARDON.

But, O thou tyrant!
Do not repent these things; for they are heavier
Than all thy woes can stir; therefore betake thee
To nothing but despair. A thousand knees
Ten thousand years together, naked, fasting,

* Spiders were esteemed poisonous in our author's time.
† Heavings.

Upon a barren mountain, and still winter
In storm perpetual, could not move the gods
To look that way thou wert.

DESCRIPTION OF A GHOST APPEARING IN A DREAM.

I have heard (but not believ'd) the spirits of the dead
May walk again: if such thing be, thy mother
Appear'd to me last night; for ne'er was dream
So like a waking. To me comes a creature,
Sometimes her head on one side, some another;
I never saw a vessel of like sorrow,
So fill'd, and so becoming: in pure white robes,
Like very sanctity, she did approach
My cabin where I lay: thrice bow'd before me:
And, gasping to begin some speech, her eyes
Became two spouts: the fury spent, anon
Did this break from her: *Good Antigonus,*
Since fate, against thy better disposition,
Hath made thy person for the thrower-out
Of my poor babe, according to thine oath,—
Places remote enough are in Bohemia,
There weep, and leave it crying; and, for the babe
Is counted lost for ever, Perdita,
I pr'ythee call't; for this ungentle business,
Put on thee by my lord, thou ne'er shalt see
Thy wife Paulina more:—and so, with shrieks,
She melted into air. Affrighted much,
I did in time collect myself; and thought
This was so, and no slumber. Dreams are toys:
Yet for this once, yea, superstitiously,
I will be squar'd by this.

THE INFANT EXPOSED.

Poor wretch,
That, for thy mother's fault, art thus expos'd
To loss, and what may follow!—Weep I cannot,
But my heart bleeds: and most accurs'd am I,
To be by oath enjoin'd to this.—Farewell!
The day frowns more and more; thou art like to have
A lullaby too rough.

A CLOWN'S DESCRIPTION OF A WRECK.

I would you did but see how it chafes, how it rages, how it takes up the shore! but that's not to the point: O, the most piteous cry of the poor souls! sometimes to see 'em, and not to see 'em: now the ship boring the moon with her mainmast; and anon, swallowed with yest and froth, as you'd thrust a cork into a hogshead. And then for the land service,—To see how the bear tore out his shoulder-bone; how he cried to me for help, and said, his name was Antigonus, a nobleman: But to make an end of the ship:—to see how the sea flap-dragoned* it:—but, first, how the poor souls roared, and the sea mocked them;—and how the poor gentleman roared, and the bear mocked him, both roaring louder than the sea, or weather.

ACT IV.

A GARLAND FOR OLD MEN.

Reverend sirs,
For you there's rosemary, and rue; these keep
Seeming, and savour†, all the winter long;
Grace, and remembrance, be to you both,
And welcome to our shearing!

NATURE AND ART.

Per. Sir, the year growing ancient,—
Not yet on summer's death, nor on the birth
Of trembling winter,—the fairest flowers o' the season
Are our carnations, and streak'd gillyflowers,
Which some call nature's bastards: of that kind
Our rustic garden's barren; and I care not
To get slips of them.
Pol. Wherefore, gentle maiden,
Do you neglect them?

* Swallowed. † Likeness and smell.

Per. For* I have heard it said,
There is an art, which, in their piedness, shares
With great creating nature.
Pol. Say, there be;
Yet nature is made better by no mean,
But nature makes that mean: so, o'er that art,
Which, you say, adds to nature, is an art
That nature makes. You see, sweet maid, we marry
A gentler scion to the wildest stock;
And make conceive a bark of baser kind
By bud of nobler race; This is an art
Which does mend nature,—change it rather: but
The art itself is nature.

A GARLAND FOR MIDDLE-AGED MEN.

I'll not put
The dibble † in earth to set one slip of them;
No more than, were I painted, I would wish
This youth should say, 'twere well; and only therefore
Desire to breed by me.—Here's flowers for you;
Hot lavender, mints, savory, marjoram;
The marigold, that goes to bed with the sun,
And with him rises weeping; these are flowers
Of middle summer, and, I think, they are given
To men of middle age.

A GARLAND FOR YOUNG MEN.

Cam. I should leave grazing, were I of your flock,
And only live by gazing.
Per. Out, alas!
You'd be so lean, that blasts of January
Would blow you through and through.—Now, my fairest friend,
I would I had some flowers o' the spring, that might
Become your time of day; and yours, and yours;
That wear upon your virgin branches yet
Your maidenheads growing:—O Proserpina,
For the flowers now, that, frighted, thou let'st fall

* Because that. † A tool to set plants.

From Dis's* waggon! daffodils,
That come before the swallow dares, and take
The winds of March with beauty; violets dim,
But sweeter than the lids of Juno's eyes,
Or Cytherea's breath; pale primroses,
That die unmarried, ere they can behold
Bright Phœbus in his strength, a malady
Most incident to maids; bold oxlips, and
The crown-imperial; liles of all kinds,
The flower-de-luce being one! O, these I lack,
To make you garlands of; and, my sweet friend,
To strew him o'er and o'er.

A LOVER'S COMMENDATION.

What you do,
Still betters what is done. When you speak, sweet,
I'd have you do it ever: when you sing,
I'd have you buy and sell so; so give alms;
Pray so; and, for the ordering your affairs,
To sing them too: When you do dance, I wish you
A wave o' the sea, that you might ever do
Nothing but that; move still, still so, and own
No other function: Each your doing,
So singular in each particular,
Crowns what you are doing in the present deeds,
That all your acts are queens.

TRUE LOVE.

He says, he loves my daughter:
I think so too; for never gaz'd the moon
Upon the water, as he'll stand, and read,
As 'twere, my daughter's eyes: and, to be plain,
I think there is not half a kiss to choose,
Who loves another best.

PRESENTS LIGHTLY REGARDED BY REAL LOVERS.

Pol. How now, fair shepherd?
Your heart is full of something, that does take
Your mind from feasting. Sooth, when I was young,
And handed love, as you do, I was wont

* Pluto.

To load my she with knacks: I would have ransack'd
The pedlar's silken treasury, and have pour'd it
To her acceptance: you have let him go,
And nothing marted * with him: if your lass
Interpretation should abuse; and call this
Your lack of love, or bounty: you were straited †
For a reply, at least, if you make a care
Of happy holding her.

Flo. Old sir, I know
She prizes not such trifles as these are:
The gifts, she looks from me, are pack'd and lock'd
Up in my heart; which I have given already,
But not deliver'd.—O, hear me breathe my life
Before this ancient sir, who, it should seem,
Hath sometime lov'd: I take thy hand; this hand,
As soft as dove's down, and as white as it;
Or Ethiopian's tooth, or the fann'd snow,
That's bolted ‡ by the northern blasts twice o'er.

A FATHER THE BEST GUEST AT HIS SON'S NUPTIALS.

Pol. Methinks, a father
Is, at the nuptial of his son, a guest
That best becomes the table. Pray you, once more:
Is not your father grown incapable
Of reasonable affairs? is he not stupid
With age, and altering rheums? Can he speak? hear?
Know man from man? dispute his own estate §?
Lies he not bedrid? and again does nothing,
But what he did being childish?

Flo. No, good sir:
He has his health, and ampler strength, indeed,
Than most have of his age.

Pol. By my white beard,
You offer him, if this be so, a wrong
Something unfilial: Reason, my son,
Should choose himself a wife; but as good reason,
The father (all whose joy is nothing else

* Bought, trafficked. † Put to difficulties.

‡ The sieve used to separate flour from bran is called a bolting-cloth. § Talk over his affairs.

But fair posterity), should hold some counsel
In such a business.

RURAL SIMPLICITY.

I was not much afeard: for once, or twice,
I was about to speak;—and tell him plainly,
The selfsame sun, that shines upon his court,
Hides not his visage from our cottage, but
Looks on alike.

LOVE CEMENTED BY PROSPERITY, BUT LOOSENED BY ADVERSITY.

Prosperity's the very bond of love;
Whose fresh complexion and whose heart together
Affliction alters.

ACT V.

WONDER PROCEEDING FROM SUDDEN JOY.

There was speech in their dumbness, language in their very gesture: they looked, as they had heard of a world ransomed, or one destroyed: A notable passion of wonder appear'd in them: but the wisest beholder, that knew no more but seeing, could not say, if the importance* were joy, or sorrow: but in the extremity of the one, it must needs be.

A STATUE.

What was he, that did make it?—See, my lord,
Would you not deem, it breath'd? and that those veins
Did verily bear blood?
Pol. Masterly done:
The very life seems warm upon her lip.
Leon. The fixure of her eye has motion in't†
As‡ we are mock'd with art.

* The thing imported.
† *i. e.* Though her eye be fixed, it seems to have motion in it.
‡ As if.

Still, methinks
There is an air comes from her; What fine chisel
Could ever yet cut breath? Let no man mock me,
For I will kiss her.

A WIDOW COMPARED TO A TURTLE.

I, an old turtle,
Will wing me to some wither'd bow; and there
My mate, that's never to be found again,
Lament till I am lost.

THE

Beauties of Shakspeare.

PART II.

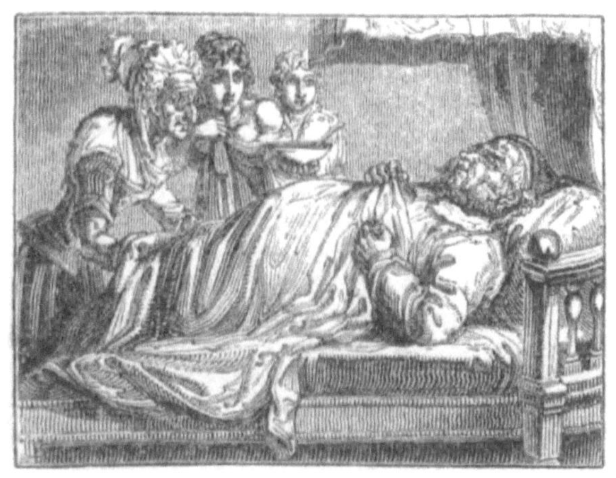

HISTORICAL PLAYS.

CHRONOLOGICALLY ARRANGED.

KING JOHN.

ACT I.

NEW TITLES.

GOOD *den* *, *sir Richard,—God-a-mercy, fellow;*—
And if his name be George, I'll call him Peter:
For new-made honour doth forget men's names;
'Tis too respective †, and too sociable,
For your conversion ‡. Now your traveller,—
He and his tooth-pick at my worship's mess;
And when my knightly stomach is suffic'd,
Why then I suck my teeth, and catechise
My picked man of countries §:——*My dear sir,*
(Thus, leaning on mine elbow, I begin),
I shall beseech you—That is question now:
And then comes answer like an ABC-book ‖:—
O sir, says answer, *at your best command;*
At your employment; at your service, sir:——
No, sir, says question, *I, sweet sir, at yours:*
And so, ere answer knows what question would
(Saving in dialogue of compliment;
And talking of the Alps, and Apennines,
The Pyrenean, and the river Po),
It draws toward supper in conclusion so.
But this is worshipful society,
And fits the mounting spirit, like myself:
For he is but a bastard to the time,
That doth not smack of observation.

* Good evening.
† Respectable.
‡ Change of condition.
§ My traveled fop.
‖ Catechism.

ACT II.

DESCRIPTION OF ENGLAND.

That pale, that white-fac'd shore,
Whose foot spurns back the ocean's roaring tides,
And coops from other lands her islanders,
Even till that England, hedg'd in with the main,
That water-walled bulwark, still secure
And confident from foreign purposes,
Even till that utmost corner of the west
Salute thee for her king.

DESCRIPTION OF AN ENGLISH ARMY.

His marches are expedient * to this town,
His forces strong, his soldiers confident.
With him along is come the mother-queen,
An Ate †, stirring him to blood and strife;
With her her niece, the lady Blanch of Spain;
With them a bastard of the king deceas'd:
And all the unsettled humours of the land,—
Rash, inconsiderate, fiery voluntaries,
With ladies' faces, and fierce dragons' spleens,—
Have sold their fortunes at their native homes,
Bearing their birthrights proudly on their backs,
To make a hazard of new fortunes here,
In brief, a braver choice of dauntless spirits,
Than now the English bottoms have waft o'er,
Did never float upon the swelling tide,
To do offence and scath ‡ in Christendom.
The interruption of their churlish drums
Cuts off more circumstance: they are at hand.

COURAGE.

By how much unexpected, by so much
We must awake endeavour for defence:
For courage mounteth with occasion.

A BOASTER.

What cracker is this same, that deafs our ears
With this abundance of superfluous breath?

* Immediate, expeditious. † The Goddess of Revenge.
‡ Mischief.

DESCRIPTION OF VICTORY BY THE FRENCH.

You men of Angiers, open wide your gates,
And let young Arthur, duke of Bretagne, in;
Who, by the hand of France, this day hath made
Much work for tears in many an English mother,
Whose sons lie scatter'd on the bleeding ground:
Many a widow's husband groveling lies,
Coldly embracing the discolour'd earth;
And victory, with little loss, doth play
Upon the dancing banners of the French;
Who are at hand, triumphantly display'd,
To enter conquerors.

VICTORY DESCRIBED BY THE ENGLISH.

Rejoice, you men of Angiers, ring your bells;
King John, your king and England's doth approach,
Commander of this hot malicious day!
Their armours, that march'd hence so silver bright,
Hither return all gilt with Frenchmen's blood;
There stuck no plume in any English crest,
That is removed by a staff of France;
Our colours do return in those same hands
That did display them when we first march'd forth;
And, like a jolly troop of huntsmen, come
Our lusty English, all with purpled hands,
Dyed in the dying slaughter of their foes.

A COMPLETE LADY.

If lusty love should go in quest of beauty,
Where should he find it fairer than in Blanch?
If zealous* love should go in search of virtue,
Where should he find it purer than in Blanch?
If love ambitious sought a match of birth,
Whose veins bound richer blood than lady Blanch?

POWERFUL EFFECTS OF SELF-INTEREST.

Rounded † in the ear
With that same purpose-changer, that sly devil;
That broker, that still breaks the pate of faith;

* Pious. † Conspired.

That daily break-vow; he that wins of all,
Of kings, of beggars, old men, young men, maids;—
Who, having no external thing to lose
But the word maid,—cheats the poor maid of that;
That smooth-faced gentleman, tickling commodity*,—
Commodity, the bias of the world:
The world, who of itself is peised† well,
Made to run even, upon even ground;
Till this advantage, this vile drawing bias,
This sway of motion, this commodity,
Makes it take head from all indifferency,
From all direction, purpose, course, intent:
And this same bias, &c.

ACT III.

A WOMAN'S FEARS.

Thou shalt be punish'd for thus frighting me,
For I am sick, and capable‡ of fears;
Oppress'd with wrongs, and therefore full of fears;
A widow, husbandless, subject to fears;
A woman, naturally born to fears;
And though thou now confess, thou didst but jest,
With my vex'd spirits I cannot take a truce,
But they will quake and tremble all this day.

TOKENS OF GRIEF.

What dost thou mean by shaking of thy head?
Why dost thou look so sadly on my son?
What means that hand upon that breast of thine?
Why holds thine eye that lamentable rheum,
Like a proud river peering§ o'er his bounds?
Be these sad signs confirmers of thy words?
Then speak again; not all thy former tale,
But this one word, whether thy tale be true.

* Interest. † Poised, balanced.
‡ Susceptible. § Appearing.

A MOTHER'S FONDNESS FOR A BEAUTIFUL CHILD.

If thou, that bidst me be content, wert grim,
Ugly, and sland'rous to thy mother's womb,
Full of unpleasing blots, and sightless* stains,
Lame, foolish, crooked, swart, prodigious†,
Patch'd with foul moles, and eye-offending marks,
I would not care, I then would be content;
For then I should not love thee; no, nor thou
Become thy great birth, nor deserve a crown.
But thou art fair; and at thy birth, dear boy!
Nature and fortune join'd to make thee great;
Of nature's gifts thou mayst with lilies boast,
And with the half-blown rose.

GRIEF.

I will instruct my sorrows to be proud;
For grief is proud, and makes his owner stout,

COWARDICE AND PERJURY.

O Lymoges! O Austria! thou dost shame
That bloody spoil: Thou slave, thou wretch, thou coward:
Thou little valiant, great in villany!
Thou ever strong upon the stronger side!
Thou fortune's champion, that dost never fight
But when her humorous ladyship is by
To teach thee safety! thou art perjur'd too,
And sooth'st up greatness. What a fool art thou,
A ramping fool; to brag, and stamp, and swear,
Upon my party! Thou cold-blooded slave,
Hast thou not spoke like thunder on my side?
Been sworn my soldier? bidding me depend
Upon thy stars, thy fortune, and thy strength?
And dost thou now fall over to my foes?
Thou wear a lion's hide! doff‡ it for shame,
And hang a calf's skin on those recreant limbs.

* Unsightly. † Portentous. ‡ Do off.

THE HORRORS OF A CONSPIRACY.

I had a thing to say,—But let it go:
The sun is in the heaven, and the proud day,
Attended with the pleasures of the world,
Is all too wanton, and too full of gawds*,
To give me audience:—If the midnight bell
Did, with his iron tongue and brazen mouth,
Sound out unto the drowsy race of night;
If this same were a churchyard where we stand,
And thou possessed with a thousand wrongs;
Or if that surly spirit, melancholy,
Had bak'd thy blood, and made it heavy thick
(Which else, runs tickling up and down the veins,
Making that idiot, laughter, keep men's eyes,
And strain their cheeks to idle merriment,
A passion hateful to my purposes);
Or if that thou couldst see me without eyes,
Hear me without thine ears, and make reply
Without a tongue, using conceit† alone,
Without eyes, ears, and harmful sound of words;
Then, in despite of brooded watchful day,
I would into thy bosom pour my thoughts:
But, ah, I will not.

APOSTROPHE TO DEATH.

O amiable, lovely death!
Thou odoriferous stench! sound rottenness!
Arise forth from the couch of lasting night,
Thou hate and terror to prosperity,
And I will kiss thy detestable bones;
And put my eyeballs in thy vaulty brows;
And ring these fingers with thy household worms;
And stop this gap of breath with fulsome dust,
And be a carrion monster like thyself:
Come, grin on me; and I will think thou smil'st,
And buss thee as thy wife! Misery's love,
O, come to me!

* Showy ornaments. † Conception.

A MOTHER'S RAVINGS.

I am not mad: this hair I tear, is mine;
My name is Constance; I was Geffrey's wife;
Young Arthur is my son, and he is lost:
I am not mad;—I would to heaven I were!
For then, 'tis like I should forget myself:
O, if I could, what grief should I forget!—
Preach some philosophy to make me mad,
And thou shalt be canoniz'd, cardinal;
For, being not mad, but sensible of grief,
My reasonable part produces reason
How I may be deliver'd of these woes,
And teaches me to kill or hang myself:
If I were mad, I should forget my son;
Or madly think, a babe of clouts were he:
I am not mad; too well, too well I feel
The different plague of each calamity.

A MOTHER'S GRIEF FOR THE LOSS OF A SON.

Father cardinal, I have heard you say,
That we shall see and know our friends in heaven:
If that be true, I shall see my boy again;
For, since the birth of Cain, the first male child,
To him that did but yesterday suspire*,
There was not such a gracious† creature born.
But now will canker sorrow eat my bud,
And chase the native beauty from his cheek,
And he will look as hollow as a ghost;
As dim and meagre as an ague's fit;
And so he'll die; and, rising so again,
When I shall meet him in the court of heaven
I shall not know him: therefore never, never
Must I behold my pretty Arthur more.
Pand. You hold too heinous a respect of grief.
Const. He talks to me, that never had a son.
K. Phi. You are as fond of grief, as of your child.
Const. Grief fills the room up of my absent child,
Lies in his bed, walks up and down with me;

* Breathe. † Graceful.

Puts on his pretty looks, repeats his words,
Remembers me of all his gracious parts,
Stuffs out his vacant garments with his form;
Then, have I reason to be fond of grief.

DESPONDENCY.

There's nothing in this world can make me joy:
Life is as tedious as a twice-told tale,
Vexing the dull ear of a drowsy man.

STRENGTH OF DEPARTING DISEASES.

Before the curing of a strong disease,
Even in the instant of repair and health,
The fit is strongest; evils that take leave,
On their departure most of all show evil.

DANGER TAKES HOLD OF ANY SUPPORT.

He, that stands upon a slippery place,
Makes nice of no vile hold to stay him up.

ACT IV.

ARTHUR'S PATHETIC SPEECHES TO HUBERT.

Methinks, nobody should be sad but I:
Yet, I remember, when I was in France,
Young gentlemen would be as sad as night,
Only for wantonness. By my christendom,
So I were out of prison, and kept sheep,
I should be as merry as the day is long.

* * * * *

Have you the heart? When your head did but ache,
I knit my handkerchief about your brows
(The best I had, a princess wrought it me),
And I did never ask it you again:
And with my hand at midnight held your head;
And like the watchful minutes to the hour,
Still and anon cheer'd up the heavy time;
Saying, What lack you? and, Where lies your grief?
Or, What good love may I perform for you?
Many a poor man's son would have lain still,

And ne'er have spoke a loving word to you;
But you at your sick service had a prince..
Nay, you may think, my love was crafty love,
And call it cunning: Do, an if you will:
If heaven be pleas'd that you must use me ill,
Why, then you must.—Will you put out mine eyes?
These eyes, that never did, nor never shall,
So much as frown on you?

* * * * *

Alas, what need you be so boist'rous rough?
I will not struggle, I will stand stone still.
For heaven's sake Hubert, let me not be bound!
Nay, hear me, Hubert! drive these men away,
And I will sit as quiet as a lamb;
I will not stir, nor wince, nor speak a word,
Nor look upon the iron angerly:
Thrust but these men away, and I'll forgive you,
Whatever torment you do put me to.
Is there no remedy?

Hub. None, but to lose your eyes.

Arth. O heaven!—that there were but a mote in yours,
A grain, a dust, a gnat, a wand'ring hair,
Any annoyance in that precious sense!
Then, feeling what small things are boist'rous there,
Your vile intent must needs seem horrible.

PERFECTION ADMITS OF NO ADDITION.

To gild refined gold, to paint the lily,
To throw a perfume on the violet,
To smooth the ice, or add another hue
Unto the rainbow, or with taper-light
To seek the beauteous eye of heaven to garnish*,
Is wasteful and ridiculous excess.

* * * * *

In this, the antique and well-noted face
Of plain old form is much disfigured:
And, like a shifted wind unto a sail,
It makes the course of thoughts to fetch about:

* Decorate.

Startles and frights consideration;
Makes sound opinion sick, and truth suspected,
For putting on so new a fashion'd robe.

THE COUNTENANCE OF A MURDERER.

This is the man should do the bloody deed;
The image of a wicked heinous fault
Lives in his eye; that close aspect of his
Does show the mood of a much-troubled breast.

A STRUGGLING CONSCIENCE.

The colour of the king doth come and go,
Between his purpose and his conscience,
Like heralds 'twixt two dreadful battles set:
His passion is so ripe, it needs must break.

NEWS-BEARERS.

Old men, and beldams, in the streets
Do prophesy upon it dangerously:
Young Arthur's death is common in their mouths:
And when they talk of him they shake their heads,
And whisper one another in the ear;
And he, that speaks, doth gripe the hearer's wrist;
Whilst he, that hears, makes fearful action,
With wrinkled brows, with nods, with rolling eyes.
I saw a smith stand with his hammer, thus,
The whilst his iron did on the anvil cool,
With open mouth swallowing a tailor's news;
Who, with his shears and measure in his hand,
Standing on slippers (which his nimble haste
Had falsely thrust upon contrary feet);
Told of a many thousand warlike French,
That were embattled and rank'd in Kent:
Another lean unwash'd artificer
Cuts off his tale, and talks of Arthur's death.

THE EVIL PURPOSES OF KINGS TOO SERVILELY EXECUTED.

It is the curse of kings, to be attended
By slaves, that take their humours for a warrant
To break within the bloody house of life:
And, on the winking of authority,

To understand a law; to know the meaning
Of dangerous majesty, when, perchance, it frowns
More upon humour than advis'd respect*.

A VILLAIN'S LOOK, AND READY ZEAL.

How oft the sight of means to do ill deeds,
Makes deeds ill done! Hadst not thou been by,
A fellow by the hand of nature mark'd,
Quoted†, and sign'd, to do a deed of shame,
This murder had not come into my mind.
Hadst thou but shook thy head, or made a pause,
When I spake darkly what I purposed;
Or turn'd an eye of doubt upon my face,
As bid me tell my tale in express words;
Deep shame had struck me dumb, made me break off,
And those thy fears might have wrought fears in me.

HYPOCRISY.

Trust not those cunning waters of his eyes,
For villany is not without such rheum‡;
And he, long traded in it, makes it seem
Like rivers of remorse§ and innocency.

DESPAIR.

If thou didst but consent
To this most cruel act, do but despair,
And, if thou want'st a cord, the smallest thread
That ever spider twisted from her womb
Will serve to strangle thee; a rush will be
A beam to hang thee on; or wouldst thou drown thy-
self,
Put but a little water in a spoon,
And it shall be as all the ocean,
Enough to stifle such a villain up.

* Deliberate consideration. † Observed.
‡ Moisture. § Pity.

ACT V.

A MAN IN TEARS.

Let me wipe off this honourable dew,
That silverly doth progress on thy cheeks:
My heart hath melted at a lady's tears,
Being an ordinary inundation;
But this effusion of such manly drops,
This shower, blown up by tempest of the soul,
Startles mine eyes, and makes me more amaz'd
Than had I seen the vaulty top of heaven
Figur'd quite o'er with burning meteors.
Lift up thy brow, renowned Salisbury,
And with a great heart heave away this storm:
Commend these waters to those baby eyes,
That never saw the giant world enrag'd;
Nor met with fortune other than at feasts,
Full warm of blood, of mirth, of gossiping.

DRUMS.

Strike up the drums: and let the tongue of war
Plead for our interest.
* * * * *
Do but start
An echo with the clamour of thy drum,
And even at hand a drum is ready brac'd,
That shall reverberate all as loud as thine;
Sound but another, and another shall,
As loud as thine, rattle the welkin's * ear,
And mock the deep-mouth'd thunder.

APPROACH OF DEATH.

It is too late; the life of all his blood
Is touch'd corruptibly; and his pure brain
(Which some suppose the soul's frail dwellinghouse)
Doth, by the idle comments that it makes,
Foretell the ending of mortality.

* Sky.

MADNESS OCCASIONED BY POISON.

Ay, marry, now my soul hath elbow-room ;
It would not out at windows, nor at doors.
There is so hot a summer in my bosom,
That all my bowels crumble up to dust:
I am a scribbled form, drawn with a pen
Upon a parchment; and against this fire
Do I shrink up,
Poison'd,—ill-fare:—dead, forsook, cast off:
And none of you will bid the winter come,
To thrust his icy fingers in my maw ;
Nor let my kingdom's rivers take their course
Through my burn'd bosom ; nor entreat the north
To make his bleak winds kiss my parched lips,
And comfort me with cold.

ENGLAND INVINCIBLE IF UNANIMOUS.

England never did (nor never shall)
Lie at the proud foot of a conqueror,
But when it first did help to wound itself.
Now these her princes are come home again,
Come the three corners of the world in arms,
And we shall shock them: Nought shall make us rue,
If England to itself do rest but true.

KING RICHARD II.

ACT I.

REPUTATION.

The purest treasure mortal times afford,
Is—spotless reputation ; that away,
Men are but gilded loam, or painted clay.

COWARDICE.

That which in mean men we entitle—patience,
Is pale cold cowardice in noble breasts.

CONSOLATION UNDER BANISHMENT.

All places that the eye of heaven visits,
Are to a wise man ports and happy havens:
Teach thy necessity to reason thus;
There is no virtue like necessity.
Think not, the king did banish thee;
But thou the king: Woe doth the heavier sit,
Where it perceives it is but faintly borne.
Go, say—I sent thee forth to purchase honour,
And not—the king exiled thee: or suppose
Devouring pestilence hangs in our air,
And thou art flying to a fresher clime.
Look, what thy soul holds dear, imagine it
To lie that way thou go'st, not whence thou com'st:
Suppose the singing birds, musicians;
The grass whereon thou tread'st, the presence* strew'd;
The flowers, fair ladies; and thy steps, no more
Than a delightful measure, or a dance:
For gnarling† sorrow hath less power to bite
The man that mocks at it, and sets it light.

THOUGHTS INEFFECTUAL TO MODERATE AFFLICTION.

O, who can hold a fire in his hand,
By thinking on the frosty Caucasus?
Or cloy the hungry edge of appetite,
By bare imagination of a feast!
Or wallow naked in December snow,
By thinking on fantastic summer's heat?
O, no! the apprehension of the good,
Gives but the greater feeling to the worse:
Fell sorrow's tooth doth never rankle more,
Than when it bites but lanceth not the sore.

POPULARITY.

Ourself, and Bushy, Bagot here, and Green,
Observ'd his courtship to the common people:
How he did seem to dive into their hearts,
With humble and familiar courtesy,

* Presence-chamber at court. † Growling.

What reverence he did throw away on slaves;
Wooing poor craftsmen, with the craft of smiles,
And patient underbearing of his fortune,
As 'twere, to banish their affects with him.
Off goes his bonnet to an oyster wench;
A brace of draymen bid—God speed him well,
And had the tribute of his supple knee,
With—*Thanks, my countrymen, my loving friends*;—
As were our England in reversion his,
And he our subjects' next degree in hope.

ACT II.

ENGLAND PATHETICALLY DESCRIBED.

This royal throne of kings, this sceptred isle,
This earth of majesty, this seat of Mars,
This other Eden, demi-paradise;
This fortress, built by nature for herself,
Against infection, and the hand of war;
This happy breed of men, this little world;
This precious stone set in the silver sea,
Which serves it in the office of a wall,
Or as a moat defensive to a house,
Against the envy of less happier lands.

* * * * *

England, bound in with the triumphant sea,
Whose rocky shore beats back the envious siege
Of watery Neptune, is now bound in with shame,
With inky blots and rotten parchment bonds;
That England, that was wont to conquer others,
Hath made a shameful conquest of itself.

GRIEF.

Each substance of a grief hath twenty shadows,
Which show like grief itself, but are not so:
For sorrow's eye, glazed with blinding tears,
Divides one thing entire to many objects;

Like perspectives *, which, rightly gaz'd upon,
Show nothing but confusion; eyed awry,
Distinguish form.

HOPE DECEITFUL.

I will despair, and be at enmity
With cozening hope; he is a flatterer,
A parasite, a keeper back of death,
Who gently would dissolve the bands of life,
Which false hope lingers in extremity.

PROGNOSTICS OF WAR.

The baytrees in our country are all wither'd,
And meteors fright the fixed stars of heaven;
The pale-faced moon looks bloody on the earth,
And lean-look'd prophets whisper fearful change.;
Rich men look sad, and ruffians dance and leap.

ACT III.

APOSTROPHE TO ENGLAND.

As a long parted mother with her child
Plays fondly with her tears, and smiles in meeting;
So weeping, smiling, greet I thee, my earth,
And do thee favour with my royal hands.
Feed not thy sovereign's foe, my gentle earth,
Nor with thy sweets comfort his rav'nous sense:
But let thy spiders, that suck up thy venom,
And heavy gaited toads, lie in their way;
Doing annoyance to the treacherous feet,
Which with usurping steps do trample thee.
Yield stinging nettles to mine enemies:
And when they from thy bosom pluck a flower,
Guard it, I pray thee, with a lurking adder;
Whose double tongue may with a mortal touch
Throw death upon thy sovereign's enemies.—
Mock not my senseless conjuration, lords;
This earth shall have a feeling, and these stones

* Pictures.

Prove armed soldiers, ere her native king
Shall falter under foul rebellious arms.

SUN RISING AFTER A DARK NIGHT.

Know'st thou not,
That when the searching eye of heaven is hid
Behind the globe, and lights the lower world,
Then thieves and robbers range abroad unseen,
In murders and in outrage, bloody here;
But when, from under this terrestrial ball,
He fires the proud tops of the eastern pines,
And darts his light through every guilty hole,
Then murders, treasons, and detested sins,
The cloak of night being pluck'd from off their backs,
Stand bare and naked, trembling at themselves.

VANITY OF POWER AND MISERY OF KINGS.

No matter where; of comfort no man speak:
Let's talk of graves, of worms, and epitaphs;
Make dust our paper, and with rainy eyes
Write sorrow on the bosom of the earth.
Let's choose executors, and talk of wills:
And yet not so,--for what can we bequeath,
Save our deposed bodies to the ground?
Our lands, our lives, and all are Bolingbroke's,
And nothing can we call our own, but death;
And that small model of the barren earth,
Which serves as paste and cover to our bones.
For heaven's sake, let us sit upon the ground,
And tell sad stories of the death of kings:—
How some have been depos'd, some slain in war;
Some haunted by the ghosts they have depos'd;
Some poison'd by their wives, some sleeping kill'd;
All murder'd:—For within the hollow crown
That rounds the mortal temples of a king,
Keeps death his court: and there the antic sits,
Scoffing his state, and grinning at his pomp;
Allowing him a breath, a little scene,
To monarchize, be fear'd, and kill with looks;
Infusing him with self and vain conceit,—
As if this flesh, which walls about our life,

Were brass impregnable; and humour'd thus,
Comes at the last, and with a little pin
Bores through his castle wall, and—farewell king!
Cover your heads, and mock not flesh and blood
With solemn reverence; throw away respect,
Tradition, form, and ceremonious duty,
For you have but mistook me all this while:
I live with bread like you, feel want, taste grief,
Need friends:—Subjected thus,
How can you say to me—I am a king?

ACT V.

MELANCHOLY STORIES.

In winter's tedious nights, sit by the fire
With good olk folks; and let them tell thee tales
Of woful ages long ago betid *:
And ere thou bid good night, to quit † their grief,
Tell thou the lamentable fall of me,
And send the hearers weeping to their beds.

PUBLIC ENTRY.

York. Then, as I said, the duke, great Bolingbroke,—
Mounted upon a hot and fiery steed,
Which his aspiring rider seem'd to know,—
With slow, but stately pace, kept on his course,
While all tongues cried—God save thee, Bolingbroke!
You would have thought the very windows spake,
So many greedy looks of young and old
Through casements darted their desiring eyes
Upon his visage: and that all the walls,
With painted imag'ry ‡, had said at once,—
Jesu preserve thee! welcome, Bolingbroke!
Whilst he, from one side to the other turning,
Bare-headed, lower than his proud steed's neck,

* Passed. † Be even with them.
‡ Tapestry hung from the windows.

Bespake them thus,—*I thank you, countrymen:*
And thus still doing, thus he pass'd along.
Duch. Alas, poor Richard, where rides he the while?
York. As in a theatre, the eyes of men,
After a well-grac'd actor leaves the stage,
Are idly bent* on him that enters next,
Thinking his prattle to be tedious:
Even so, or with much more contempt, men's eyes
Did scowl on Richard; no man cried, God save him;
No joyful tongue gave him his welcome home:
But dust was thrown upon his sacred head;
Which with such gentle sorrow he shook off,—
His face still combating with tears and smiles,
The badges of his grief and patience,—
That had not God for some strong purpose steel'd
The hearts of men, they must perforce have melted,
And barbarism itself have pitied him.

VIOLETS.

Who are the violets now,
That strew the green lap of the new-come spring?

A SOLILOQUY IN PRISON.

I have been studying how I may compare
This prison, where I live, unto the world:
And, for because the world is populous,
And here is not a creature but myself,
I cannot do it;—Yet I'll hammer it out.
My brain I'll prove the female to my soul;
My soul, the father: and these two beget
A generation of still-breeding thoughts,
And these same thoughts people this little world†
In humours, like the people of this world,
For no thought is contented.

* * * * *

Thoughts tending to content, flatter themselves,—
That they are not the first of fortune's slaves,
Nor shall not be the last; like silly beggars,

* Carelessly turned. † His own body.

Who, sitting in the stocks, refuge their shame,—
That many have, and others must sit there:
And in this thought they find a kind of ease,
Bearing their own misfortune on the back
Of such as have before endur'd the like,
Thus play I, in one person, many people,
And none contented: Sometimes am I king,
Then treason makes me wish myself a beggar,
And so I am: Then crushing penury
Persuades me I was better when a king;
Then am I king'd again: and, by-and-by,
Think that I am unking'd by Bolingbroke,
And straight am nothing:—But, whate'er I am,
Nor I, nor any man, that but man is,
With nothing shall be pleased, till he be eased
With being nothing.

KING HENRY IV.

PART I.

ACT I.

PEACE AFTER CIVIL WAR.

So shaken as we are, so wan with care,
Find we a time for frighted peace to pant,
And breathe short-winded accents of new broils
To be commenc'd in stronds * afar remote.
No more the thirsty Erinnys † of this soil
Shall daub her lips with her own children's blood;
No more shall trenching war channel her fields,
Nor bruise her flow'rets with the armed hoofs
Of hostile paces: those opposed eyes,
Which,—like the meteors of a troubled heaven,

* Strands, banks of the sea. † The fury of discord.

All of one nature, of one substance bred,——
Did lately meet in the intestine shock
And furious close of civil butchery,
Shall now, in mutual, well-beseeming ranks,
March all one way; and be no more oppos'd
Against acquaintance, kindred, and allies:
The edge of war, like an ill-sheathed knife,
No more shall cut his master.

KING HENRY'S CHARACTER OF PERCY, AND OF HIS SON PRINCE HENRY.

Yea, there thou mak'st me sad, and mak'st me sin
In envy that my lord Northumberland
Should be the father of so bless'd a son:
A son, who is the theme of honour's tongue;
Amongst a grove, the very straightest plant;
Who is sweet fortune's minion, and her pride:
Whilst I, by looking on the praise of him,
See riot and dishonour stain the brow
Of my young Harry.

PRINCE HENRY'S SOLILOQUY.

I know you all, and will a while uphold
The unyok'd humour of your idleness:
Yet herein will I imitate the sun;
Who doth permit the base contagious clouds
To smother up his beauty from the world,
That, when he please again to be himself,
Being wanted, he may be more wonder'd at,
By breaking through the foul and ugly mists
Of vapours that did seem to strangle him.
If all the year were playing holidays,
To sport would be as tedious as to work;
But, when they seldom come, they wish'd-for come,
And nothing pleaseth but rare accidents.
So, when this loose behaviour I throw off,
And pay the debt I never promised,
By how much better than my word I am,
By so much shall I falsify men's hopes*;

* Expectations.

And like bright metal on a sullen * ground,
My reformation, glittering o'er my fault,
Shall show more goodly, and attract more eyes,
Than that which hath no foil to set it off.
I'll so offend, to make offence a skill;
Redeeming time, when men think least I will.

HOTSPUR'S DESCRIPTION OF A FINICAL COURTIER.

But I remember, when the fight was done,
When I was dry with rage and extreme toil,
Breathless and faint, leaning upon my sword,
Came there a certain lord, neat, trimly dress'd,
Fresh as a bridegroom; and his chin new reap'd,
Show'd like a stubble land at harvest home;
He was perfumed like a milliner;
And 'twixt his finger and his thumb he held
A pouncet box †, which ever and anon
He gave his nose and took't away again;
Who, therewith angry, when it next came there,
Took it in snuff:—and still he smil'd, and talk'd;
And, as the soldiers bore dead bodies by,
He call'd them—untaught knaves, unmannerly,
To bring a slovenly unhandsome corse
Betwixt the wind and his nobility.
With many holiday and lady terms
He question'd me; among the rest demanded
My prisoners, in your majesty's behalf.
I then, all smarting, with my wounds being cold,
To be so pester'd with a popinjay ‡,
Out of my grief§ and my impatience,
Answer'd neglectingly, I know not what;
He should, or he should not;—for he made me mad,
To see him shine so brisk, and smell so sweet,
And talk so like a waiting gentlewoman,
Of guns, and drums, and wounds, (God save the mark!)
And telling me, the sovereign'st thing on earth
Was parmaceti, for an inward bruise;

* Dull. † A small box for musk or other perfumes.
‡ Parrot. § Pain.

And that it was great pity, so it was,
That villanous saltpetre should be digg'd
Out of the bowels of the harmless earth,
Which many a good tall* fellow had destroy'd
So cowardly: and, but for these vile guns,
He would himself have been a soldier.

DANGER.

I'll read you matter deep and dangerous;
As full of peril, and advent'rous spirit,
As to o'erwalk a current, roaring loud,
On the unsteadfast footing of a spear.

HONOUR.

By heaven, methinks, it were an easy leap,
To pluck bright honour from the pale-fac'd moon;
Or dive into the bottom of the deep,
Where fathom-line could never touch the ground,
And pluck up drowned honour by the locks;
So he, that doth redeem her thence, might wear,
Without corrival †, all her dignities:
But out upon this half-fac'd fellowship ‡!

ACT II.

LADY PERCY'S PATHETIC SPEECH TO HER HUSBAND.

O my good lord, why are you thus alone?
For what offence have I, this fortnight, been
A banish'd woman from my Harry's bed?
Tell me, sweet lord, what is't that takes from thee
Thy stomach, pleasure, and thy golden sleep?
Why dost thou bend thine eyes upon the earth;
And start so often when thou sit'st alone?
Why hast thou lost the fresh blood in thy cheeks;
And given my treasures, and my rights of thee,
To thick-ey'd musing, and curs'd melancholy?
In thy faint slumbers, I by thee have watch'd,
And heard thee murmur tales of iron wars:
Speak terms of manage to thy bounding steed;

* Brave. † A rival. ‡ Friendship.

Cry, *Courage!—to the field!* And thou hast talk'd
Of sallies, and retires; of trenches, tents,
Of palisadoes, frontiers, parapets;
Of basilisks, of cannon, culverin;
Of prisoners' ransom, and of soldiers slain,
And all the 'currents* of a heady fight.
Thy spirit within thee hath been so at war,
And thus hath so bestirr'd thee in thy sleep,
That beads† of sweat have stood upon thy brow,
Like bubbles in a late disturbed stream;
And in thy face strange motions have appear'd,
Such as we see when men restrain their breath
On some great sudden haste. O, what portents are these?
Some heavy business hath my lord in hand,
And I must know it, else he loves me not.

ACT III.

PRODIGIES RIDICULED.

I cannot blame him: at my nativity
The front of heaven was full of fiery shapes,
Of burning cressets‡: and, at my birth,
The frame and huge foundation of the earth
Shak'd like a coward.
Hot. Why, so it would have done
At the same season, if your mother's cat had
But kitten'd, though yourself had ne'er been born.

* * * * *

Diseased nature oftentimes breaks forth
In strange eruptions: oft the teeming earth
Is with a kind of colic pinch'd and vex'd
By the imprisoning of unruly wind
Within her tomb; which, for enlargement striving,
Shakes the old beldame earth, and topples§ down
Steeples and moss-grown towers.

* Occurrences. † Drops.
‡ Lights set crossways upon beacons, and also upon poles, which were used in processions, &c. § Tumbles.

ON MISERABLE RHYMERS.

Marry, and I am glad of it with all my heart;
I had rather be a kitten, and cry—mew,
Than one of these same metre balladmongers:
I had rather hear a brazen canstick * turn'd,
Or a dry wheel grate on an axletree;
And that would set my teeth nothing on edge,
Nothing so much as mincing poetry;
'Tis like the forc'd gait of a shuffling nag.

PUNCTUALITY IN BARGAINS.

I'll give thrice so much land
To any well-deserving friend;
But, in the way of bargain, mark ye me,
I'll cavil on the ninth part of a hair.

A HUSBAND SUNG TO SLEEP BY HIS WIFE.

She bids you
Upon the wanton rushes lay you down,
And rest your gentle head upon her lap,
And she will sing the song that pleaseth you,
And on your eyelids crown the god of sleep,
Charming your blood with pleasing heaviness;
Making such difference 'twixt wake and sleep,
As is the difference 'twixt day and night,
The hour before the heavenly harness'd team
Begins his golden progress in the east.

KING HENRY'S PATHETIC ADDRESS TO HIS SON.

Had I so lavish of my presence been,
So common-hackney'd in the eyes of men,
So stale and cheap to vulgar company;
Opinion, that did help me to the crown,
Had still kept loyal to possession †;
And left me in reputeless banishment,
A fellow of no mark, nor likelihood.
By being seldom seen, I could not stir,
But, like a comet, I was wonder'd at:

* Candlestick.
† True to him that had then possession of the crown.

That men would tell their children, *This is he;*
Others would say,—*Where?—which is Bolingbroke?*
And then I stole all courtesy from heaven,
And dress'd myself in such humility,
That I did pluck allegiance from men's hearts,
Loud shouts and salutations from their mouths,
Even in the presence of the crowned king.
Thus did I keep my person fresh, and new;
My presence, like a robe pontifical,
Ne'er seen, but wonder'd at: and so my state,
Seldom, but sumptuous, showed like a feast;
And won, by rareness, such solemnity.
The skipping king, he ambled up and down
With shallow jesters, and rash bavin * wits,
Soon kindled, and soon burn'd: carded his state;
Mingled his royalty with capering fools;
Had his great name profaned with their scorns
And gave his countenance against his name,
To laugh at gibing boys, and stand the push
Of every beardless vain comparative †:
Grew a companion to the common streets,
Enfeoff'd ‡ himself to popularity:
That being daily swallow'd by men's eyes,
They surfeited with honey; and began
To loathe the taste of sweetness, whereof a little
More than a little is by much too much.
So, when he had occasion to be seen,
He was but as the cuckoo is in June,
Heard, not regarded; seen, but with such eyes,
As, sick and blunted with community,
Afford no extraordinary gaze,
Such as is bent on sun-like majesty
When it shines seldom in admiring eyes:
But rather drowz'd, and hung their eyelids down,
Slept in his face, and render'd such aspect
As cloudy men use to their adversaries;
Being with his presence glutted, gorg'd, and full.

* Brushwood. † Rival. ‡ Possessing.

PRINCE HENRY'S MODEST DEFENCE OF HIMSELF.

God forgive them, that have so much sway'd
Your majesty's good thoughts away from me!
I will redeem all this on Percy's head,
And, in the closing of some glorious day,
Be bold to tell you, that I am your son;
When I will wear a garment all of blood,
And stain my favours in a bloody mask,
Which, wash'd away, shall scour my shame with it.
And that shall be the day, whene'er it lights,
That this same child of honour and renown,
This gallant Hotspur, this all-praised knight,
And your unthought-of Harry, chance to meet:
For every honour sitting on his helm,
'Would they were multitudes; and on my head
My shames redoubled! for the time will come
That I shall make this northern youth exchange
His glorious deeds for my indignities.
Percy is but my factor, good my lord,
To engross up glorious deeds on my behalf;
And I will call him to so strict account,
That he shall render every glory up,
Yea, even the slightest worship of his time,
Or I will tear the reckoning from his heart.
This, in the name of God, I promise here:
The which if he be pleased I shall perform,
I do beseech your majesty, may salve
The long-grown wounds of my intemperance:
If not, the end of life cancels all bands *;
And I will die a hundred thousand deaths,
Ere break the smallest parcel † of this vow.

* Bonds. † Part.

ACT IV.

A GALLANT WARRIOR.

I saw young Harry,—with his beaver on,
His cuisses* on his thighs, gallantly armed,—
Rise from the ground like feather'd Mercury,
And vaulted with such ease into his seat,
As if an angel dropp'd down from the clouds,
To turn and wind a fiery Pegasus,
And witch† the world with noble horsemanship.

HOTSPUR'S IMPATIENCE FOR THE BATTLE.

Let them come;
They come like sacrifices in their trim,
And to the fire-ey'd maid of smoky war,
All hot, and bleeding, will we offer them:
The mailed Mars shall on his altar sit,
Up to the ears in blood. I am on fire,
To hear this rich reprisal is so nigh,
And yet not ours:—Come, let me take my horse,
Who is to bear me, like a thunderbolt,
Against the bosom of the prince of Wales:
Harry to Harry shall, hot horse to horse,
Meet, and ne'er part, till one drop down a corse.—
O, that Glendower were come!

ACT V.

PRINCE HENRY'S MODEST CHALLENGE.

Tell your nephew,
The prince of Wales doth join with all the world
In praise of Henry Percy: By my hopes,—
This present enterprise set off his head,—
I do not think a braver gentleman,
More active-valiant, or more valiant-young,

* Armour. † Bewitch, charm.

More daring, or more bold, is now alive,
To grace this latter age with noble deeds.
For my part I may speak it to my shame,
I have a truant been to chivalry;
And so, I hear, he doth account me too:
Yet this before my father's majesty,—
I am content, that he shall take the odds
Of his great name and estimation;
And will, to save the blood on either side,
Try fortune with him in a single fight.

FALSTAFF'S CATECHISM.

Well, 'tis no matter: Honour pricks me on. Yea, but how if honour prick me off when I come on? how then? Can honour set to a leg? No. Or an arm? No. Or take away the grief of a wound? No. Honour hath no skill in surgery then? No. What is honour? A word. What is in that word? Honour. What is that honour? Air. A trim reckoning.—Who hath it? He that died o' Wednesday. Doth he feel it? No. Doth he hear it? No. Is it insensible then? Yea, to the dead. But will it not live with the living? No. Why? Detraction will not suffer it:—therefore I'll none of it. Honour is a mere escutcheon *, and so ends my catechism.

LIFE DEMANDS ACTION.

O gentlemen, the time of life is short;
To spend that shortness basely, were too long,
If life did ride upon a dial's point,
Still ending at the arrival of an hour.

PRINCE HENRY'S PATHETIC SPEECH ON THE DEATH OF HOTSPUR.

Brave Percy, fare thee well.
Ill-weav'd ambition, how much art thou shrunk!
When that this body did contain a spirit,
A kingdom for it was too small a bound;

* Painted heraldry in funerals.

But now, two paces of the vilest earth
Is room enough:—This earth, that bears thee dead,
Bears not alive so stout a gentleman.
If thou wert sensible of courtesy,
I should not make so dear a show of zeal:
But let my favours * hide thy mangled face;
And even, in thy behalf, I'll thank myself
For doing these fair rites of tenderness.
Adieu, and take thy praise with thee to heaven!
Thy ignominy sleep with thee in the grave,
But not remember'd in thy epitaph!

KING HENRY IV.

PART II.

INDUCTION.

RUMOUR.

I, FROM the orient to the drooping west,
Making the wind my post-horse, still unfold
The acts commenced on this ball of earth:
Upon my tongues continual slanders ride;
The which in every language I pronounce,
Stuffing the ears of men with false reports.
I speak of peace, while covert enmity,
Under the smile of safety, wounds the world:
And who but Rumour, who but only I,
Make fearful musters, and prepar'd defence;
Whilst the big year, swoln with some other grief,
Is thought with child by the stern tyrant war,
And no such matter? Rumour is a pipe
Blown by surmises, jealousies, conjectures;
And of so easy and so plain a stop,

* Scarf, with which he covers Percy's face.

That the blunt monster with uncounted heads,
The still-discordant wavering multitude,
Can play upon it.

ACT I.

CONTENTION.

Contention, like a horse
Full of high feeding, madly hath broke loose,
And bears down all before him.

POST MESSENGER.

After him, came, spurring hard,
A gentleman almost forspent* with speed,
That stopp'd by me to breathe his bloodied horse:
He ask'd the way to Chester; and of him
I did demand, what news from Shrewsbury.
He told me, that rebellion had bad luck,
And that young Harry Percy's spur was cold:
With that, he gave his able horse the head,
And, bending forward, struck his armed heels
Against the panting sides of his poor jade
Up to the rowel-head; and, starting so,
He seem'd in running to devour the way,
Staying no longer question.

MESSENGER WITH ILL NEWS.

This man's brow, like to a title-leaf,
Foretells the nature of a tragic volume:
So looks the strond, whereon the imperious flood
Hath left a witness'd usurpation†.——
Thou tremblest; and the whiteness in thy cheek
Is apter than thy tongue to tell thy errand.
Even such a man, so faint, so spiritless,
So dull, so dead in look, so woe-begone,
Drew Priam's curtain in the dead of night,
And would have told him, half his Troy was burn'd.—
I see a strange confession in thine eye:
Thou shak'st thy head, and hold'st it fear, or sin,

* Exhausted. † An attestation of its ravage.

To speak a truth. If he be slain, say so:
The tongue offends not that reports his death:
And he doth sin that does belie the dead;
Not he, which says the dead is not alive.
Yet the first bringer of unwelcome news
Hath but a losing office; and his tongue
Sounds ever after as a sullen bell,
Remember'd knolling a departing friend.

GREATER GRIEFS DESTROY THE LESS.

As the wretch, whose fever-weaken'd joints,
Like strengthless hinges buckle under life,
Impatient of his fit, breaks like a fire
Out of his keeper's arms; even so my limbs,
Weaken'd with grief, being now enraged with grief,
Are thrice themselves: hence therefore, thou nice * crutch;
A scaly gauntlet now, with joints of steel,
Must glove this hand: and hence, thou sickly quoif †,
Thou art a guard too wanton for the head,
Which princes, flesh'd with conquest, aim to hit.
Now bind my brows with iron; and approach
The ragged'st hour that time and spite dare bring,
To frown upon the enrag'd Northumberland!
Let heaven kiss earth! Now let not nature's hand
Keep the wild flood confin'd! let order die!
And let this world no longer be a stage,
To feed contention in a lingering act;
But let one spirit of the first-born Cain
Reign in all bosoms, that, each heart being set
On bloody courses, the rude scene may end,
And darkness be the burier of the dead!

THE FICKLENESS OF THE VULGAR.

An habitation giddy and unsure
Hath he that buildeth on the vulgar heart.
O thou fond many ‡! with what loud applause
Didst thou beat heaven with blessing Bolingbroke,
Before he was what thou wouldst have him be?

* Trifling. † Cap. ‡ Multitude.

And being now trimm'd * in thine own desires,
Thou, beastly feeder, art so full of him,
That thou provok'st thyself to cast him up.

ACT III.

APOSTROPHE TO SLEEP.

Sleep, gentle sleep,
Nature's soft nurse, how have I frighted thee,
That thou no more wilt weigh my eyelids down,
And steep my senses in forgetfulness?
Why rather, sleep, liest thou in smoky cribs,
Upon uneasy pallets stretching thee,
And hush'd with buzzing night-flies to thy slumber:
Than in the perfum'd chambers of the great,
Under the canopies of costly state,
And lull'd with sounds of sweetest melody.
O thou dull god, why liest thou with the vile,
In loathsome beds; and leav'st the kingly couch,
A watch-case, or a common 'larum bell?
Wilt thou upon the high and giddy mast
Seal up the ship-boy's eyes, and rock his brains
In cradle of the rude imperious surge;
And in the visitation of the winds,
Who take the ruffian billows by the top,
Curling their monstrous heads, and hanging them
With deaf'ning clamours on the slippery clouds,
That, with the hurly †, death itself awakes?
Canst thou, O partial sleep! give thy repose
To the wet sea-boy, in an hour so rude;
And, in the calmest and most stillest night,
With all appliances and means to boot,
Deny it to a king?

* Dressed. † Noise.

ACT IV.

THE CHARACTER OF KING HENRY V. BY HIS FATHER.

He is gracious, if he be observ'd *;
He hath a tear for pity, and a hand
Open as day for melting charity:
Yet notwithstanding, being incens'd, he's flint;
As humorous as winter, and as sudden
As flaws congealed in the spring of day,
His temper, therefore, must be well observ'd;
Chide him for faults, and do it reverently,
When you perceive his blood inclin'd to mirth:
But, being moody, give him line and scope;
Till that his passions, like a whale on ground,
Confound themselves with working.

ON FORTUNE.

Will fortune never come with both hands full,
But write her fair words still in foulest letters?
She either gives a stomach, and no food,—
Such are the poor, in health; or else a feast,
And takes away the stomach,—such are the rich,
That have abundance, and enjoy it not.

REFLECTIONS ON A CROWN.

O polish'd perturbation! golden care!
That keep'st the ports † of slumber open wide
To many a watchful night!—sleep with it now!
Yet not so sound, and half so deeply sweet,
As he, whose brow, with homely biggin ‡ bound,
Snores out the watch of night. O majesty!
When thou dost pinch thy bearer, thou dost sit
Like a rich armour worn in heat of day,
That scalds with safety.

REFLECTIONS ON GOLD.

How quickly nature falls into revolt,
When gold becomes her object!

* Has an attention shown him. † Gates. ‡ Cap.

For this the foolish over-careful fathers
Have broke their sleep with thoughts, their brains with care,
Their bones with industry;
For this they have engrossed and pil'd up
The canker'd heaps of strange-achieved gold;
For this they have been thoughtful to invest
Their sons with arts and martial exercises:
When, like the bee, tolling* from every flower
The virtuous sweets;
Our thighs pack'd with wax, our mouths with honey,
We bring it to the hive; and, like the bees,
Are murder'd for our pains.

SCENE BETWEEN PRINCE HENRY AND HIS FATHER.

Come hither to me, Harry:—
Depart the chamber, leave us here alone.
P. Hen. I never thought to hear you speak again.
K. Hen. Thy wish was father, Harry, to that thought:
I stay too long by thee, I weary thee.
Dost thou so hunger for my empty chair,
That thou wilt needs invest thee with mine honours
Before thy hour be ripe? O foolish youth!
Thou seek'st the greatness that will overwhelm thee.
Stay but a little; for my cloud of dignity
Is held from falling with so weak a wind,
That it will quickly drop: my day is dim.
Thou hast stol'n that, which, after some few hours,
Were thine without offence; and, at my death,
Thou hast seal'd up my expectation†:
Thy life did manifest, thou lov'dst me not,
And thou wilt have me die assured of it.
Thou hid'st a thousand daggers in thy thoughts:
Which thou hast whetted on thy stony heart,
To stab at half an hour of my life.
What! canst thou not forbear me half an hour?
Then get thee gone; and dig my grave thyself;

* Taking toll. † Confirmed my opinion.

And bid the merry bells ring to thine ear,
That thou art crowned, not that I am dead.
Let all the tears that should bedew my hearse,
Be drops of balm, to sanctify thy head:
Only compound me with forgotten dust;
Give that, which gave thee life, unto the worms.
Pluck down my officers, break my decrees;
For now a time is come to mock at form,
Harry the fifth is crown'd:—Up, vanity!
Down, royal state! all you sage counsellors, hence!
And to the English court assemble now,
From every region, apes of idleness!
Now, neighbour confines, purge you of your scum:
Have you a ruffian, that will swear, drink, dance,
Revel the night; rob, murder, and commit
The oldest sins the newest kind of ways?
Be happy, he will trouble you no more:
England shall double gild his treble guilt;
England shall give him office, honour, might;
For the fifth Harry from curb'd licence plucks
The muzzle of restraint, and the wild dog
Shall flesh his tooth in every innocent.
O my poor kingdom, sick with civil blows!
When that my care could not withhold thy riots,
What wilt thou do, when riot is thy care?
O, thou wilt be a wilderness again,
Peopled with wolves, thy old inhabitants!

P. Hen. O, pardon me, my liege! but for my tears, [*Kneeling.*
The moist impediments unto my speech,
I had forestall'd this dear and deep rebuke,
Ere you with grief had spoke, and I had heard
The course of it so far. There is your crown,
And He that wears the crown immortally,
Long guard it yours! If I affect it more,
Than as your honour, and as your renown,
Let me no more from this obedience rise,
(Which my most true and inward-duteous spirit
Teacheth) this prostrate and exterior bending!
Heaven witness with me, when I here came in,
And found no course of breath within your majesty,

How cold it struck my heart! if I do feign,
O, let me in my present wildness die;
And never live to show the incredulous world
The noble change that I have purposed?
Coming to look on you, thinking you dead,
(And dead almost, my liege, to think you were,)
I spake unto the crown as having sense,
And thus upbraided it. *The care on thee depending*
Hath fed upon the body of my father;
Therefore, thou, best of gold, art worst of gold.
*Other, less fine in carat**, *is more precious,*
Preserving life in med'cine potable†:
But thou, most fine, most honour'd, most renown'd,
Hast eat thy bearer up. Thus, my most royal liege,
Accusing it, I put it on my head;
To try with it,—as with an enemy,
That had before my face murder'd my father,—
The quarrel of a true inheritor.
But if it did infect my blood with joy,
Or swell my thoughts to any strain of pride;
If any rebel or vain spirit of mine
Did, with the least affection of a welcome,
Give entertainment to the might of it,
Let God for ever keep it from my head!
And make me as the poorest vassal is,
That doth with awe and terror kneel to it!
K. Hen. O my son!
Heaven put it in thy mind, to take it hence,
That thou might'st win the more thy father's love,
Pleading so wisely in excuse of it.
Come hither, Harry, sit thou by my bed;
And hear, I think, the very latest counsel
That ever I shall breathe. Heaven knows, my son,
By what bye-paths, and indirect crook'd ways,
I met this crown; and I myself know well,
How troublesome it sat upon my head:
To thee it shall descend with better quiet,
Better opinion, better confirmation;
For all the soil‡ of the achievement goes

* Weight. † To be taken. ‡ Spot, dirt.

With me into the earth. It seem'd in me,
But as an honour snatch'd with boisterous hand:
And I had many living to upbraid
My gain of it by their assistances;
Which daily grew to quarrel and to bloodshed,
Wounding supposed peace: all these bold fears *,
Thou see'st, with peril I have answered:
For all my reign hath been but as a scene
Acting that argument; and now my death
Changes the mode †: for what in me was purchas'd ‡,
Falls upon thee in a more fairer sort;
So thou the garland wear'st successively.
Yet, though thou stand'st more sure than I could do,
Thou art not firm enough, since griefs are green;
And all thy friends, which thou must make thy friends,
Have but their stings and teeth newly ta'en out;
By whose fell working I was first advanc'd,
And by whose power I well might lodge a fear
To be again displac'd; which to avoid,
I cut them off; and had a purpose now
To lead out many to the Holy Land;
Lest rest, and lying still, might make them look
Too near unto my state. Therefore, my Harry,
Be it thy course, to busy giddy minds
With foreign quarrels; that action, hence borne out,
May waste the memory of the former days.
More would I, but my lungs are wasted so,
That strength of speech is utterly denied me.
How I came by the crown, O God, forgive!
And grant it may with thee in true peace live!
P. Hen. My gracious liege,
You won it, wore it, kept it, gave it me;
Then plain and right must my possession be:
Which I, with more than with a common pain,
'Gainst all the world will rightfully maintain.

* Frights. † State of things.
‡ Purchase, in Shakspeare, frequently means *stolen goods.*

ACT V.

ADDRESS OF THE CHIEF JUSTICE TO KING HENRY V. WHOM HE HAD IMPRISONED.

If the deed were ill,
Be you contented, wearing now the garland *,
To have a son set your decrees at nought;
To pluck down justice from your awful bench;
To trip the course of law, and blunt the sword
That guards the peace and safety of your person:
Nay, more; to spurn at your most royal image,
And mock your workings in a second body †.
Question your royal thoughts, make the case yours;
Be now the father, and propose a son:
Hear your own dignity so much profan'd,
See your most dreadful laws so loosely slighted,
Behold yourself so by a son disdained;
And then imagine me taking your part,
And, in your power, soft silencing your son.

KING HENRY V.

CHORUS.

INVOCATION TO THE MUSE.

O, FOR a muse of fire, that would ascend
The brightest heaven of invention!
A kingdom for a stage, princes to act,
And monarchs to behold the swelling scene!
Then should the warlike Harry, like himself,

* Crown.
† Treat with contempt your acts executed by a representative.

Assume the port of Mars; and, at his heels,
Leash'd in like hounds, should famine, sword, and fire,
Crouch for employment.

ACT I.

CONSIDERATION.

Consideration like an angel came,
And whipp'd the offending Adam out of him;
Leaving his body as a paradise,
To envelop and contain celestial spirits.

PERFECTIONS OF KING HENRY V.

Hear him but reason in divinity,
And, all-admiring, with an inward wish
You would desire, the king were made a prelate;
Hear him debate of commonwealth affairs,
You would say,—it hath been all-in-all his study:
List* his discourse of war, and you shall hear
A fearful battle render'd you in music:
Turn him to any cause of policy,
The Gordian knot of it he will unloose,
Familiar as his garter; that, when he speaks,
The air, a charter'd libertine, is still,
And the mute wonder lurketh in men's ears,
To steal his sweet and honeyed sentences.

THE COMMONWEALTH OF BEES.

So work the honey bees;
Creatures, that, by a rule in nature, teach
The act of order to a peopled kingdom.
They have a king, and officers of sorts†:
Where some, like magistrates, correct at home;
Others, like merchants, venture trade abroad;
Others, like soldiers, armed in their stings,
Make boot upon the summer's velvet buds;
Which pillage they with merry march bring home
To the tent-royal of their emperor:

* Listen to. † Different degrees.

Who, busied in his majesty, surveys
The singing masons building roofs of gold;
The civil * citizens kneading up the honey;
The poor mechanic porters crowding in
Their heavy burdens at his narrow gate;
The sad-ey'd justice, with his surly hum,
Delivering o'er to executors † pale
The lazy yawning drone.

ACT II.

CHORUS.

WARLIKE SPIRIT.

Now all the youth of England are on fire,
And silken dalliance in the wardrobe lies;
Now thrive the armourers, and honour's thought
Reigns solely in the breast of every man:
They sell the pasture now, to buy the horse;
Following the mirror of all Christian kings,
With winged heels, as English Mercuries.
For now sits Expectation in the air;
And hides a sword, from hilts unto the point,
With crowns imperial, crowns, and coronets,
Promis'd to Harry, and his followers.

APOSTROPHE TO ENGLAND.

O England!—model to thy inward greatness,
Like little body with a mighty heart,—
What mightst thou do, that honour would thee do,
Were all thy children kind and natural!
But see thy fault! France hath in thee found out
A nest of hollow bosoms, which he ‡ fills
With treacherous crowns.

* Sober, grave. † Executioners.
‡ *i. e.* The king of France.

FALSE APPEARANCES.

O, how hast thou with jealousy infected
The sweetness of affiance! Show men dutiful?
Why, so didst thou: Seem they grave and learned?
Why, so didst thou: Come they of noble family?
Why, so didst thou: Seem they religious?
Why, so didst thou: Or are they spare in diet;
Free from gross passion, or of mirth, or anger;
Constant in spirit, not swerving with the blood;
Garnish'd and deck'd in modest complement*;
Not working with the eye, without the ear,
And, but in purged judgment, trusting neither?
Such, and so finely bolted†, didst thou seem:
And thus thy fall hath left a kind of blot,
To mark the full fraught man, and best indued‡,
With some suspicion.

DAME QUICKLY'S ACCOUNT OF FALSTAFF'S DEATH.

'A made a finer end, and went away, and it had been any christom § child; 'a parted even just between twelve and one, e'en at turning o'the tide; for after I saw him fumble with the sheets, and play with flowers, and smile upon his fingers' ends, I knew there was but one way; for his nose was as sharp as a pen, and 'a babbled of green fields. How now, Sir John? quoth I: what, man! be of good cheer. So 'a cried out—God, God, God! three or four times: now I, to comfort him, bid him, 'a should not think of God; I hoped there was no need to trouble himself with any such thoughts yet: So, 'a bade me lay more clothes on his feet: I put my hand into the bed, and felt them, and they were as cold as any stone.

KING HENRY'S CHARACTER BY THE CONSTABLE OF FRANCE.

You are too much mistaken in this king;
Question your grace the late ambassadors,—

* Accomplishment. † Sifted. ‡ Endowed.
§ A child not more than a month old.

With what great state he heard their embassy,
How well supplied with noble counsellors,
How modest in exception *, and, withal,
How terrible in constant resolution,—
And you shall find his vanities forespent †
Were but the outside of the Roman Brutus,
Covering discretion with a coat of folly;
As gardeners do with ordure hide those roots
That shall first spring, and be most delicate.

ACT III.

CHORUS.

DESCRIPTION OF A FLEET SETTING SAIL.

Suppose, that you have seen
The well-appointed king at Hampton pier
Embark his royalty; and his brave fleet
With silken streamers the young Phœbus fanning,
Play with your fancies; and in them behold,
Upon the hempen tackle, ship-boys climbing:
Hear the shrill whistle, which doth order give
To sounds confus'd: behold the threaden sails,
Borne with the invisible and creeping wind,
Draw the huge bottoms through the furrow'd sea,
Breasting the lofty surge.

ACT IV.

CHORUS.

DESCRIPTION OF NIGHT IN A CAMP.

From camp to camp, through the foul womb of night,
The hum of either army stilly ‡ sounds,

* In making objections. † Wasted, exhausted.
‡ Gently, lowly.

That the fix'd sentinels almost receive
The secret whispers of each other's watch:
Fire answers fire, and through their paly flames
Each battle sees the other's umber'd * face:
Steed threatens steed, in high and boastful neighs
Piercing the night's dull ear; and from the tents,
The armourers, accomplishing the knights,
With busy hammers closing rivets up,
Give dreadful note of preparation.
The country cocks do crow, the clocks do toll,
And the third hour of drowsy morning name.
Proud of their numbers, and secure in soul,
The confident and over-lusty † French
Do the low-rated English play at dice;
And chide the cripple tardy-gaited night,
Who, like a foul and ugly witch, doth limp
So tediously away. The poor condemned English,
Like sacrifices, by their watchful fires
Sit patiently, and inly ruminate
The morning's danger; and their gesture sad,
Investing lank-lean cheeks, and war-worn coats,
Presenteth them unto the gazing moon
So many horrid ghosts. O, now, who will behold
The royal captain of this ruin'd band,
Walking from watch to watch, from tent to tent,
Let him cry—Praise and glory on his head!
For forth he goes, and visits all his host;
Bids them good-morrow, with a modest smile;
And calls them—brothers, friends, and countrymen.
Upon his royal face there is no note,
How dread an army hath enrounded him;
Nor doth he dedicate one jot of colour
Unto the weary and all-watched night:
But freshly looks, and overbears attaint,
With cheerful semblance, and sweet majesty;
That every wretch, pining and pale before,
Beholding him, plucks comfort from his looks:
A largess universal, like the sun,
His liberal eye doth give to every one,
Thawing cold fear.

* Discoloured by the gleam of the fires. † Over-saucy.

Enter BATES, COURT, *and* WILLIAMS.

Court. Brother John Bates, is not that the morning which breaks yonder?

Bates. I think it be: but we have no great cause to desire the approach of day.

Will. We see yonder the beginning of the day, but, I think, we shall never see the end of it.—Who goes there?

K. Hen. A friend.

Will. Under what captain serve you?

K. Hen. Under Sir Thomas Erpingham.

Will. A good old commander, and a most kind gentleman: I pray you, what thinks he of our estate?

K. Hen. Even as men wrecked upon a sand, that look to be washed off the next tide.

Bates. He hath not told his thought to the king.

K. Hen. No; nor it is not meet he should. For, though I speak it to you, I think, the king is but a man, as I am: the violet smells to him, as it doth to me; the element shows to him, as it doth to me; all his senses have but human conditions *; his ceremonies laid by, in his nakedness he appears but a man; and though his affections are higher mounted than ours, yet, when they stoop, they stoop with the like wing; therefore, when he sees reason of fears, as we do, his fears, out of doubt, be of the same relish as ours are: Yet, in reason, no man should possess him with any appearance of fear, lest he, by showing it, should dishearten his army.

Bates. He may show what outward courage he will: but, I believe, as cold a night as 'tis, he could wish himself in the Thames up to the neck; and so I would he were, and I by him, at all adventures, so we were quit here.

K. Hen. By my troth, I will speak my conscience of the king; I think he would not wish himself any where but where he is.

Bates. Then, 'would he were here alone; so should

* Qualities.

he be sure to be ransomed, and a many poor men's lives saved.

K. Hen. I dare say, you love him not so ill, to wish him here alone; howsoever you speak this, to feel other men's minds: Methinks, I could not die any where so contented, as in the king's company: his cause being just, and his quarrel honourable.

Will. That's more than we know.

Bates. Ay, or more than we should seek after; for we know enough, if we know we are the king's subjects; if his cause be wrong, our obedience to the king wipes the crime of it out of us.

Will. But if the cause be not good, the king himself hath a heavy reckoning to make; when all those legs, and arms, and heads chopped off in a battle shall join together at the latter day*, and cry all—We died at such a place; some, swearing; some, crying for a surgeon; some, upon their wives left poor behind them; some, upon the debts they owe; some, upon their children rawly† left. I am afeard there are few die well, that die in battle; for how can they charitably dispose of any thing, when blood is their argument? Now, if these men do not die well, it will be a black matter for the king that led them to it: whom to disobey, were against all proportion of subjection.

K. Hen. So, if a son, that is by his father sent about merchandise, do sinfully miscarry upon the sea, the imputation of his wickedness, by your rule, should be imposed upon his father that sent him: or if a servant, under his master's command, transporting a sum of money, be assailed by robbers, and die in many irreconciled iniquities, you may call the business of the master the author of the servant's damnation:—But this is not so: the king is not bound to answer the particular endings of his soldiers, the father of his son, nor the master of his servant; for they purpose not their death, when they purpose their services. Besides, there is no king, be his cause never

* The last day, the day of judgment. † Suddenly.

so spotless, if it come to the arbitrement of swords, can try it out with all unspotted soldiers. Some, peradventure, have on them the guilt of premeditated and contrived murder; some, of beguiling virgins with the broken seals of perjury; some, making the wars their bulwark, that have before gored the gentle bosom of peace with pillage and robbery. Now, if these men have defeated the law, and outrun native punishment*, though they can outstrip men, they have no wings to fly from God: war is his beadle, war is his vengeance; so that here men are punished, for before-breach of the king's laws, in now the king's quarrel: where they feared the death, they have borne life away; and where they would be safe, they perish: Then if they die unprovided, no more is the king guilty of their damnation, than he was before guilty of those impieties for the which they are now visited. Every subject's duty is the king's; but every subject's soul is his own. Therefore should every soldier in the wars do as every sick man in his bed, wash every mote out of his conscience: and dying so, death is to him advantage; or not dying, the time was blessedly lost, wherein such preparation was gained: and in him that escapes, it were not sin to think, that making God so free an offer, he let him outlive that day to see his greatness, and to teach others how they should prepare.

Will. 'Tis certain, every man that dies ill, the ill is upon his own head, the king is not to answer for it.

THE MISERIES OF ROYALTY.

O hard condition! twin-born with greatness,
Subjected to the breath of every fool,
Whose sense no more can feel but his own wringing!
What infinite heart's ease must kings neglect,
That private men enjoy?
And what have kings, that privates have not too,
Save ceremony, save general ceremony?

* *i. e.* Punishment in their native country.

And what art thou, thou idol ceremony?
What kind of god art thou, that suffer'st more
Of mortal griefs, than do thy worshippers?
What are thy rents? what are thy comings-in?
O ceremony, show me but thy worth!
What is the soul of adoration *?
Art thou aught else but place, degree, and form,
Creating awe and fear in other men?
Wherein thou art less happy being fear'd
Than they in fearing.
What drink'st thou oft, instead of homage sweet,
But poison'd flattery? O, be sick, great greatness,
And bid thy ceremony give thee cure!
Think'st thou, the fiery fever will go out
With titles blown from adulation?
Will it give place to flexure and low bending?
Canst thou, when thou command'st the beggar's knee,
Command the health of it? No, thou proud dream,
That play'st so subtly with a king's repose;
I am a king, that find thee; and I know,
'Tis not the balm, the sceptre, and the ball,
The sword, the mace, the crown imperial,
The enter-tissued robe of gold and pearl,
The farced † title running 'fore the king,
The throne he sits on, nor the tide of pomp,
That beats upon the high shore of this world,
No, not all these, thrice gorgeous ceremony,
Not all these, laid in bed majestical,
Can sleep so soundly as the wretched slave;
Who, with a body fill'd, and vacant mind,
Gets him to rest, cramm'd with distressful bread;
Never sees horrid night, the child of hell;
But, like a lackey, from the rise to set,
Sweats in the eye of Phœbus, and all night
Sleeps in Elysium; next day, after dawn,
Doth rise, and help Hyperion ‡ to his horse;

* "What is the real worth and intrinsic value of adoration?"

† Farced is stuffed. The tumid puffy titles with which a king's name is introduced.

‡ The sun.

And follows so the ever-running year
With profitable labour, to his grave:
And, but for ceremony, such a wretch,
Winding up days with toil, and nights with sleep,
Had the fore-hand and 'vantage of a king.

DESCRIPTION OF THE MISERABLE STATE OF THE ENGLISH ARMY.

Yon island carrions, desperate of their bones,
Ill-favour'dly become the morning field:
Their ragged curtains * poorly are let loose,
And our air shakes them passing scornfully.
Big Mars seems bankrupt in their beggar'd host,
And faintly through a rusty beaver peeps.
Their horsemen sit like fixed candlesticks,
With torch-staves in their hand: and their poor jades
Lob down their heads, dropping the hides and hips;
The gum down-roping from their pale-dead eyes;
And in their pale dull mouths the gimmal † bit
Lies foul with chew'd grass still and motionless;
And their executors, the knavish crows,
Fly o'er them all, impatient for their hour.

KING HENRY'S SPEECH BEFORE THE BATTLE OF AGINCOURT.

He that outlives this day, and comes safe home,
Will stand a tip-toe when this day is nam'd,
And rouse him at the name of Crispian.
He, that shall live this day, and see old age,
Will yearly on the vigil feast his friends,
And say—to-morrow is Saint Crispian:
Then will he strip his sleeve and show his scars,
And say, these wounds I had on Crispian's day.
Old men forget: yet all shall be forgot,
But he'll remember, with advantages,
What feats he did that day: Then shall our names,
Familiar in their mouths as household words,—
Harry the king, Bedford, and Exeter,

* Colours. † Ring.

Warwick and Talbot, Salisbury and Gloster,—
Be in their flowing cups freshly remember'd.

DESCRIPTION OF THE DUKE OF YORK'S DEATH.

He smil'd me in the face, raught* me his hand,
And, with a feeble gripe, says,—*Dear my lord,*
Commend my service to my sovereign.
So did he turn, and over Suffolk's neck
He threw his wounded arm, and kiss'd his lips;
And so, espous'd to death, with blood he seal'd
A testament of noble-ending love.
The pretty and sweet manner of it forc'd
Those waters from me, which I would have stopp'd;
But I had not so much of man in me,
But all my mother came into mine eyes,
And gave me up to tears.

ACT V.

THE MISERIES OF WAR.

Her vine, the merry cheerer of the heart,
Unpruned dies: her hedges even-pleached,—
Like prisoners wildly overgrown with hair,
Put forth disorder'd twigs: her fallow leas
The darnel, hemlock, and rank fumitory,
Doth root upon; while that the coulter† rusts,
That should deracinate‡ such savagery:
The even mead, that erst brought sweetly forth
The freckled cowslip, burnet, and green clover,
Wanting the scythe, all uncorrected, rank,
Conceives by idleness; and nothing teems,
But hateful docks, rough thistles, kecksies, burs,
Losing both beauty and utility.
And as our vineyards, fallows, meads, and hedges,
Defective in their natures, grow to wildness.

* Reached. † Ploughshare.
‡ To deracinate is to force up the roots.

KING HENRY VI.

PART I.

ACT I.

GLORY.

GLORY is like a circle in the water,
Which never ceaseth to enlarge itself,
Till, by broad spreading, it disperse to nought.

ACT V.

MARRIAGE.

Marriage is a matter of more worth
Than to be dealt in by attorneyship*.
* * * * *

For what is wedlock forced, but a hell,
An age of discord and continual strife?
Whereas the contrary bringeth forth bliss,
And is a pattern of celestial peace.

KING HENRY VI.

PART II.

ACT I.

A RESOLVED AND AMBITIOUS WOMAN.

FOLLOW I must, I cannot go before,
While Gloster bears this base and humble mind.
Were I a man, a duke, and next of blood,
I would remove these tedious stumbling-blocks,

* By the discretional agency of another.

And smooth my way upon their headless necks:
And, being a woman, I will not be slack
To play my part in fortune's pageant.

ACT II.

GOD'S GOODNESS EVER TO BE REMEMBERED.

Let never day nor night unhallow'd pass,
But still remember what the Lord hath done.

THE DUCHESS OF GLOSTER'S REMONSTRANCE TO HER HUSBAND, WHEN DOING PENANCE.

For, whilst I think I am thy married wife,
And, thou a prince, protector of this land,
Methinks, I should not thus be led along,
Mail'd up in shame *, with papers on my back;
And follow'd with a rabble, that rejoice
To see my tears, and hear my deep-fet † groans.
The ruthless flint doth cut my tender feet;
And, when I start, the envious people laugh,
And bid me be advised how I tread.

ACT III.

SILENT RESENTMENT DEEPEST.

Smooth runs the water, where the brook is deep;
And in his simple show he harbours treason.

A GUILTY COUNTENANCE.

Upon thy eyeballs murderous tyranny
Sits in grim majesty, to fright the world.

DESCRIPTION OF A MURDERED PERSON.

See, how the blood is settled in his face!
Oft have I seen a timely parted ghost ‡,

* Wrapped up in disgrace; alluding to the sheet of penance.

† Deep-fetched.

‡ A body become inanimate in the common course of nature; to which violence has not brought a timeless end.

Of ashy semblance, meagre, pale, and bloodless,
Being all descended to the labouring heart;
Who, in the conflict that it holds with death,
Attracts the same for aidance 'gainst the enemy;
Which with the heart there cools and ne'er returneth
To blush and beautify the cheek again.
But, see, his face is black, and full of blood;
His eyeballs further out than when he liv'd,
Staring full ghastly, like a strangled man:
His hair uprear'd, his nostrils stretch'd with struggling;
His hands abroad display'd, as one that grasp'd
And tugg'd for life, and was by strength subdu'd.
Look on the sheets, his hair, you see, is sticking:
His well-proportion'd beard made rough and rugged,
Like to the summer's corn by tempest lodg'd.
It cannot be, but he was murder'd here;
The least of all these signs were probable.

A GOOD CONSCIENCE.

What stronger breast-plate than a heart untainted?
Thrice is he arm'd, that hath his quarrel just;
And he but naked, though lock'd up in steel,
Whose conscience with injustice is corrupted.

REMORSELESS HATRED.

A plague upon them! Wherefore should I curse them?
Would curses kill, as doth the mandrake's groan,
I would invent as bitter-searching terms,
As curst, as harsh, and horrible to hear,
Deliver'd strongly through my fixed teeth,
With full as many signs of deadly hate,
As lean-fac'd Envy in her loathsome cave:
My tongue should stumble in mine earnest words:
Mine eyes should sparkle like the beaten flint:
My hair be fix'd on end, as one distract:
Ay, every joint should seem to curse and ban:
And even now my burden'd heart would break,
Should I not curse them. Poison be their drink!
Gall, worse than gall, the daintiest that they taste!

Their sweetest shade, a grove of cypress trees!
Their chiefest prospect, murdering basilisks!
Their softest touch, as smart as lizard's stings!
Their music, frightful as the serpent's hiss;
And boding screech-owls make the concert full!
All the foul terrors in dark-seated hell.

* * * * *

Now, by the ground that I am banish'd from,
Well could I curse away a winter's night,
Though standing naked on a mountain top,
Where biting cold would never let grass grow.

PARTING LOVERS.

And banished I am, if but from thee.
Go, speak not to me; even now be gone.—
O, go not yet!—Even thus two friends condemn'd
Embrace, and kiss, and take ten thousand leaves,
Loather a hundred times to part than die.
Yet now farewell; and farewell life with thee!
Suf. Thus is poor Suffolk ten times banished,
Once by the king, and three times thrice by thee.
'Tis not the land I care for, wert thou hence;
A wilderness is populous enough,
So Suffolk had thy heavenly company:
For where thou art, there is the world itself,
With every several pleasure in the world;
And where thou art not, desolation.

DYING WITH THE PERSON BELOVED PREFERABLE TO PARTING.

If I depart from thee, I cannot live:
And in thy sight to die, what were it else,
But like a pleasant slumber in thy lap?
Here could I breathe my soul into the air,
As mild and gentle as the cradle-babe,
Dying with mother's dug between its lips.

THE DEATH-BED HORRORS OF A GUILTY CONSCIENCE.

Bring me unto my trial when you will.
Died he not in his bed? where should he die?
Can I make men live, whe'r they will or no?

O! torture me no more, I will confess.—
Alive again? then show me where he is;
I'll give a thousand pound to look upon him,—
He hath no eyes, the dust hath blinded them.—
Comb down his hair; look! look! it stands upright,
Like lime-twigs set to catch my winged soul!—
Give me some drink; and bid the apothecary
Bring the strong poison that I bought of him.

ACT IV.

NIGHT.

The gaudy, blabbing, and remorseful* day
Is crept into the bosom of the sea;
And now loud-howling wolves arouse the jades
That drag the tragic melancholy night;
Who with their drowsy, slow, and flagging wings
Clip dead men's graves, and from their misty jaws
Breathe foul contagious darkness in the air.

KENT.

Kent, in the commentaries Cæsar writ,
Is term'd the civil'st place of all this isle:
Sweet is the country, because full of riches;
The people liberal, valiant, active, wealthy.

LORD SAY'S APOLOGY FOR HIMSELF.

Justice with favour have I always done;
Prayers and tears have mov'd me, gifts could never.
When have I aught exacted at your hands,
Kent to maintain, the king, the realm, and you?
Large gifts have I bestow'd on learned clerks,
Because my book preferr'd me to the king:
And—seeing ignorance is the curse of God,
Knowledge the wing wherewith we fly to heaven,—
Unless you be possess'd with devilish spirits,
You cannot but forbear to murder me.

* Pitiful.

KING HENRY VI.

PART III.

ACT I.

THE TRANSPORTS OF A CROWN.

Do but think,
How sweet a thing it is to wear a crown;
Within whose circuit is Elysium,
And all that poets feign of bliss and joy.

A HUNGRY LION.

So looks the pent-up lion o'er the wretch
That trembles under his devouring paws:
And so he walks, insulting o'er his prey;
And so he comes to rend his limbs asunder.

THE DUKE OF YORK ON THE GALLANT BEHAVIOUR OF HIS SONS.

My sons—God knows, what hath bechanced them:
But this I know,—they have demean'd themselves
Like men born to renown, by life, or death.
Three times did Richard make a lane to me;
And thrice cried,—*Courage, father, fight it out!*
And full as oft came Edward to my side,
With purple falchion, painted to the hilt
In blood of those that had encounter'd him;
And when the hardiest warriors did retire,
Richard cried—*Charge! and give no foot of ground!*
And cried,—*A Crown, or else a glorious tomb!*
A sceptre, or an earthly sepulchre!
With this, we charg'd again; but out, alas!
We bodg'd* again; as I have seen a swan

* *i. e.* We boggled, made bad, or bungling work of our attempt to rally.

With bootless labour swim against the tide,
And spend her strength with over-matching waves.

A FATHER'S PASSION ON THE MURDER OF A FAVOURITE CHILD.

O, tiger's heart, wrapp'd in a woman's hide!
How couldst thou drain the life-blood of the child,
To bid the father wipe his eyes withal,
And yet be seen to bear a woman's face?
Women are soft, mild, pitiful, and flexible;
Thou stern, obdurate, flinty, rough, remorseless.

* * * * *

That face of his the hungry cannibals
Would not have touch'd, would not have stain'd with blood:
But you are more inhuman, more inexorable,—
O, ten times more,—than tigers of Hyrcania.
See, ruthless queen, a hapless father's tears:
This cloth thou dipp'dst in blood of my sweet boy,
And I with tears do wash the blood away.
Keep thou the napkin, and go boast of this:
And, if thou tell'st the heavy story right,
Upon my soul, the hearers will shed tears;
Yea, even my foes will shed fast-falling tears,
And say,—Alas, it was a piteous deed!

ACT II.

THE DUKE OF YORK IN BATTLE.

Methought, he bore him* in the thickest troop,
As doth a lion in a herd of neat†;
Or as a bear, encompass'd round with dogs;
Who having pinch'd a few, and made them cry,
The rest stand all aloof, and bark at him.

* Demeaned himself. † Neat cattle, cows, oxen, &c.

MORNING.

See, how the morning opes her golden gates,
And takes her farewell of the glorious sun*!
How well resembles it the prime of youth,
Trimm'd like a younker, prancing to his love!

THE MORNING'S DAWN.

This battle fares like to the morning's war,
When dying clouds contend with growing light;
What time the shepherd, blowing of his nails,
Can neither call it perfect day, nor night.

THE BLESSINGS OF A SHEPHERD'S LIFE.

O God! methinks, it were a happy life,
To be no better than a homely swain;
To sit upon a hill, as I do now,
To carve out dials quaintly, point by point,
Thereby to see the minutes how they run:
How many make the hour full complete,
How many hours bring about the day,
How many days will finish up the year,
How many years a mortal man may live.
When this is known, then to divide the times:
So many hours must I tend my flock;
So many hours must I take my rest;
So many hours must I contemplate;
So many hours must I sport myself;
So many days my ewes have been with young;
So many weeks ere the poor fools will yean;
So many years ere I shall shear the fleece:
So minutes, hours, days, weeks, months, and years,
Pass'd over to the end they were created,
Would bring white hairs unto a quiet grave.
Ah! what a life were this! how sweet! how lovely!
Gives not the hawthorn bush a sweeter shade
To shepherds, looking on their silly sheep,
Than doth a rich embroider'd canopy
To kings, that fear their subjects' treachery?

* Aurora takes for a time her farewell of the sun, when she dismisses him to his diurnal course.

O, yes it doth: a thousand fold it doth.
And to conclude,—the shepherd's homely curds,
His cold thin drink out of his leather bottle,
His wonted sleep under a fresh tree's shade,
All which secure and sweetly he enjoys,
Is far beyond a prince's delicates,
His viands sparkling in a golden cup,
His body couched in a curious bed,
When care, mistrust, and treason wait on him.

ACT III.

NO STABILITY IN A MOB.

Look, as I blow this feather from my face,
And as the air blows it to me again,
Obeying with my wind when I do blow,
And yielding to another when it blows,
Commanded always by the greater gust;
Such is the likeness of you common men.

A SIMILE ON AMBITIOUS THOUGHTS.

Why, then I do but dream on sovereignty;
Like one that stands upon a promontory,
And spies a far-off shore where he would tread,
Wishing his foot were equal with his eye;
And chides the sea that sunders him from thence,
Saying—he'll lade it dry to have his way.

GLOSTER'S DEFORMITY.

Why, love forswore me in my mother's womb:
And, for I should not deal in her soft laws
She did corrupt frail nature with some bribe
To shrink mine arm up like a wither'd shrub;
To make an envious mountain on my back,
Where sits deformity to mock my body;
To shape my legs of an unequal size;
To disproportion me in every part,
Like to a chaos, or an unlick'd bear-whelp,
That carries no impression like the dam.
And am I then a man to be belov'd?

GLOSTER'S DISSIMULATION.

Why, I can smile, and murder while I smile;
And cry, content, to that which grieves my heart;
And wet my cheeks with artificial tears,
And frame my face to all occasions.
I'll drown more sailors than the mermaid shall;
I'll slay more gazers than the basilisk;
I'll play the orator as well as Nestor,
Deceive more slily than Ulysses could,
And, like a Sinon, take another Troy:
I can add colours to the cameleon;
Change shapes, with Proteus, for advantages,
And set the murd'rous Machiavel to school.
Can I do this, and cannot get a crown?

ACT IV.

HENRY VI. ON HIS OWN LENITY.

I have not stopp'd mine ears to their demands,
Nor posted off their suits with slow delays;
My pity hath been balm to heal their wounds,
My mildness hath allay'd their swelling griefs,
My mercy dry'd their water-flowing tears:
I have not been desirous of their wealth,
Nor much oppress'd them with great subsidies,
Nor forward of revenge, though they much err'd.

ACT V.

DYING SPEECH OF THE EARL OF WARWICK.

Ah, who is nigh? come to me, friend, or foe,
And tell me, who is victor, York, or Warwick?
Why ask I that? my mangled body shows,
My blood, my want of strength, my sick heart shows,
That I must yield my body to the earth,
And, by my fall, the conquest to my foe.

Thus yields the cedar to the axe's edge,
Whose arms gave shelter to the princely eagle,
Under whose shade the ramping lion slept;
Whose top-branch over-peer'd Jove's spreading tree,
And kept low shrubs from winter's powerful wind.
These eyes, that now are dimm'd with death's black veil,
Have been as piercing as the mid-day sun,
To search the secret treasons of the world:
The wrinkles in my brows, now fill'd with blood,
Were liken'd oft to kingly sepulchres;
For who liv'd king, but I could dig his grave?
And who durst smile, when Warwick bent his brow?
Lo, now my glory smear'd in dust and blood!
My parks, my walks, my manors that I had,
Even now forsake me: and, of all my lands,
Is nothing left me, but my body's length!

QUEEN MARGARET'S SPEECH BEFORE THE BATTLE OF TEWKSBURY.

Lords, knights, and gentlemen, what I should say,
My tears gainsay *; for every word I speak,
Ye see, I drink the water of mine eyes.
Therefore, no more but this:—Henry, your sovereign,
Is prisoner to the foe; his state usurp'd,
His realm a slaughter-house, his subjects slain,
His statutes cancell'd, and his treasure spent;
And yonder is the wolf, that makes this spoil.
You fight in justice: then, in God's name, lords,
Be valiant, and give signal to the fight.

OMENS ON THE BIRTH OF RICHARD III.

The owl shriek'd at thy birth, an evil sign;
The night-crow cried, aboding luckless time;
Dogs howl'd, and hideous tempests shook down trees;
The raven rook'd † her on the chimney's top,
And chattering pies in dismal discords sung.

* Unsay, deny.
† To rook, signified to squat down or lodge on any thing.

Thy mother felt more than a mother's pain,
And yet brought forth less than a mother's hope;
To wit,—an indigest deformed lump,
Not like the fruit of such a goodly tree.
Teeth hadst thou in thy head, when thou wast born,
To signify,—thou cam'st to bite the world.

KING RICHARD III.

ACT I.

THE DUKE OF GLOSTER ON HIS OWN DEFORMITY.

Now are our brows bound with victorious wreaths;
Our bruised arms hung up for monuments;
Our stern alarums chang'd to merry meetings,
Our dreadful marches to delightful measures *.
Grim-visag'd war hath smooth'd his wrinkled front;
And now,—instead of mounting barbed † steeds
To fright the souls of fearful adversaries,—
He capers nimbly in a lady's chamber,
To the lascivious pleasing of a lute.
But I,—that am not shap'd for sportive tricks,
Nor made to court an amorous looking-glass:
I, that am rudely stamp'd, and want love's majesty,
To strut before a wanton ambling nymph;
I, that am curtail'd of this fair proportion,
Cheated of feature by dissembling nature,
Deform'd, unfinish'd, sent before my time
Into this breathing world, scarce half made up,
And that so lamely and unfashionable,
That dogs bark at me, as I halt by them;—

* Dances. † Armèd.

Why I, in this weak piping time of peace,
Have no delight to pass away the time,
Unless to spy my shadow in the sun,
And descant on mine own deformity;
And therefore,—since I cannot prove a lover,
To entertain these fair well-spoken days,—
I am determined to prove a villain,
And hate the idle pleasures of these days.

GLOSTER'S LOVE FOR LADY ANNE.

Those eyes of thine from mine have drawn salt tears,
Sham'd their aspects with store of childish drops:
These eyes, which never shed remorseful * tear,—
Not, when my father York and Edward wept,
To hear the piteous moan that Rutland made,
When black-fac'd Clifford shook his sword at him:
Nor when thy warlike father, like a child,
Told the sad story of my father's death;
And twenty times made pause, to sob, and weep,
That all the standers-by had wet their cheeks,
Like trees bedash'd with rain: in that sad time,
My manly eyes did scorn an humble tear;
And what these sorrows could not thence exhale,
Thy beauty hath, and made them blind with weeping.
I never su'd to friend, nor enemy;
My tongue could never learn sweet soothing word;
But now thy beauty is propos'd my fee,
My proud heart sues, and prompts my tongue to speak.

GLOSTER'S PRAISES OF HIS OWN PERSON, AFTER HIS SUCCESSFUL ADDRESSES.

My dukedom to a beggarly denier †,
I do mistake my person all this while:
Upon my life, she finds, although I cannot,
Myself to be a marvellous proper man.
I'll be at charges for a looking glass;

* Pitiful. † A small French coin.

And entertain a score or two of tailors,
To study fashions to adorn my body:
Since I am crept in favour with myself,
I will maintain it with some little cost.

QUEEN MARGARET'S EXECRATIONS ON GLOSTER.

The worm of conscience still be-gnaw thy soul!
Thy friends suspect for traitors while thou liv'st,
And take deep traitors for thy dearest friends!
No sleep close up that deadly eye of thine,
Unless it be while some tormenting dream
Affrights thee with a hell of ugly devils!
Thou elvish-mark'd, abortive, rooting hog!
Thou that wast seal'd in thy nativity
The slave of nature, and the son of hell!
Thou slander of thy mother's heavy womb!
Thou loathed issue of thy father's loins!
Thou rag of honour! thou detested——

HIGH BIRTH.

I was born so high,
Our aiery * buildeth in the cedar's top,
And dallies with the wind, and scorns the sun.

GLOSTER'S HYPOCRISY.

But then I sigh, and, with a piece of scripture,
Tell them—that God bids us do good for evil:
And thus I clothe my naked villany
With old odd ends, stol'n forth of holy writ:
And seem a saint, when most I play the devil.

CLARENCE'S DREAM.

What was your dream, my lord? I pray you, tell me.
Clar. Methought, that I had broken from the Tower,
And was embark'd to cross to Burgundy:
And, in my company, my brother Gloster;
Who from my cabin tempted me to walk
Upon the hatches; thence we look'd toward England,

* Nest.

And cited up a thousand heavy times,
During the wars of York and Lancaster
That had befall'n us. As we pac'd along
Upon the giddy footing of the hatches,
Methought that Gloster stumbled; and, in falling,
Struck me, that thought to stay him, overboard,
Into the tumbling billows of the main.
O Lord! methought what pain it was to drown!
What dreadful noise of water in mine ears!
What sights of ugly death within mine eyes!
Methought I saw a thousand fearful wrecks;
A thousand men, that fishes gnaw'd upon;
Wedges of gold, great anchors, heaps of pearl,
Inestimable stones, unvalued jewels,
All scatter'd in the bottom of the sea,
Some lay in dead men's skulls; and, in those holes
Where eyes did once inhabit, there were crept
(As 'twere in scorn of eyes,) reflecting gems,
That woo'd the slimy bottom of the deep,
And mock'd the dead bones that lay scatter'd by.

Brak. Had you such leisure in the time of death,
To gaze upon these secrets of the deep?

Clar. Methought, I had; and often did I strive
To yield the ghost: but still the envious flood
Kept in my soul, and would not let it forth
To seek the empty, vast, and wand'ring air:
But smother'd it within my panting bulk *,
Which almost burst to belch it in the sea.

Brak. Awak'd you not with this sore agony?

Clar. O no, my dream was lengthen'd after life;
O, then began the tempest to my soul!
I pass'd methought, the melancholy flood,
With that grim ferryman which poets write of,
Unto the kingdom of perpetual night.
The first that there did greet my stranger soul,
Was my great father-in-law, renowned Warwick,
Who cried aloud,—*What scourge for perjury*
Can this dark monarchy afford false Clarence?
And so he vanish'd: Then came wand'ring by

* Body.

A shadow, like an angel, with bright hair
Dabbled in blood: and he shriek'd out aloud,—
Clarence is come,—false, fleeting, perjur'd Clarence,—
That stabb'd me in the field by Tewksbury;—
Seize on him, furies, take him to your torments!
With that, methought, a legion of foul fiends
Environ'd me, and howled in mine ears
Such hideous cries, that, with the very noise,
I trembling waked, and, for a season after,
Could not believe but that I was in hell;
Such terrible impression made my dream.
Brak. No marvel, lord, though it affrighted you!
I am afraid, methinks, to hear you tell it.
Clar. O, Brakenbury, I have done these things—
That now give evidence against my soul,—
For Edward's sake; and see how he requites me!—
O God! if my deep prayers cannot appease thee,
But thou wilt be avenged on my misdeeds,
Yet execute thy wrath on me alone:
O, spare my guiltless wife, and my poor children!

SORROW.

Sorrow breaks seasons, and reposing hours,
Makes the night morning, and the noontide night.

THE CARES OF GREATNESS.

Princes have but their titles for their glories,
An outward honour for an inward toil;
And, for my unfelt imaginations,
They often feel a world of restless cares:
So that, between their titles and low name,
There's nothing differs but the outward fame.

A MURDERER'S ACCOUNT OF CONSCIENCE.

I'll not meddle with it, it is a dangerous thing, it makes a man a coward: a man cannot steal, but it accuseth him; a man cannot swear, but it checks him; a man cannot lie with his neighbour's wife, but it detects him: 'Tis a blushing shame-faced spirit, that mutinies in a man's bosom; it fills one full of obstacles; it made me once restore a purse of gold, that by chance I found; it beggars any man that keeps it; it is turned out of all towns and cities for a dangerous thing; and every man, that means to live well, endeavours to trust to himself, and live without it.

ACT II.

DECEIT.

Ah, that deceit should steal such gentle shapes,
And with a virtuous visor hide deep vice!

SUBMISSION TO HEAVEN OUR DUTY.

In common worldly things, 'tis call'd—ungrateful,
With dull unwillingness to repay a debt,
Which with a bounteous hand was kindly lent;
Much more to be thus opposite with heaven,
For it requires the royal debt it lent you.

THE DUCHESS OF YORK'S LAMENTATION ON THE MISFORTUNES OF HER FAMILY.

Duch. Accursed and unquiet wrangling days!
How many of you have mine eyes beheld?
My husband lost his life to get the crown;
And often up and down my sons were tost,
For me to joy, and weep, their gain, and loss:
And being seated, and domestic broils
Clean overblown, themselves, the conquerors,
Make war upon themselves: brother to brother,
Blood to blood, self 'gainst self: O, preposterous
And frantic courage, end thy damned spleen;
Or let me die, to look on death no more!

ACT III.

THE VANITY OF TRUST IN MAN.

O momentary grace of mortal men,
Which we more hunt for than the grace of God.
Who builds his hope in air of your fair looks,

Lives like a drunken sailor on a mast;
Ready, with every nod, to tumble down
Into the fatal bowels of the deep.

CONTEMPLATION.

When holy and devout religious men
Are at their beads, 'tis hard to draw them thence;
So sweet is zealous contemplation.

ACT IV.

DESCRIPTION OF THE MURDER OF THE TWO YOUNG PRINCES IN THE TOWER.

The tyrannous and bloody act is done;
The most arch deed of piteous massacre,
That ever yet this land was guilty of.
Dighton and Forrest, whom I did suborn
To do this piece of ruthless* butchery,
Albeit they were flesh'd villains, bloody dogs,
Melting with tenderness and mild compassion,
Wept like two children, in their death's sad story.
O thus, quoth Dighton, *lay the gentle babes,—*
Thus, thus, quoth Forrest, *girdling one another*
Within their alabaster innocent arms;
Their lips were four red roses on a stalk,
Which, in their summer beauty, kiss'd each other.
A book of prayers on their pillow lay:
Which once, quoth Forrest, *almost chang'd my mind;*
But, O, the devil—there the villain stopp'd;
When Dighton thus told on,—*we smothered*
The most replenished sweet work of nature,
That, from the prime creation, e'er she fram'd.—
Hence, both are gone with conscience and remorse,
They could not speak; and so I left them both,
To bear this tidings to the bloody king.

EXPEDITION.

Come.—I have learn'd, that fearful commenting
Is leaden servitor to dull delay;

* Merciless.

Delay leads impotent and snail-pac'd beggary:
Then fiery expedition be my wing,
Jove's Mercury, and herald for a king!

QUEEN MARGARET'S EXPROBATION.

I call'd thee then, vain flourish of my fortune;
I call'd thee then, poor shadow, painted queen:
The presentation of but what I was,
The flattering index* of a direful pageant,
One heav'd a high to be hurl'd down below:
A mother only mock'd with two fair babes;
A dream of what thou wast; a garish† flag,
To be the aim of every dangerous shot;
A sign of dignity, a breath, a bubble;
A queen in jest, only to fill the scene.
Where is thy husband now? Where be thy brothers?
Where be thy two sons? wherein dost thou joy?
Who sues, and kneels, and says—God save the queen?
Where be the bending peers that flatter'd thee?
Where be the thronging troops that follow'd thee?
Decline all this, and see what now thou art.
For happy wife, a most distressed widow;
For joyful mother, one that wails the name;
For one being sued to, one that humbly sues;
For queen, a very caitiff crown'd with care;
For one that scorn'd at me, now scorn'd of me;
For one being fear'd of all, now fearing one;
For one commanding all, obey'd of none.
Thus hath the course of justice wheel'd about,
And left thee but a very prey to time;
Having no more but thought of what thou wert,
To torture thee the more, being what thou art.

CHARACTER OF KING RICHARD BY HIS MOTHER.

Tetchy‡ and wayward was thy infancy;
Thy school-days, frightful, desperate, wild, and furious;
Thy prime of manhood, daring, bold, and venturous;
Thy age confirm'd, proud, subtle, sly, and bloody.

* Indexes were anciently placed at the beginning of books.
† Flaring. ‡ Touchy, fretful.

ACT V.

HOPE.

True hope is swift, and flies with swallow's wings,
Kings it makes gods, and meaner creatures kings.

A FINE EVENING.

The weary sun hath made a golden set,
And, by the bright track of his fiery car,
Gives token of a goodly day to-morrow.

DAYBREAK.

The silent hours steal on,
And flaky darkness breaks within the east.

RICHMOND'S PRAYER.

O Thou! whose captain I account myself,
Look on my forces with a gracious eye;
Put in their hands thy bruising irons of wrath,
That they may crush down with a heavy fall
The usurping helmets of our adversaries!
Make us thy ministers of chastisement,
That we may praise thee in thy victory!
To thee I do commend my watchful soul,
Ere I let fall the windows of mine eyes;
Sleeping, and waking, O defend me still!

RICHARD STARTING OUT OF HIS DREAM.

Give me another horse,—bind up my wounds,—
Have mercy, Jesu!—Soft; I did but dream.—
O coward conscience, how dost thou afflict me!
The lights burn blue,—It is now dead midnight.
Cold fearful drops stand on my trembling flesh.
What do I fear? myself?

CONSCIENCE.

Conscience is but a word that cowards use,
Devis'd at first to keep the strong in awe.

RICHARD'S ADDRESS BEFORE THE BATTLE.

A thousand hearts are great within my bosom:
Advance our standards, set upon our foes;
Our ancient word of courage, fair Saint George,
Inspire us with the spleen of fiery dragons!
Upon them! Victory sits on our helms.

RICHARD'S BEHAVIOUR AFTER AN ALARUM.

A horse! a horse! my kingdom for a horse!
Cate. Withdraw, my lord, I'll help you to a horse.
K. Rich. Slave, I have set my life upon a cast,
And I will stand the hazard of the die:
I think, there be six Richmonds in the field;
Five have I slain to-day, instead of him:—
A horse! a horse! my kingdom for a horse!

KING HENRY VIII.

ACT I.

ANGER.

To climb steep hills,
Requires slow pace at first: Anger is like
A full hot-horse; who being allow'd his way,
Self-mettle tires him.

ACTION TO BE CARRIED ON WITH RESOLUTION.

If I am traduc'd by tongues, which neither know
My faculties, nor person, yet will be
The chronicles of my doing,—let me say,
'Tis but the fate of place, and the rough brake *

* Thicket of thorns.

That virtue must go through. We must not stint *
Our necessary actions, in the fear
To cope † malicious censurers; which ever,
As ravenous fishes do a vessel follow
That is new trimm'd; but benefit no further
Than vainly longing. What we oft do best,
By sick interpreters, once ‡ weak ones, is
Not ours, or not allow'd §; what worst, as oft,
Hitting a grosser quality, is cried up
For our best act. If we shall stand still,
In fear our motion will be mock'd or carp'd at,
We should take root here where we sit, or sit
State statues only.

NEW CUSTOMS.

New customs,
Though they be never so ridiculous,
Nay, let them be unmanly, yet are follow'd.

ACT II.

THE DUKE OF BUCKINGHAM'S PRAYER FOR THE KING.

May he live
Longer than I have time to tell his years!
Ever belov'd and loving may his rule be!
And, when old time shall lead him to his end,
Goodness and he fill up one monument!

DEPENDENTS NOT TO BE TOO MUCH TRUSTED BY GREAT MEN.

This from a dying man receive as certain:
Where you are liberal of your loves, and counsels,
Be sure, you be not loose: for those you make friends,
And give your hearts to, when they once perceive
The least rub in your fortunes, fall away
Like water from ye, never found again
But where they mean to sink ye.

* Retard. † Encounter. ‡ Sometime. § Approved.

A GOOD WIFE.

A loss of her,
That, like a jewel, has hung twenty years
About his neck, yet never lost her lustre;
Of her, that loves him with that excellence
That angels love good men with; even of her
That, when the greatest stroke of fortune falls,
Will bless the king.

THE BLESSINGS OF A LOW STATION.

'Tis better to be lowly born,
And range with humble livers in content,
Than to be perk'd up in a glistering grief,
And wear a golden sorrow.

QUEEN KATHARINE'S SPEECH TO HER HUSBAND.

Alas, sir,
In what have I offended you? what cause
Hath my behaviour given to your displeasure,
That thus you should proceed to put me off,
And take your good grace from me? Heaven witness,
I have been to you a true and humble wife,
At all times to your will conformable:
Ever in fear to kindle your dislike,
Yea, subject to your countenance: glad, or sorry,
As I saw it inclin'd. When was the hour,
I ever contradicted your desire,
Or made it not mine too? Or which of your friends
Have I not strove to love, although I knew
He were mine enemy? what friend of mine
That had to him deriv'd your anger, did I
Continue in my liking? nay, gave notice
He was from thence discharg'd? Sir, call to mind
That I have been your wife, in this obedience,
Upward of twenty years, and have been blest
With many children by you: If, in the course
And process of this time, you can report,
And prove it too, against mine honour aught,
My bond to wedlock, or my love and duty,
Against your sacred person, in God's name,

Turn me away; and let the foul'st contempt
Shut door upon me, and so give me up
To the sharpest kind of justice.

QUEEN KATHARINE'S SPEECH TO CARDINAL WOLSEY.

You are meek, and humble mouth'd;
You sign your place and calling, in full seeming *,
With meekness and humility: but your heart
Is cramm'd with arrogancy, spleen, and pride.
You have, by fortune, and his highness' favours,
Gone slightly o'er low steps; and now are mounted
Where powers are your retainers: and your words,
Domestics to you, serve your will, as't please
Yourself pronounce their office. I must tell you,
You tender more your person's honour, than
Your high profession spiritual.

KING HENRY'S CHARACTER OF QUEEN KATHARINE.

That man i' the world, who shall report he has
A better wife, let him in nought be trusted,
For speaking false in that; Thou art, alone
(If thy rare qualities, sweet gentleness,
Thy meekness saint-like, wife-like government,—
Obeying in commanding,—and thy parts
Sovereign and pious else, could speak thee out †),
The queen of earthly queens.

ACT III.

QUEEN KATHARINE ON HER OWN MERIT.

Have I liv'd thus long—(let me speak myself,
Since virtue finds no friends),—a wife, a true one?
A woman (I dare say, without vainglory),
Never yet branded with suspicion?
Have I with all my full affections
Still met the king? lov'd him next heaven? obey'd him?

* Appearance. † Speak out thy merits.

Been, out of fondness, superstitious to him*?
Almost forgot my prayers to content him?
And am I thus rewarded? 'tis not well, lords.
Bring me a constant woman to her husband,
One that ne'er dream'd a joy beyond his pleasure;
And to that woman, when she has done most,
Yet will I add an honour,—a great patience.

QUEEN KATHARINE COMPARED TO A LILY.

Like the lily,
That once was mistress of the field, and flourish'd,
I'll hang my head, and perish.

OBEDIENCE TO PRINCES.

The hearts of princes kiss obedience,
So much they love it; but to stubborn spirits,
They swell, and grow as terrible as storms.

OUTWARD EFFECTS OF HORROR.

Some strange commotion
Is in his brain: he bites his lip, and starts;
Stops on a sudden, looks upon the ground,
Then lays his finger on his temple; straight,
Springs out into fast gait†; then, stops again,
Strikes his breast hard; and anon, he casts
His eye against the moon: in most strange postures
We have seen him set himself.

FIRM ALLEGIANCE.

Though perils did
Abound, as thick as thought could make them, and
Appear in forms more horrid; yet my duty,
As doth a rock against the chiding flood,
Should the approach of this wild river break,
And stand unshaken yours.

EXTERNAL EFFECTS OF ANGER.

What sudden anger's this? how have I reap'd it?
He parted frowning from me, as if ruin

* Served him with superstitious attention. † Steps.

Leap'd from his eyes: So looks the chafèd lion
Upon the daring huntsman that has gall'd him;
Then makes him nothing,

FALLING GREATNESS.

Nay then, farewell!
I have touch'd the highest point of all my greatness;
And, from that full meridian of my glory,
I haste now to my setting: I shall fall
Like a bright exhalation in the evening,
And no man see me more.

THE VICISSITUDES OF LIFE.

So farewell to the little good you bear me.
Farewell, a long farewell, to all my greatness!
This is the state of man; To-day he puts forth
The tender leaves of hope, to-morrow blossoms,
And bears his blushing honours thick upon him;
The third day, comes a frost, a killing frost;
And,—when he thinks, good easy man, full surely
His greatness is a ripening,—nips his root,
And then he falls, as I do. I have ventur'd,
Like little wanton boys that swim on bladders,
This many summers in a sea of glory;
But far beyond my depth: my high-blown pride
At length broke under me; and now has left me,
Weary, and old with service, to the mercy
Of a rude stream, that must for ever hide me.
Vain pomp, and glory of this world, I hate ye;
I feel my heart new open'd: O, how wretched
Is that poor man, that hangs on princes' favours!
There is, betwixt that smile we would aspire to,
That sweet aspect of princes, and their ruin,
More pangs and fears than wars or women have;
And when he falls, he falls like Lucifer,
Never to hope again.

CARDINAL WOLSEY'S SPEECH TO CROMWELL.

Cromwell, I did not think to shed a tear
In all my miseries; but thou hast forc'd me
Out of thy honest truth to play the woman.

Let's dry our eyes: and thus far hear me, Cromwell;
And,—when I am forgotten, as I shall be;
And sleep in dull cold marble, where no mention
Of me more must be heard of,—say, I taught thee,
Say, Wolsey,—that once trod the ways of glory,
And sounded all the depths and shoals of honour,—
Found thee a way, out of his wreck, to rise in;
A sure and safe one, though thy master miss'd it.
Mark but my fall, and that that ruin'd me.
Cromwell, I charge thee, fling away ambition;
By that sin fell the angels, how can man then,
The image of his Maker, hope to win by't?
Love thyself last: cherish those hearts that hate thee;
Corruption wins not more than honesty.
Still in thy right hand carry gentle peace,
To silence envious tongues. Be just, and fear not!
Let all the ends, thou aim'st at, be thy country's.
Thy God's, and truth's; then if thou fall'st, O Cromwell,
Thou fall'st a blessed martyr. Serve the king;
And,—Pr'ythee, lead me in:
There take an inventory of all I have,
To the last penny: 'tis the king's: my robe,
And my integrity to heaven, is all
I dare now call mine own. O Cromwell, Cromwell,
Had I but serv'd my God with half the zeal
I serv'd my king, he would not in mine age
Have left me naked to mine enemies.

ACT IV.

APPLAUSE.

Such a noise arose
As the shrouds make at sea in a stiff tempest,
As loud, and to as many tunes: hats, cloaks,
(Doublets, I think), flew up; and had their faces
Been loose, this day they had been lost. Such joy

I never saw before. Great-bellied women,
That had not half a week to go, like rams
In the old time of war, would shake the press,
And make them reel before them. No man living
Could say, *This is my wife*, there ; all were woven
So strangely in one piece.

CARDINAL WOLSEY'S DEATH.

At last, with easy roads*, he came to Leicester,
Lodg'd in the abbey ; where the reverend abbot,
With all his convent, honourably receiv'd him ;
To whom he gave these words,—*O, father abbot,*
An old man, broken with the storms of state,
Is come to lay his weary bones among ye ;
Give him a little earth for charity!
So went to bed : where eagerly his sickness
Pursu'd him still ; and, three nights after this,
About the hour of eight (which he himself
Foretold, should be his last), full of repentance,
Continual meditations, tears, and sorrows,
He gave his honours to the world again,
His blessed part to heaven, and slept in peace.

WOLSEY'S VICES AND VIRTUES.

So may he rest : his faults lie gently on him !
Yet thus far, Griffith, give me leave to speak him,
And yet with charity,—He was a man
Of an unbounded stomach †, ever ranking
Himself with princes ; one, that by suggestion
Ty'd all the kingdom : simony was fair play ;
His own opinion was his law : I' the presence ‡
He would say untruths ; and be ever double,
Both in his words and meaning : He was never,
But where he meant to ruin, pitiful :
His promises were, as he then was, mighty ;
But his performance, as he is now, nothing.

* By short stages. † Price. ‡ Of the king.

Of his own body he was ill, and gave
The clergy ill example.
Grif. Noble madam,
Men's evil manners live in brass; their virtues
We write in water.
* * * * *

This cardinal,
Though from an humble stock, undoubtedly
Was fashion'd to * much honour. From his cradle,
He was a scholar, and a ripe, and good one;
Exceeding wise, fair spoken, and persuading:
Lofty, and sour, to them that lov'd him not;
But, to those men that sought him, sweet as summer.
And though he were unsatisfied in getting
(Which was a sin), yet in bestowing, madam,
He was most princely: Ever witness for him
Those twins of learning, that he rais'd in you,
Ipswich and Oxford! one † of which fell with him,
Unwilling to outlive the good that did it;
The other, though unfinish'd, yet so famous,
So excellent in art, and still so rising,
That Christendom shall ever speak his virtue.
His overthrow heap'd happiness upon him;
For then, and not till then, he felt himself,
And found the blessedness of being little;
And, to add greater honours to his age
Than man could give him, he died, fearing God.

ACT V.

MALICIOUS MEN.

Men, that make
Envy, and crooked malice, nourishment,
Dare bite the best.

* Formed for. † Ipswich.

A CHURCHMAN.

Love, and meekness, lord,
Become a churchman better than ambition;
Win straying souls with modesty again,
Cast none away.

INHUMANITY.

'Tis a cruelty,
To load a falling man.

ARCHBISHOP CRANMER'S PROPHECY.

Let me speak, sir,
For heaven now bids me; and the words I utter
Let none think flattery, for they'll find them truth.
This royal infant (heaven still move about her!)
Though in her cradle, yet now promises
Upon this land a thousand thousand blessings,
Which time shall bring to ripeness: She shall be
(But few now living can behold that goodness),
A pattern to all princes living with her,
And all that shall succeed: Sheba was never
More covetous of wisdom, and fair virtue,
Than this pure soul shall be: all princely graces,
That mould up such a mighty piece as this is,
With all the virtues that attend the good,
Shall still be doubled on her: truth shall nurse her,
Holy and heavenly thoughts still counsel her:
She shall be lov'd and fear'd: Her own shall bless her:
Her foes shake like a field of beaten corn,
And hang their heads with sorrow: Good grows with
her:
In her days, every man shall eat in safety
Under his own vine, what he plants; and sing
The merry songs of peace to all his neighbours:
God shall be truly known; and those about her
From her shall read the perfect ways of honour,
And by those claim their greatness, not by blood.

Nor shall this peace sleep with her: But as when
The bird of wonder dies, the maiden phœnix,
Her ashes new create another heir,
As great in admiration as herself;
So shall she leave her blessedness to one,
(When heaven shall call her from this cloud of darkness),
Who, from the sacred ashes of her honour,
Shall star-like rise, as great in fame as she was,
And so stand fix'd: Peace, plenty, love, truth, terror,
That were the servants to this chosen infant,
Shall then be his, and like a vine grow to him;
Wherever the bright sun of heaven shall shine,
His honour, and the greatness of his name
Shall be, and make new nations: He shall flourish,
And, like a mountain cedar, reach his branches
To all the plains about him:——Our children's children
Shall see this, and bless Heaven.

THE

Beauties of Shakspeare.

PART III.

TRAGEDIES.

ANTONY AND CLEOPATRA.

ACT I.

LOVE THE NOBLENESS OF LIFE.

Let Rome in Tyber melt! and the wide arch
Of the rang'd empire fall! Here is my space;
Kingdoms are clay: our dungy earth alike
Feeds beast as man: the nobleness of life
Is, to do thus, when such a mutual pair, [*Embracing.*
And such a twain can do't, in which, I bind,
On pain of punishment, the world to weet *,
We stand up peerless.
Why did he marry Fulvia, and not love her?—
I'll seem the fool I am not; Antony
Will be himself.
Ant. But stirr'd by Cleopatra.—
Now, for the love of Love, and her soft hours.

ANTONY'S VICES AND VIRTUES.

I must not think, there are
Evils enough to darken all his goodness:
His faults, in him, seem as the spots of heaven,
More fiery by night's blackness; hereditary,
Rather than purchas'd †; what he cannot change,
Than what he chooses.
Cæs. You are too indulgent: Let us grant, it is not
Amiss to tumble on the bed of Ptolemy;
To give a kingdom for a mirth; to sit
And keep the turn of tippling with a slave;
To reel the streets at noon, and stand the buffet
With knaves that smell of sweat: say, this becomes him,

* Know. † Procured by his own fault.

(As his composure must be rare indeed,
Whom these things cannot blemish), yet must Antony
No way excuse his soils, when we do bear
So great weight in his lightness *. If he fill'd
His vacancy with his voluptuousness,
Full surfeits, and the dryness of his bones,
Call on him † for't: but, to confound ‡ such time,
That drums him from his sport, and speaks as loud
As his own state, and ours,—'tis to be chid
As we rate boys; who, being mature in knowledge,
Pawn their experience to their present pleasure,
And so rebel to judgment.
Antony,
Leave thy lascivious wassals §. When thou once
Wast beaten from Modena, where thou slew'st
Hirtius and Pansa, consuls, at thy heel
Did famine follow; whom thou fought'st against,
Though daintily brought up, with patience more
Than savages can suffer: Thou didst drink
The stale ‖ of horses, and the gilded puddle ¶
Which beasts would cough at: thy palate then did deign
The roughest berry on the rudest hedge;
Yea, like the stag, when snow the pasture sheets,
The barks of trees thou browsed'st; on the Alps
It is reported, thou didst eat strange flesh,
Which some did die to look on: And all this
(It wounds thine honour, that I speak it now),
Was borne so like a soldier, that thy cheek
So much as lank'd not.

CLEOPATRA'S SOLICITUDE ON THE ABSENCE OF ANTONY.

O Charmian,
Where think'st thou he is now? Stands he, or sits he?
Or does he walk? or is he on his horse?
O happy horse, to bear the weight of Antony!

* Levity. † Visit him. ‡ Consume.
§ Feastings; in the old copy it is *vaissailes*, i. e. vassals.
‖ Urine. ¶ Stagnant, slimy water.

Do bravely, horse! for wot'st thou whom thou mov'st?
The demi-Atlas of this earth, the arm
And burgonet* of men.—He's speaking now,
Or murmuring, *Where's my serpent of old Nile?*
For so he calls me: Now I feed myself
With most delicious poison:—Think on me,
That am with Phœbus' amorous pinches black,
And wrinkled deep in time? Broad-fronted Cæsar,
When thou wast here above the ground, I was
A morsel for a monarch: and great Pompey
Would stand, and make his eyes grow in my brow;
There would he anchor his aspéct, and die
With looking on his life.

ACT II.

THE VANITY OF HUMAN WISHES.

We, ignorant of ourselves,
Beg often our own harms, which the wise powers
Deny us for our good; so find we profit,
By losing of our prayers.

DESCRIPTION OF CLEOPATRA SAILING DOWN THE CYDNUS.

The barge she sat in, like a burnish'd throne,
Burn'd on the water: the poop was beaten gold;
Purple the sails, and so perfumed, that
The winds were love-sick with them: the oars were silver;
Which to the tune of flutes kept stroke, and made
The water, which they beat, to follow faster,
As amorous of their strokes. For her own person,
It beggar'd all description: she did lie
In her pavilion (cloth of gold, of tissue),
O'er-picturing that Venus, where we see,
The fancy out-work nature: on each side her,

* A helmet.

Stood pretty dimpled boys, like smiling Cupids,
With diverse-colour'd fans, whose wind did seem
To glow the delicate cheeks which they did cool,
And what they undid, did *.
Agr. O, rare for Antony!
Eno. Her gentlewomen, like the Nereides,
So many mermaids, tended her i' the eyes,
And made their bends adornings: at the helm
A seeming mermaid steers; the silken tackle
Swell with the touches of those flower-soft hands,
That yarely frame † the office. From the barge
A strange invisible perfume hits the sense
Of the adjacent wharfs. The city cast
Her people out upon her; and Antony,
Enthron'd in the market-place, did sit alone,
Whistling to the air; which, but for vacancy,
Had gone to gaze on Cleopatra too,
And made a gap in nature.

CLEOPATRA'S INFINITE POWER IN PLEASING.

Age cannot wither her, nor custom stale
Her infinite variety: Other women
Cloy th' appetites they feed; but she makes hungry
Where most she satisfies. For vilest things
Become themselves in her; that the holy priests
Bless her, when she's riggish ‡.

THE UNSETTLED HUMOURS OF LOVERS.

Enter CLEOPATRA, CHARMIAN, IRAS, *and* ALEXAS.

Cleo. Give me some music; music, moody § food
Of us that trade in love.
Attend. The music, ho!

Enter MARDIAN.

Cleo. Let it alone; let us to billiards:
Come, Charmian.

* Added to the warmth they were intended to diminish.
† Readily perform. ‡ Wanton. § Melancholy.

Char. My arm is sore, best play with Mardian.
Cleo. As well a woman with an eunuch play'd,
As with a woman:—Come, you'll play with me, sir?
Mar. As well as I can, madam.
Cleo. And when good will is show'd, though it come too short,
The actor may plead pardon. I'll none now:—
Give me mine angle,—We'll to the river: there,
My music playing far off, I will betray
Tawny-finn'd fishes; my bended hook shall pierce
Their slimy jaws; and, as I draw them up,
I'll think them every one an Antony,
And say, Ah, ha! you're caught.
Char. 'Twas merry, when
You wager'd on your angling; when your diver
Did hang a salt-fish on his hook, which he
With fervency drew up.
Cleo. That time!—O times!—
I laugh'd him out of patience; and that night
I laugh'd him into patience: and next morn,
Ere the ninth hour, I drunk him to his bed;
Then put my tires* and mantles on him, whilst
I wore his sword Philippan.

ACT III.

AMBITION JEALOUS OF A TOO SUCCESSFUL FRIEND.

O Silius, Silius,
I have done enough: A lower place, note well,
May make too great an act: For learn this, Silius;
Better leave undone, than by our deeds acquire
Too high a fame, when him we serve's away.

WHAT OCTAVIA'S ENTRANCE SHOULD HAVE BEEN.

Why have you stol'n upon us thus? You come not
Like Cæsar's sister: The wife of Antony
Should have an army for an usher, and

* Head-dress.

The neighs of horse to tell of her approach,
Long ere she did appear; the trees by the way,
Should have borne men; and expectation fainted,
Longing for what it had not: nay, the dust,
Should have ascended to the roof of heaven,
Rais'd by your populous troops: But you are come
A market-maid to Rome; and have prevented
The ostent* of our love, which, left unshown
Is often left unlov'd: we should have met you
By sea, and land; supplying every stage
With an augmented greeting.

WOMEN.

Women are not,
In their best fortunes, strong; but want will perjure
The ne'er-touch'd vestal.

FORTUNE FORMS OUR JUDGMENTS.

I see men's judgments are
A parcel † of their fortunes: and things outward
Do draw the inward quality after them,
To suffer all alike.

LOYALTY.

Mine honesty, and I, begin to square ‡.
The loyalty, well held to fools, does make
Our faith mere folly:—Yet, he, that can endure
To follow with allegiance a fallen lord,
Does conquer him that did his master conquer,
And earns a place i' the story.

WISDOM SUPERIOR TO FORTUNE.

Wisdom and fortune combating together,
If that the former dare but what it can,
No chance may shake it.

VICIOUS PERSONS INFATUATED BY HEAVEN.

Good, my lord,—
But when we in our viciousness grow hard,
(O misery on't!) the wise gods seal § our eyes;

* Show, token.
† Are of a piece with them.
‡ Quarrel.
§ Close up.

In our own filth drop our clear judgments; make us
Adore our errors; laugh at us, while we strut
To our confusion.

FURY EXPELS FEAR.

Now he'll out-stare the lightning. To be furious,
Is, to be frighted out of fear: and, in that mood,
The dove will peck the estridge*; and I see still,
A diminution in our captain's brain
Restores his heart: When valour preys on reason,
It eats the sword it fights with.

ACT IV.

A MASTER TAKING LEAVE OF HIS SERVANTS.

Tend me to-night;
May be, it is the period of your duty:
Haply†, you shall not see me more; or if,
A mangled shadow: perchance, to-morrow
You'll serve another master. I look on you,
As one that takes his leave. Mine honest friends,
I turn you not away; but, like a master
Married to your good service, stay till death:
Tend me to-night two hours, I ask no more,
And the gods yield‡ you for't!

EARLY RISING THE WAY TO EMINENCE.

This morning, like the spirit of a youth
That means to be of note, begins betimes.

ANTONY TO CLEOPATRA, AT HIS RETURN WITH VICTORY.

O thou day o' the world,
Chain mine arm'd neck; leap thou, attire and all,
Through proof of harness§ to my heart, and there
Ride on the pants triumphing.

* Ostrich. † Perhaps. ‡ Reward.
§ Armour of proof.

LOATHED LIFE.

O sovereign mistress of true melancholy,
The poisonous damp of night disponge * upon me;
That life, a very rebel to my will,
May hang no longer on me.

ANTONY'S DESPONDENCY.

O sun, thy uprise shall I see no more:
Fortune and Antony part here; even here
Do we shake hands.—All come to this?—The hearts
That spaniel'd me at heels, to whom I gave
Their wishes, do discandy, melt their sweets
On blossoming Cæsar; and this pine is bark'd,
That overtopp'd them all.

DEPARTING GREATNESS.

The soul and body rive † not more in parting,
Than greatness going off.

ANTONY'S REFLECTIONS ON HIS FADED GLORY.

Sometime, we see a cloud that's dragonish:
A vapour, sometime, like a bear, or lion,
A tower'd citadel, a pendent rock,
A forked mountain, or blue promontory
With trees upon't, that nod unto the world,
And mock our eyes with air: Thou hast seen these signs;
They are black vesper's pageants.

Eros. Ay, my lord.

Ant. That, which is now a horse, even with a thought,
The rack ‡ dislimns; and makes it indistinct,
As water is in water.

Eros. It does, my lord.

Ant. My good knave § Eros, now thy captain is
Even such a body: here I am Antony;
Yet cannot hold this visible shape, my knave.
I made these wars for Egypt; and the queen,—

* Discharge, as a sponge when squeezed discharges the moisture it had imbibed. † Split.
‡ The fleeting clouds. § Servant.

Whose heart, I thought, I had, for she had mine;
Which, while it was mine, had annex'd unto't
A million more, now lost,—she, Eros, has
Pack'd cards with Cæsar, and false play'd my glory
Unto an enemy's triumph.—
Nay, weep not, gentle Eros; there is left us
Ourselves to end ourselves.

DESCRIPTION OF CLEOPATRA'S SUPPOSED DEATH.

Death of one person can be paid but once;
And that she has discharg'd: What thou wouldst do,
Is done unto thy hand; the last she spake
Was Antony! most noble Antony!
Then in the midst a tearing groan did break
The name of Antony; it was divided
Between her heart and lips: she render'd life,
Thy name so buried in her.

CLEOPATRA'S REFLECTIONS ON THE DEATH OF ANTONY.

It were for me
To throw my sceptre at the injurious gods;
To tell them, that this world did equal theirs,
Till they had stolen our jewel. All's but naught;
Patience is sottish; and impatience does
Become a dog that's mad: Then is it sin,
To rush into the secret house of death,
Ere death dare come to us?—How do you, women?
What, what? good cheer? Why, how now, Charmian?
My noble girls!—Ah, women, women! look,
Our lamp is spent, it's out:—Good sirs, take heart:—
We'll bury him: and then, what's brave, what's noble,
Let's do it after the high Roman fashion,
And make death proud to take us. Come away:
This case of that huge spirit now is cold.

ACT V.

DEATH.

My desolation does begin to make
A better life: 'Tis paltry to be Cæsar;
Not being fortune, he's but fortune's knave *,
A minister of her will: And it is great
To do that thing that ends all other deeds;
Which shackles accidents, and bolts up change;
Which sleeps, and never palates more the dung,
The beggar's nurse and Cæsar's.

CLEOPATRA'S DREAM, AND DESCRIPTION OF ANTONY.

Cleo. I dream'd, there was an emperor Antony;—
O, such another sleep, that I might see
But such another man!
Dol. If it might please you,—
Cleo. His face was as the heavens; and therein stuck
A sun, and moon; which kept their course, and lighted
The little O, the earth.
Dol. Most sovereign creature,—
Cleo. His legs bestrid the ocean: his rear'd arm
Crested the world: his voice was propertied
As all the tuned spheres, and that to friends;
But when he meant to quail † and shake the orb,
He was as rattling thunder. For his bounty,
There was no winter in't; an autumn 'twas,
That grew the more by reaping: His delights
Were dolphinlike; they show'd his back above
The element they liv'd in: In his livery
Walk'd crowns, and crownets; realms and islands were
As plates ‡ dropp'd from his pocket.

* Servant. † Crush. ‡ Silver money.

FIRM RESOLUTION.

How poor an instrument
May do a noble deed! he brings me liberty.
My resolution's plac'd, and I have nothing
Of woman in me: Now from head to foot
I am marble-constant: now the fleeting* moon
No planet is of mine.

CLEOPATRA'S SPEECH ON APPLYING THE ASP.

Give me my robe, pnt on my crown; I have
Immortal longings in me: Now no more
The juice of Egypt's grape shall moist this lip:—
Yare, yare†, good Iras; quick.—Methinks I hear
Antony call; I see him rouse himself
To praise my noble act; I hear him mock
The luck of Cæsar, which the gods give men
To excuse their after wrath: Husband, I come:
Now to that name my courage prove my title!
I am fire, and air; my other elements
I give to baser life.—So, have you done?
Come, then, and take the last warmth of my lips.
Farewell, kind Charmian;—Iras, long farewell.
Have I the aspic in my lips? Dost fall?
If thou and nature can so gently part,
The stroke of death is as a lover's pinch,
Which hurts and is desir'd. Dost thou lie still?
If thus thou vanishest, thou tell'st the world
It is not worth leave-taking.

Char. Dissolve, thick cloud, and rain; that I may say,
The gods themselves do weep!

Cleo. This proves me base:
If she first meet the curled Antony,
He'll make demand of her; and spend that kiss,
Which is my heaven to have. Come, mortal wretch,
[*To the asp, which she applies to her breast.*
With thy sharp teeth this knot intrinsicate
Of life at once untie: poor venomous fool,

* Inconstant. † Make haste.

Be angry, and despatch. O, couldst thou speak!
That I might hear thee call great Cæsar, ass
Unpolicied *!
Char. O eastern star!
Cleo. Peace, peace!
Dost thou not see my baby at my breast,
That sucks the nurse asleep?
Char. O, break! O, break!
Cleo. As sweet as balm, as soft as air, as gentle,—
O Antony!—Nay, I will take thee too:—
[*Applying another asp to her arm.*
What should I stay— [*Falls on a bed, and dies.*
Char. In this wild world?—So, fare thee well.—
Now boast thee, death! in thy possession lies
A lass unparallel'd.

CORIOLANUS.

ACT I.

A MOB.

WHAT would you have, you curs,
That like nor peace nor war? the one affrights you,
The other makes you proud. He that trusts you,
Where he should find you lions, finds you hares;
Where foxes, geese: You are no surer, no,
Than is the coal of fire upon the ice,
Or hailstone in the sun. Your virtue is,
To make him worthy, whose offence subdues him,
And curse that justice did it. Who deserves greatness,
Deserves your hate: and your affections are
A sick man's appetite, who desires most that
Which would increase his evil. He that depends

* Unpolitic, to leave me to myself.

Upon your favours, swims with fins of lead,
And hews down oaks with rushes. Hang ye! Trust ye?
With every minute you do change your mind;
And call him noble, that was now your hate,
Him vile, that was your garland.

AN IMAGINARY DESCRIPTION OF CORIOLANUS WARRING.

Methinks I hear hither your husband's drum;
See him pluck Aufidius down by the hair;
As children from a bear, the Volces shunning him:
Methinks, I see him stamp thus, and call thus,—
Come on, you cowards, you were got in fear,
Though you were born in Rome: His bloody brow
With his mail'd hand then wiping, forth he goes;
Like to a harvest-man, that's task'd to mow
Or all, or lose his hire.
Vir. His bloody brow! O, Jupiter, no blood!
Vol. Away, you fool! it more becomes a man,
Than gilt his trophy. The breasts of Hecuba,
When she did suckle Hector, look'd not lovelier
Than Hector's forehead, when it spit forth blood
At Grecian swords contending.

DOING OUR DUTY MERITS NOT PRAISE.

Pray, now, no more: my mother,
Who has a charter * to extol her blood,
When she does praise me, grieves me. I have done,
As you have done; that's what I can; induc'd
As you have been; that's for my country:
He, that has but effected his good will,
Hath overta'en mine act.

AUFIDIUS'S HATRED TO CORIOLANUS.

Nor sleep, nor sanctuary,
Being naked, sick: nor fane, nor Capitol,
The prayers of priests, nor times of sacrifice,
Embarquements all of fury, shall lift up

* Privilege.

Their rotten privilege and custom 'gainst
My hate to Marcius: where I find him, were it
At home, upon my brother's guard *, even there
Against the hospitable canon, would I
Wash my fierce hand in his heart.

ACT II.

POPULARITY.

All tongues speak of him, and the bleared sights
Are spectacled to see him: Your prattling nurse
Into a rapture † lets her baby cry,
While she chats him: the kitchen malkin ‡ pins
Her richest lockram § 'bout her reechy ‖ neck,
Clambering the walls to eye him: stalls, bulks, windows,
Are smother'd up, leads fill'd, and ridges hors'd
With variable complexions; all agreeing
In earnestness to see him: seld ¶-shown flamens **
Do press among the popular throngs, and puff
To win a vulgar station ††: our veil'd dames
Commit the war of white and damask, in
Their nicely-gawded ‡‡ cheeks, to the wanton spoil
Of Phœbus' burning kisses: such a pother,
As if that whatsoever god, who leads him,
Were slily crept into his human powers,
And gave him graceful posture.

COMINIUS'S PRAISE OF CORIOLANUS IN THE SENATE.

I shall lack voice: the deeds of Coriolanus
Should not be utter'd feebly.—It is held,
That valour is the chiefest virtue, and
Most dignifies the haver §§: if it be,

* My brother posted to protect him. † Fit.
‡ Maid. § Best linen. ‖ Soiled with sweat and smoke.
¶ Seldom. ** Priests. †† Common standing-place.
‡‡ Adorn'd. §§ Possessor.

The man I speak of cannot in the world
Be singly counterpois'd. At sixteen years,
When Tarquin made a head for Rome, he fought
Beyond the mark of others: our then dictator,
Whom with all praise I point at, saw him fight,
When with his Amazonian chin* he drove
The bristled† lips before him: he bestrid
An o'er-press'd Roman, and i' the consul's view
Slew three opposers: Tarquin's self he met,
And struck him on his knee: in that day's feats,
When he might act the woman in the scene‡,
He prov'd best man i' the field, and for his meed§
Was brow-bound with the oak. His pupil age
Man entered thus, he waxed like a sea;
And, in the brunt of seventeen battles since,
He lurch'd‖ all swords o' the garland. For this last,
Before and in Corioli, let me say,
I cannot speak him home: He stopp'd the fliers;
And, by his rare example, made the coward
Turn terror into sport: as waves before
A vessel under sail, so men obey'd,
And fell below his stem: his sword (death's stamp)
Where it did mark, it took; from face to foot
He was a thing of blood, whose every motion¶
Was timed** with dying cries: alone he enter'd
The mortal gate o' the city, which he painted
With shunless destiny, aidless came off,
And with a sudden reinforcement struck
Corioli, like a planet: now all's his:
When by and by the din of war 'gan pierce
His ready sense: then straight his doubled spirit
Requicken'd what in flesh was fatigate††,
And to the battle came he; where he did
Run reeking o'er the lives of men, as if
'Twere a perpetual spoil: and till we call'd
Both field and city ours, he never stood
To ease his breast with panting.

* Without a beard. † Bearded.
‡ Smooth-faced enough to act a woman's part.
§ Reward. ‖ Won. ¶ Stroke. ** Followed.
†† Wearied.

ACT III.

THE MISCHIEF OF ANARCHY.

My soul aches,
To know, when two authorities are up,
Neither supreme, how soon confusion
May enter 'twixt the gap of both, and take
The one by the other.

CHARACTER OF CORIOLANUS.

His nature is too noble for the world:
He would not flatter Neptune for his trident,
Or Jove for his power to thunder. His heart's his mouth:
What his breast forges that his tongue must vent;
And, being angry, does forget that ever
He heard the name of death.

HONOUR AND POLICY.

I have heard you say,
Honour and policy, like unsever'd friends,
I' the war do grow together: Grant that, and tell me,
In peace, what each of them by th' other lose,
That they combine not there.

THE METHOD TO GAIN POPULAR FAVOUR.

Go to them, with this bonnet in thy hand;
And thus far having stretch'd it (here be with them),
Thy knee bussing the stones (for in such business
Action is eloquence, and the eyes of the ignorant
More learned than the ears), waving thy head,
Which often, thus, correcting thy stout heart,
That humble, as the ripest mulberry,
Now will not hold the handling: Or, say to them,
Thou art their soldier, and being bred in broils,
Hast not the soft way, which, thou dost confess,
Were fit for thee to use, as they to claim,
In asking their good loves; but thou wilt frame
Thyself, forsooth, hereafter theirs, so far
As thou hast power, and person.

CORIOLANUS'S ABHORRENCE OF FLATTERY.

Well, I must do't:
Away my disposition, and possess me
Some harlot's spirit! My throat of war be turn'd,
Which quired with my drum, into a pipe
Small as an eunuch, or the virgin voice
That babies lulls asleep! The smiles of knaves
Tent* in my cheeks; and school-boys' tears take up
The glasses of my sight! A beggar's tongue
Make motion through my lips; and my arm'd knees,
Who bow'd but in my stirrup, bend like his
That hath receiv'd an alms!—I will not do't:
Lest I surcease to honour mine own truth,
And, by my body's action, teach my mind
A most inherent baseness.

VOLUMNIA'S RESOLUTION ON THE PRIDE OF CORIOLANUS.

At thy choice then:
To beg of thee it is my more dishonour,
Than thou of them. Come all to ruin; let
Thy mother rather feel thy pride, than fear
Thy dangerous stoutness; for I mock at death
With as big heart as thou. Do as thou list.
Thy valiantness was mine, thou suck'dst it from me;
But owe † thy pride thyself.

CORIOLANUS'S DETESTATION OF THE VULGAR.

You common cry ‡ of curs! whose breath I hate
As reek § o' the rotten fens, whose loves I prize
As the dead carcasses of unburied men
That do corrupt my air, I banish you;
And here remain with your uncertainty!
Let every feeble rumour shake your hearts!
Your enemies, with nodding of their plumes,
Fan you into despair; Have the power still
To banish your defenders; till, at length,
Your ignorance (which finds not till it feels),

* Dwell. † Own. ‡ Pack. § Vapour.

Making not reservation of yourselves
(Still your own foes), deliver you, as most
Abated* captives, to some nation
That won you without blows!

ACT IV.

PRECEPTS AGAINST ILL FORTUNE.

You were us'd
To say, extremity was the trier of spirits;
That common chances common men could bear;
That, when the sea was calm, all boats alike
Show'd mastership in floating: fortune's blows,
When most struck home, being gentle wounded, craves
A noble cunning: you were us'd to load me
With precepts, that would make invincible
The heart that conn'd them.

ON COMMON FRIENDSHIPS.

O, world, thy slippery turns! Friends now fast sworn,
Whose double bosoms seem to wear one heart,
Whose hours, whose bed, whose meal, and exercise,
Are still together, who twin, as 'twere, in love
Unseparable, shall within this hour,
On a dissension of a doit†, break out
To bitterest enmity: So fellest foes,
Whose passions and whose plots have broke their sleep,
To take the one the other, by some chance,
Some trick not worth an egg, shall grow dear friends,
And interjoin their issues.

MARTIAL FRIENDSHIP.

Let me twine
Mine arms about that body, where against

* Subdued. † A small coin.

My grained ash a hundred times hath broke,
And scared the moon with splinters! Here I clip *
The anvil of my sword; and do contest
As hotly and as nobly with thy love,
As ever in ambitious strength I did
Contend against thy valour. Know thou first,
I loved the maid I married; never man
Sigh'd truer breath; but that I see thee here,
Thou noble thing! more dances my rapt heart,
Than when I first my wedded mistress saw
Bestride my threshold. Why, thou Mars! I tell thee,
We have a power on foot; and I had purpose
Once more to hew thy target from thy brawn †
Or lose mine arm for't: Thou hast beat me out ‡
Twelve several times, and I have nightly since
Dreamt of encounters 'twixt thyself and me;
We have been down together in my sleep,
Unbuckling helms, fisting each other's throat,
And wak'd half dead with nothing.

ACT V.

THE SEASON OF SOLICITATION.

He was not taken well; he had not din'd:
The veins unfill'd, our blood is cold, and then
We pout upon the morning, are unapt
To give or to forgive; but when we have stuff'd
These pipes and these conveyances of our blood
With wine and feeding, we have suppler souls
Than in our priestlike fasts: therefore I'll watch him
Till he be dieted to my request.

OBSTINATE RESOLUTION.

My wife comes foremost; then the honour'd mould
Wherein this trunk was fram'd, and in her hand
The grandchild to her blood. But, out, affection!
All bond and privilege of nature, break!

* Embrace. † Arm. ‡ Full.

Let it be virtuous, to be obstinate.—
What is that curt'sey worth, or those doves' eyes,
Which can make gods forsworn?—I melt, and am not
Of stronger earth than others.—My mother bows;
As if Olympus to a molehill should
In supplication nod: and my young boy
Hath an aspect of intercession, which
Great nature cries, *Deny not*—Let the Volsces
Plough Rome, and harrow Italy; I'll never
Be such a gosling* to obey instinct; but stand,
As if a man were author of himself,
And knew no other kin.

RELENTING TENDERNESS.

Like a dull actor now,
I have forgot my part, and I am out,
Even to a full disgrace. Best of my flesh,
Forgive my tyranny; but do not say,
For that, *Forgive our Romans.*—O, a kiss
Long as my exile, sweet as my revenge!
Now by the jealous queen† of heaven, that kiss
I carried from thee, dear; and my true lip
Hath virgin'd it e'er since.—You gods, I prate,
And the most noble mother of the world
Leave unsaluted: Sink, my knee, i'the earth;
Of thy deep duty more impressions show
Than that of common sons.

CHASTITY.

The noble sister of Publicola,
The moon of Rome; chaste as the icicle,
That's curded by the frost from purer snow,
And hangs on Dian's temple: Dear Valeria!

CORIOLANUS'S PRAYER FOR HIS SON.

The god of soldiers,
With the consent of supreme Jove, inform
Thy thoughts with nobleness; that thou mayst prove
To shame unvulnerable, and stick i'the wars
Like a great seamark, standing every flaw‡,
And saving those that eye thee!

* A young goose. † Juno. ‡ Gust, storm.

VOLUMNIA'S PATHETIC SPEECH TO HER SON CORIOLANUS.

Think with thyself,
How more unfortunate than all living women
Are we come hither: since that thy sight, which should
Make our eyes flow with joy, hearts dance with comforts,
Constrains them weep, and shake with fear and sorrow:
Making the mother, wife, and child, to see
The son, the husband, and the father, tearing
His country's bowels out. And to poor we,
Thine enmity's most capital: thou barr'st us
Our prayers to the gods, which is a comfort
That all but we enjoy.

* * * * *

We must find
An evident calamity, though we had
Our wish, which side should win: for either thou
Must, as a foreign recreant, be led,
With manacles through our streets, or else
Triumphantly tread on thy country's ruin;
And bear the palm, for having bravely shed
Thy wife and children's blood. For myself, son,
I purpose not to wait on fortune, till
These wars determine*: if I cannot persuade thee
Rather to show a noble grace to both parts,
Than seek the end of one, thou shalt no sooner
March to assault thy country, than to tread
(Trust to't, thou shalt not) on thy mother's womb,
That brought thee to this world.

PEACE AFTER A SIEGE.

Ne'er through an arch so hurried the blown tide,
As the recomforted through the gates. Why, hark you;
The trumpets, sackbuts, psalteries, and fifes,
Tabors and cymbals, and the shouting Romans,
Make the sun dance.

* Conclude.

CYMBELINE.

ACT I.

PARTING LOVERS.

Imo. THOU shouldst have made him
As little as a crow, or less, ere left
To after-eye him.
Pisa. Madam, so I did.
Imo. I would have broke mine eye-strings; crack'd them, but
To look upon him: till the diminution
Of space had pointed him sharp as my needle:
Nay, follow'd him, till he had melted from
The smallness of a gnat to air; and then
Have turn'd mine eye, and wept.—But, good Pisanio,
When shall we hear from him?
Pisa. Be assur'd, madam,
With his next vantage *.
Imo. I did not take my leave of him, but had
Most pretty things to say: ere I could tell him,
How I would think on him, at certain hours,
Such thoughts, and such; or I could make him swear
The she's of Italy should not betray
Mine interest, and his honour; or have charg'd him,
At the sixth hour of morn, at noon, at midnight,
To encounter me with orisons †, for then
I am in heaven for him: or ere I could
Give him that parting kiss, which I had set
Betwixt two charming words, comes in my father,
And, like the tyrannous breathing of the north,
Shakes all our buds from growing.

* Opportunity. † Meet me with reciprocal prayer.

THE BASENESS OF FALSEHOOD TO A WIFE.

Doubting things go ill, often hurts more
Than to be sure they do: For certainties
Either are past remedies: or, timely knowing,
The remedy then born; discover to me
What both you spur and stop*.
Iach. Had I this cheek
To bathe my lips upon; this hand, whose touch,
Whose every touch, would force the feeler's soul
To the oath of loyalty; this object, which
Takes prisoner the wild motion of mine eye,
Fixing it only here; should I (damn'd then),
Slaver with lips as common as the stairs
That mount the Capitol; join gripes with hands
Made hard with hourly falsehood (falsehood, as
With labour); then lie peeping in an eye,
Base and unlustrous as the smoky light
That's fed with stinking tallow; it were fit,
That all the plagues of hell should at one time
Encounter such revolt.

ACT II.

SCENE. *A Bedchamber; in one part of it a Trunk.*

IMOGEN *reading in her Bed; a* Lady *attending.*

Imo. Mine eyes are weak:—
Fold down the leaf where I have left: To bed:
Take not away the taper, leave it burning:
And if thou canst awake by four o'the clock,
I pr'ythee, call me. Sleep hath seiz'd me wholly.
[*Exit* Lady.
To your protection I commend me, gods!
From fairies, and the tempters of the night,
Guard me, beseech ye!
[*Sleeps.* IACHIMO, *from the Trunk.*

* What you seem anxious to utter, and yet withhold.

Iach. The crickets sing, and man's o'er-labour'd sense
Repairs itself by rest: Our Tarquin thus
Did softly press the rushes *, ere he waken'd
The chastity he wounded.—Cytherea,
How bravely thou becom'st thy bed! fresh lily!
And whiter than the sheets! That I might touch!
But kiss; one kiss! Rubies unparagon'd,
How dearly they do't.—'Tis her breathing that
Perfumes the chamber thus: The flame o'the taper
Bows toward her; and would underpeep her lids,
To see the enclosed lights, now canopied
Under these windows: White and azure, lac'd
With blue of heav'n's own tinct †. But my design?
To note the chamber:—I will write all down:
Such, and such, pictures;—There the window:—Such
The adornment of her bed;—The arras ‡, figures,
Why, such, and such:—And the contents o'the story,—
Ah, but some natural notes about her body,
Above ten thousand meaner moveables
Would testify to enrich mine inventory:
O sleep, thou ape of death, lie dull upon her!
And be her sense but as a monument,
Thus in a chapel lying!—Come off, come off;—
[*Taking off her Bracelet.*
As slippery, as the Gordian knot was hard!
'Tis mine; and this will witness outwardly,
As strongly as the conscience does within,
To the madding of her lord. On her left breast
A mole cinque-spotted, like the crimson drops
I' the bottom of a cowslip: Here's a voucher,
Stronger than ever law could make: this secret
Will force him think I have pick'd the lock, and ta'en
The treasure of her honour. No more.—To what end?
Why should I write this down, that's riveted,

* It was anciently the custom to strew chambers with rushes.

† *i. e.* The white skin laced with blue veins.

‡ Tapestry.

Screw'd to my memory? She hath been reading late
The tale of Tereus; here the leaf's turn'd down,
Where Philomel gave up;—I have enough:
To the trunk again, and shut the spring of it.
Swift, swift, you dragons of the night!—that dawning
May bare the raven's eye: I lodge in fear;
Though this a heavenly angel, hell is here.
[*Goes into the Trunk. The Scene closes.*

GOLD.

'Tis gold
Which buys admittance; oft it doth; yea, and makes
Diana's rangers false themselves, yield up
Their deer to the stand of the stealer; and 'tis gold
Which makes the true man kill'd, and saves the thief;
Nay, sometime, hangs both thief and true man: What
Can it not do, and undo?

A SATIRE ON WOMEN.

Is there no way for men to be, but women
Must be half-workers? We are bastards all;
And that most venerable man, which I
Did call my father, was I know not where
When I was stamp'd; some coiner with his tools
Made me a counterfeit; Yet my mother seem'd
The Dian of that time: so doth my wife
The nonpareil of this.—O vengeance, vengeance!
Me of my lawful pleasure she restrain'd,
And pray'd me, oft, forbearance: did it with
A pudency* so rosy, the sweet view on't
Might well have warm'd old Saturn; that I thought her
As chaste as unsunn'd snow:
* * * * *

Could I find out
The woman's part in me! For there's no motion
That tends to vice in man, but I affirm
It is the woman's part: Be it lying, note it,
The woman's; flattering, hers; deceiving, hers;
Ambitions, covetings, change of prides, disdain,

* Modesty.

Nice longings, slanders, mutability,
All faults that may be nam'd, nay that hell knows,
Why, hers, in part, or all; but, rather, all:
For ev'n to vice
They are not constant, but are changing still
One vice, but of a minute old, for one
Not half so old as that. I'll write against them,
Detest them, curse them:—Yet 'tis greater skill
In a true hate, to pray they have their will:
The very devils cannot plague them better.

ACT III.

IMPATIENCE OF A WIFE TO MEET HER HUSBAND.

O, for a horse with wings!—Hear'st thou, Pisanio?
He is at Milford-Haven: Read, and tell me
How far 'tis thither. If one of mean affairs
May plod it in a week, why may not I
Glide thither in a day?—Then, true Pisanio
(Who long'st, like me, to see thy lord; who long'st,—
O, let me bate,—but not like me:—yet long'st,—
But in a fainter kind;—O, not like me;
For mine's beyond beyond), say, and speak thick *
(Love's counsellor should fill the bores of hearing,
To the smothering of the sense), how far it is
To this same blessed Milford: And, by the way,
Tell me how Wales was made so happy, as
To inherit such a haven: But, first of all,
How we may steal from hence; and, for the gap
That we shall make in time, from our hence-going,
And our return, to excuse:—but first, how get hence;
Why should excuse be born or e'er begot?
We'll talk of that hereafter. Pr'ythee, speak,
How many score of miles may we well ride
'Twixt hour and hour.

* Crowd one word on another, as fast as possible.

Pisa. One score, 'twixt sun and sun,
Madam, 's enough for you; and too much too.
Imo. Why, one that rode to his execution, man,
Could never go so slow: I have heard of riding wagers,
Where horses have been nimbler than the sands
That run i'the clock's behalf:—But this is foolery:
Go, bid my woman feign a sickness; say
She'll home to her father: and provide me, presently,
A riding suit; no costlier than would fit
A franklin's* housewife.
Pisa. Madam, you're best consider.
Imo. I see before me, man, nor here, nor here,
Nor what ensues; but have a fog in them,
That I cannot look through. Away, I pr'ythee;
Do as I bid thee: There's no more to say;
Accessible is none but Milford way. [*Exeunt.*

SCENE. Wales. *A mountainous Country, with a Cave.*

Enter Belarius, Guiderius, *and* Arviragus.

Bel. A goodly day not to keep house, with such
Whose roof's as low as ours! Stoop, boys: This gate
Instructs you how to adore the heavens; and bows you
To morning's holy office: The gates of monarchs
Are arch'd so high, that giants may jet† through
And keep their impious turbans on, without
Good morrow to the sun.—Hail, thou fair heaven!
We house i' the rock, yet use thee not so hardly
As prouder livers do.
Gui. Hail, heaven!
Arv. Hail, heaven!
Bel. Now, for our mountain sport: Up to yon hill,
Your legs are young; I'll tread these flats. Consider,
When you above perceive me like a crow,
That it is place which lessens, and sets off.
And you may then revolve what tales I have told you,

* A freeholder. † Strut, walk proudly.

Of courts, of princes, of the tricks in war:
This service is not service, so being done,
But being so allow'd: To apprehend thus,
Draws us a profit from all things we see:
And often, to our comfort, shall we find
The sharded* beetle is a safer hold
Than is the full-wing'd eagle. O, this life
Is nobler, than attending for a check;
Richer, than doing nothing for a babe;
Prouder, than rustling in unpaid-for silk:
Such gain the cap of him, that makes them fine,
Yet keeps his book uncross'd: no life to ours†.

Gui. Out of your proof you speak: we, poor unfledg'd,
Have never wing'd from view o'the nest; nor know not
What air's from home. Haply, this life is best,
If quiet life be best; sweeter to you,
That have a sharper known; well corresponding
With your stiff age; but, unto us, it is
A cell of ignorance; travelling abed;
A prison for a debtor, that not dares
To stride a limit‡.

Arv. What should we speak of,
When we are old as you? when we shall hear
The rain and wind beat dark December, how
In this our pinching cave, shall we discourse
The freezing hours away? We have seen nothing:
We are beastly; subtle as the fox, for prey;
Like warlike as the wolf, for what we eat:
Our valour is, to chase what flies; our cage
We make a quire, as doth the prison bird,
And sing our bondage freely.

Bel. How you speak!
Did you but know the city's usuries,
And felt them knowingly: the art o' the court,
As hard to leave, as keep: whose top to climb

* Scaly-winged. † *i. e.* Compared with ours.
‡ To overpass his bound.

Is certain falling, or so slippery, that
The fear's as bad as falling: the toil of the war,
A pain that only seems to seek out danger
I' the name of fame, and honour; which dies i' the
search;
And hath as oft a slanderous epitaph,
As record of fair act; nay, many times,
Doth ill deserve by doing well; what's worse,
Must court'sey at the censure:—O, boys, this story
The world may read in me: My body's mark'd
With Roman swords: and my report was once
First with the best of note: Cymbeline lov'd me;
And when a soldier was the theme, my name
Was not far off: Then was I as a tree,
Whose boughs did bend with fruit: but in one night,
A storm, or robbery, call it what you will,
Shook down my mellow hangings, nay, my leaves,
And left me bare to weather.

Gui. Uncertain favour!

Bel. My fault being nothing (as I have told you oft),
But that two villains, whose false oaths prevail'd
Before my perfect honour, swore to Cymbeline,
I was confederate with the Romans; so,
Follow'd my banishment; and, this twenty years,
This rock, and these demesnes, have been my world:
Where I have liv'd at honest freedom; paid
More pious debts to heaven, than in all
The fore-end of my time.—But, up to the mountains;
This is not hunter's language:—He, that strikes
The venison first, shall be the lord o' the feast;
To him the other two shall minister;
And we will fear no poison, which attends
In place of greater state.

THE FORCE OF NATURE.

How hard it is, to hide the sparks of nature!
These boys know little, they are sons to the king;
Nor Cymbeline dreams that they are alive.
They think they are mine: and, though train'd up thus
meanly

I' the cave, wherein they bow, their thoughts do hit
The roofs of palaces; and nature prompts them,
In simple and low things to prince it, much
Beyond the trick of others. This Polydore,—
The heir of Cymbeline and Britain, whom
The king his father call'd Guiderius,—Jove!
When on my three-foot stool I sit, and tell
The warlike feats I have done, his spirits fly out
Into my story: say, *Thus mine enemy fell;*
And thus I set my foot on his neck; even then
The princely blood flows in his cheek, he sweats,
Strains his young nerves, and puts himself in posture
That acts my words. The younger brother, Cadwal
(Once Arviragus), in as like a figure,
Strikes life into my speech, and shows much more
His own conceiving.

SLANDER.

No, 'tis slander;
Whose edge is sharper than the sword; whose tongue
Outvenoms all the worms of Nile; whose breath
Rides on the posting winds, and doth belie
All corners of the world: kings, queens, and states,
Maids, matrons, nay, the secrets of the grave
This viperous slander enters.

A WIFE'S INNOCENCY.

False to his bed! What is it, to be false?
To lie in watch there, and to think on him?
To weep 'twixt clock and clock? if sleep charge nature,
To break it with a fearful dream of him,
And cry myself awake? that's false to his bed?

WOMAN IN MAN'S APPAREL.

You must forget to be a woman; change
Command into obedience; fear, and niceness
(The handmaids of all women, or, more truly,
Woman its pretty self), to a waggish courage;
Ready in gibes, quick-answer'd, saucy, and
As quarrellous as the weasel: nay, you must

Forget that rarest treasure of your cheek,
Exposing it (but, O, the harder heart!
Alack no remedy!) to the greedy touch
Of common-kissing Titan *; and forget
Your laboursome and dainty trims, wherein
You made great Juno angry.

SCENE. *Before the Cave of* Belarius.

Enter IMOGEN, *in Boy's Clothes.*

Imo. I see, a man's life is a tedious one:
I have tir'd myself; and for two nights together
Have made the ground my bed. I should be sick,
But that my resolution helps me.—Milford,
When from the mountain-top Pisanio show'd thee,
Thou wast within a ken: O Jove! I think,
Foundations fly the wretched: such, I mean,
Where they should be reliev'd. Two beggars told me,
I could not miss my way: Will poor folks lie,
That have afflictions on them; knowing 'tis
A punishment, or trial? Yes; no wonder,
When rich ones scarce tell true: To lapse in fulness
Is sorer, than to lie for need; and falsehood
Is worse in kings than beggars.—My dear lord!
Thou art one o' the false ones: Now I think on thee,
My hunger's gone; but even before, I was
At point to sink for food.—But what is this?
Here is a path to it: 'Tis some savage hold:
I were best not call; I dare not call: yet famine,
Ere clean it o'erthrow nature, makes it valiant.
Plenty, and peace, breeds cowards; hardness ever
Of hardiness is mother.

LABOUR.

Weariness
Can snore upon the flint, when restive sloth
Finds the down pillow hard.

HARMLESS INNOCENCE.

Imo. Good masters, harm me not:
Before I enter'd here, I call'd; and thought

* The sun

To have begg'd, or bought, what I have took: Good
troth,
I have stolen nought; nor would not, though I had
found
Gold strew'd o' the floor. Here's money for my meat:
I would have left it on the board, so soon
As I had made my meal; and parted
With prayers for the provider.
Gui. Money, youth?
Arv. All gold and silver rather turn to dirt!
As 'tis no better reckon'd, but of those
Who worship dirty gods.

ACT IV.

BRAGGART.

To who? to thee? What art thou? Have not I
An arm as big as thine? a heart as big?
Thy words, I grant, are bigger; for I wear not
My dagger in my mouth.

FOOLHARDINESS.

Being scarce made up,
I mean, to man, he had not apprehension
Of roaring terrors; for the effect of judgment
Is oft the cause of fear.

INBORN ROYALTY.

O thou goddess,
Thou divine nature, how thyself thou blazon'st
In these two princely boys? They are as gentle
As zephyrs blowing below the violet,
Not wagging his sweet head: and yet as rough,
Their royal blood enchaf'd, as the rud'st wind,
That by the top doth take the mountain pine,
And make him stoop to the vale. 'Tis wonderful,
That an invisible instinct should frame them
To royalty unlearn'd; honour untaught;
Civility not seen from other; valour,

That wildly grows in them, but yields a crop
As if it had been sow'd.

Enter ARVIRAGUS, *bearing* IMOGEN, *as dead, in his Arms.*

Bel. Look, here he comes,
And brings the dire occasion in his arms,
Of what we blame him for!

Arv. The bird is dead,
That we have made so much on. I had rather
Have skipp'd from sixteen years of age to sixty,
To have turn'd my leaping time into a crutch,
Than have seen this.

Gui. O sweetest, fairest lily!
My brother wears thee not the one half so well,
As when thou grew'st thyself.

Bel. O, melancholy!
Who ever yet could sound thy bottom? find
The ooze, to show what coast thy sluggish crare*
Might easiliest harbour in?—Thou blessed thing!
Jove knows what man thou mightst have made; but I,
Thou diedst a most rare boy of melancholy!—
How found you him?

Arv. Stark†, as you see:
Thus smiling, as some fly had tickled slumber,
Not as death's dart, being laugh'd at: his right cheek
Reposing on a cushion.

Gui. Where?

Arv. O' the floor;
His arms thus leagu'd: I thought, he slept; and put
My clouted brogues‡ from off my feet, whose rudeness
Answer'd my steps too loud.

Gui. Why, he but sleeps:
If he be gone, he'll make his grave a bed;
With female fairies will his tomb be haunted,
And worms will not come to thee.

Arv. With fairest flowers,

* A slow-sailing, unweildy vessel. † Stiff.
‡ Shoes plated with iron.

Whilst summer lasts, and I live here, Fidele,
I'll sweeten thy sad grave: Thou shalt not lack
The flower, that's like thy face, pale primrose; nor
The azur'd harebell like thy veins; no, nor
The leaf of eglantine, whom not to slander,
Out-sweeten'd not thy breath; the ruddock* would
With charitable bill (O bill, sore-shaming
Those rich-left heirs, that let their fathers lie
Without a monument!) bring thee all this;
Yea, and furr'd moss besides, when flowers are none,
To winter-ground † thy corse.

* * * * *

Bel. Great griefs, I see, medicine the less; for Cloten
Is quite forgot. He was a queen's son, boys:
And, though he came our enemy, remember,
He was paid ‡ for that: Though mean and mighty, rotting
Together, have one dust; yet reverence
(That angel of the world), doth make distinction
Of place 'tween high and low. Our foe was princely;
And though you took his life, as being our foe,
Yet bury him as a prince.
Gui. Pray you, fetch him hither.
Thersites' body is as good as Ajax,
When neither are alive.

FUNERAL DIRGE.

Gui. Fear no more the heat o'the sun,
Nor the furious winter's rages;
Thou thy worldly task hast done,
Home art gone, and ta'en thy wages:
Golden lads and girls all must,
As chimney-sweepers come to dust.

Arv. Fear no more the frown o' the great,
Thou art past the tyrant's stroke;
Care no more to clothe and eat;
To thee the reed is as the oak:

* The red-breast.
† Probably a corrupt reading for *wither round* thy corse.
‡ Punished.

The sceptre, learning, physic, must
All follow this, and come to dust.

Gui. Fear no more the lightning-flash,
Arv. Nor the all-dreaded thunder-stone;
Gui. Fear not slander, censure * rash;
Arv. Thou hast finish'd joy and moan:
Both. All lovers young, all lovers must
Consign † to thee, and come to dust.

Gui. No exorciser harm thee!
Arv. Nor no witchcraft charm thee!
Gui. Ghost unlaid forbear thee!
Arv. Nothing ill come near thee!
Both. Quiet consummation have;
And renowned be thy grave!

IMOGEN, AWAKING.

Yes, sir, to Milford Haven;
Which is the way?
I thank you.—By yon bush?—Pray, how far thither?
'Ods pittikins ‡!—can it be six miles yet?
I have gone all night:—'Faith, I'll lie down and sleep.
But, soft! no bedfellow:—O, gods and goddesses!
[*Seeing the body.*
These flowers are like the pleasures of the world;
This bloody man, the care on't.—I hope, I dream;
For, so, I thought I was a cave keeper,
And cook to honest creatures: But 'tis not so;
'Twas but a bolt § of nothing, shot at nothing,
Which the brain makes of fumes: Our very eyes
Are sometimes like our judgments, blind. Good faith,
I tremble still with fear: But if there be
Yet left in heaven as small a drop of pity
As a wren's eye, fear'd gods, a part of it!
The dream's here still: even when I wake, it is
Without me, as within me; not imagin'd, felt.

* Judgment. † Seal the same contract.
‡ This diminutive adjuration is derived from *God's my pity*.
§ An arrow.

ACT V.

A ROUTED ARMY.

No blame be to you, sir; for all was lost,
But that the heavens fought: The king himself
Of his wings destitute, the army broken,
And but the backs of Britons seen, all flying
Through a strait lane; the enemy full-hearted,
Lolling the tongue with slaughtering, having work
More plentiful than tools to do't, struck down
Some mortally, some slightly touch'd, some falling
Merely through fear; that the strait pass was damm'd *
With dead men, hurt behind, and cowards living
To die with lengthen'd shame.

DEATH.

I, in mine own woe charm'd,
Could not find death, where I did hear him groan;
Nor feel him, where he struck: Being an ugly monster,
'Tis strange, he hides him in fresh cups, soft beds,
Sweet words; or hath more ministers than we
That draw his knives i' the war.

HAMLET.

ACT I.

PRODIGIES.

In the most high and palmy † state of Rome,
A little ere the mightiest Julius fell,
The graves stood tenantless, and the sheeted dead
Did squeak and gibber in the Roman streets.
— — — — — — — — — — — — — —

* Blocked up. † Victorious.

As, stars with trains of fire and dews of blood,
Disasters in the sun; and the moist star *,
Upon whose influence Neptune's empire stands,
Was sick almost to doomsday with eclipse.

GHOSTS VANISH AT THE CROWING OF A COCK.

Ber. It was about to speak, when the cock crew.
Hor. And then it started like a guilty thing
Upon a fearful summons. I have heard,
The cock, that is the trumpet of the morn,
Doth with his lofty and shrill-sounding throat
Awake the god of day; and, at his warning,
Whether in sea or fire, in earth or air,
The extravagant and erring† spirit hies
To his confine: and of the truth herein
This present object made probation ‡.

THE REVERENCE PAID TO CHRISTMAS TIME.

It faded on the crowing of the cock.
Some say, that ever 'gainst that season comes
Wherein our Saviour's birth is celebrated,
This bird of dawning singeth all night long;
And then they say no spirit dares stir abroad;
The nights are wholesome; then no planets strike,
No fairy takes, nor witch hath power to charm,
So hallow'd and so gracious is the time.

MORNING.

But, look, the morn, in russet mantle clad,
Walks o'er the dew of yon high eastern hill.

REAL GRIEF.

Seems, madam! nay, it is; I know not seems.
'Tis not alone, my inky cloak, good mother,
Nor customary suits of solemn black,
Nor windy suspiration of forc'd breath,
No, nor the fruitful river in the eye,
Nor the dejected 'haviour of the visage,
Together with all forms, modes, shows of grief,
That can denote me truly: These, indeed, seem,

* The moon. † Wandering. ‡ Proof.

For they are actions that a man might play:
But I have that within, which passeth show;
These, but the trappings and the suits of woe.

IMMODERATE GRIEF DISCOMMENDED.

'Tis sweet and commendable in your nature, Hamlet,
To give these mourning duties to your father;
But, you must know, your father lost a father;
That father lost his; and the survivor bound
In filial obligation, for some term
To do obsequious sorrow: But to perséver
In obstinate condolement, is a course
Of impious stubbornness; 'tis unmanly grief:
It shows a will most incorrect to heaven;
A heart unfortified, or mind impatient;
An understanding simple and unschool'd:
For what, we know, must be, and is as common
As any the most vulgar thing to sense,
Why should we, in our peevish opposition,
Take it to heart? Fie! 'tis a fault to heaven,
A fault against the dead, a fault to nature,
To reason most absurd; whose common theme
Is death of fathers, and who still hath cried,
From the first corse, till he that died to-day,
This must be so.

HAMLET'S SOLILOQUY ON HIS MOTHER'S MARRIAGE.

O, that this too too solid flesh would melt,
Thaw, and resolve* itself into a dew!
Or that the Everlasting had not fix'd
His canon † 'gainst self-slaughter! O God! O God!
How weary, stale, flat, and unprofitable
Seem to me all the uses of this world!
Fie on't! O fie! 'tis an unweeded garden,
That grows to seed; things rank, and gross in nature,
Possess it merely ‡. That it should come to this!
But two months dead!—nay, not so much, not two:
So excellent a king; that was, to this,

* Dissolve. † Law. ‡ Entirely.

Hyperion* to a satyr: so loving to my mother,
That he might not beteem † the winds of heaven
Visit her face too roughly. Heaven and earth!
Must I remember? why, she would hang on him,
As if increase of appetite had grown
By what it fed on: And yet, within a month,—
Let me not think on't;—Frailty, thy name is woman!—
A little month; or ere those shoes were old,
With which she follow'd my poor father's body,
Like Niobe, all tears;—why she, even she,—
O heaven! a beast, that wants discourse of reason,
Would have mourn'd longer,—married with my uncle,
My father's brother; but no more like my father,
Than I to Hercules: Within a month;
Ere yet the salt of most unrighteous tears
Had left the flushing in her galled eyes,
She married:—O most wicked speed, to post
With such dexterity to incestuous sheets!
It is not, nor it cannot come to, good.

THE EXTENT OF HUMAN PERFECTION.

He was a man, take him for all in all,
I shall not look upon his like again.

CAUTIONS TO YOUNG FEMALES.

For Hamlet, and the trifling of his favour,
Hold it a fashion, and a toy in blood:
A violet in the youth of primy nature,
Forward, not permanent, sweet, not lasting,
The perfume and suppliance of a minute:
No more.

* * * * *

Then weigh what loss your honour may sustain,
If with too credent ‡ ear you list § his songs;
Or lose your heart: or your chaste treasure open
To his unmaster'd ‖ importunity.

* Apollo. † Suffer. ‡ Believing.
§ Listen to. ‖ Licentious.

Fear it, Ophelia, fear it, my dear sister;
And keep you in the rear of your affection,
Out of the shot and danger of desire.
The chariest* maid is prodigal enough,
If she unmask her beauty to the moon:
Virtue itself 'scapes not calumnious strokes:
The canker galls the infants of the spring,
Too oft before their buttons be disclos'd;
And in the morn and liquid dew of youth
Contagious blastments are most imminent.

SATIRE ON UNGRACIOUS PASTORS.

I shall the effect of this good lesson keep,
As watchman to my heart: But, good my brother,
Do not, as some ungracious pastors do,
Show me the steep and thorny way to heaven;
Whilst, like a puff'd and reckless† libertine,
Himself the primrose path of dalliance treads,
And recks not his own read ‡.

ADVICE TO A SON GOING TO TRAVEL.

Give thy thoughts no tongue,
Nor any unproportion'd thought his act.
Be thou familiar, but by no means vulgar.
The friends thou hast, and their adoption tried,
Grapple them to thy soul with hooks of steel;
But do not dull thy palm § with entertainment
Of each new-hatch'd, unfledg'd comrade. Beware
Of entrance to a quarrel: but, being in,
Bear it that the opposer may beware of thee.
Give every man thine ear, but few thy voice:
Take each man's censure ||, but reserve thy judgment.
Costly thy habit as thy purse can buy,
But not express'd in fancy; rich, not gaudy:
For the apparel oft proclaims the man;
And they in France, of the best rank and station,

* Most cautious. † Careless.
‡ Regards not his own lessons. § Palm of the hand.
|| Opinion.

Are most select and generous *, chief † in that.
Neither a borrower, nor a lender be:
For loan oft loses both itself and friend;
And borrowing dulls the edge of husbandry ‡.
This above all,—To thine own self be true;
And it must follow, as the night the day,
Thou canst not then be false to any man.

HAMLET, ON THE APPEARANCE OF HIS FATHER'S GHOST.

Angels and ministers of grace defend us!—
Be thou a spirit of health, or goblin damn'd,
Bring with thee airs from heaven, or blasts from hell,
Be thy intents wicked, or charitable,
Thou com'st in such a questionable § shape,
That I will speak to thee; I'll call thee, Hamlet,
King, father, royal Dane: O, answer me:
Let me not burst in ignorance! but tell,
Why thy canoniz'd bones, hearsed in death,
Have burst their cerements! why the sepulchre,
Wherein we saw thee quietly inurn'd,
Hath op'd his ponderous and marble jaws,
To cast thee up again! What may this mean,
That thou, dead corse, again, in cómplete steel
Revisit'st thus the glimpses of the moon,
Making night hideous; and we fools of nature,
So horridly to shake our disposition ||,
With thoughts beyond the reaches of our souls?

THE MISCHIEFS IT MIGHT TEMPT HIM TO.

What, if it tempt you toward the flood, my lord,
Or to the dreadful summit of the cliff,
That beetles ¶ o'er his base into the sea?
And there assume some other horrible form,
Which might deprive your sovereignty of reason,
And draw you into madness? think of it:

* Noble. † Chiefly. ‡ Economy.
§ Conversible. || Frame. ¶ Hangs.

The very place puts toys* of desperation,
Without more motive, into every brain,
That looks so many fathoms to the sea,
And hears it roar beneath.

SCENE. *A more remote Part of the Platform.*

Re-enter GHOST *and* HAMLET.

Ham. Whither wilt thou lead me? speak, I'll go no further.
Ghost. Mark me.
Ham. I will.
Ghost. My hour is almost come,
When I to sulphurous and tormenting flames
Must render up myself.
Ham. Alas, poor ghost!
Ghost. Pity me not, but lend thy serious hearing
To what I shall unfold.
Ham. Speak, I am bound to hear.
Ghost. So art thou to revenge, when thou shalt hear.
Ham. What?
Ghost. I am thy father's spirit;
Doom'd for a certain term to walk the night;
And, for the day, confin'd to fast in fires,
Till the foul crimes, done in my days of nature,
Are burnt and purg'd away. But that I am forbid
To tell the secrets of my prison-house,
I could a tale unfold, whose lightest word
Would harrow up thy soul; freeze thy young blood;
Make thy two eyes, like stars, start from their spheres;
Thy knotted and combined locks to part,
And each particular hair to stand an-end,
Like quills upon the fretful porcupine:
But this eternal blazon† must not be
To ears of flesh and blood:—List, list, O list!—
If thou didst ever thy dear father love.——
Ham. O heaven!

* Whims. † Display.

Ghost. Revenge his foul and most unnatural murder.
Ham. Murder?
Ghost. Murder most foul, as in the best it is;
But this most foul, strange, and unnatural.
Ham. Haste me to know it; that I, with wings as swift
As meditation, or the thoughts of love,
May sweep to my revenge.
Ghost. I find thee apt;
And duller shouldst thou be than the fat weed
That rots itself in ease on Lethe wharf,
Wouldst thou not stir in this. Now, Hamlet, hear:
'Tis given out, that sleeping in mine orchard *,
A serpent stung me; so the whole ear of Denmark
Is by a forged process of my death
Rankly abus'd: but know, thou noble youth,
The serpent that did sting thy father's life,
Now wears his crown.
Ham. O, my prophetic soul! my uncle!
Ghost. Ay, that incestuous, that adulterate beast,
With witchcraft of his wit, with traitorous gifts,
(O wicked wit, and gifts, that have the power
So to seduce!) won to his shameful lust
The will of my most seeming virtuous queen:
O, Hamlet, what a falling-off was there!
From me, whose love was of that dignity,
That it went hand in hand even with the vow
I made to her in marriage; and to decline
Upon a wretch, whose natural gifts were poor
To those of mine!
But virtue, as it never will be mov'd,
Though lewdness court it in a shape of heaven;
So lust, though to a radiant angel link'd,
Will sate † itself in a celestial bed,
And prey on garbage.
But, soft! methinks, I scent the morning air:
Brief let me be:—Sleeping within mine orchard,
My custom always of the afternoon,
Upon my secure hour thy uncle stole,

* Garden. † Satiate.

With juice of cursed hebenon * in a vial,
And in the porches of mine ears did pour
The leperous distilment: whose effect
Holds such an enmity with blood of man,
That, swift as quicksilver, it courses through
The natural gates and alleys of the body;
And, with a sudden vigour, it doth posset
And curd, like eager droppings into milk,
The thin and wholesome blood: so did it mine;
And a most instant tetter † bark'd about,
Most lazarlike ‡, with vile and loathsome crust,
All my smooth body.
Thus was I, sleeping, by a brother's hand,
Of life, of crown, of queen, at once despatch'd §:
Cut off even in the blossoms of my sin,
Unhousel'd ||, disappointed ¶, unanel'd **;
No reckoning made, but sent to my account
With all my imperfections on my head:
O, horrible! O, horrible! most horrible!
If thou hast nature in thee, bear it not;
Let not the royal bed of Denmark be
A couch for luxury and damned incest.
But, howsoever thou pursu'st this act,
Taint not thy mind, nor let thy soul contrive
Against thy mother aught; leave her to heaven,
And to those thorns that in her bosom lodge,
To prick and sting her. Fare thee well at once!
The glowworm shows the matin to be near,
And 'gins to pale his uneffectual fire:
Adieu, adieu, adieu! remember me. [*Exit.*

Ham. O all you host of heaven! O earth! What else?
And shall I couple hell?—O fie!—Hold, hold, my heart;
And you, my sinews, grow not instant old,
But bear me stiffly up!—Remember thee?
Ay, thou poor ghost, while memory holds a seat

* Henbane. † Scab, scurf. ‡ Leprous.
§ Bereft. || Without having received the Sacrament.
¶ Unappointed, unprepared. ** Without extreme unction.

In this distracted globe *. Remember thee?
Yea, from the table of my memory
I'll wipe away all trivial fond records,
All saws † of books, all forms, all pressures past,
That youth and observation copied there;
And thy commandment all alone shall live
Within the book and volume of my brain,
Unmix'd with baser matter: yes, by heaven.
O most pernicious woman!
O villain, villain, smiling, damned villain!
My tables ‡,—meet it is, I set it down,
That one may smile, and smile, and be a villain;
At least, I am sure, it may be so in Denmark:
[*Writing.*
So, uncle, there you are. Now to my word;
It is, *Adieu, adieu! remember me.*

ACT II.

OPHELIA'S DESCRIPTION OF HAMLET'S MAD ADDRESS TO HER.

My lord, as I was sewing in my closet,
Lord Hamlet,—with his doublet all unbrac'd;
No hat upon his head; his stockings foul'd,
Ungarter'd, and down-gyved § to his ankle;
Pale as his shirt; his knees knocking each other;
And with a look so piteous in purport,
As if he had been loosed out of hell,
To speak of horrors,—he comes before me.
Pol. Mad for thy love?
Oph. My lord, I do not know;
But, truly, I do fear it.
Pol. What said he?
Oph. He took me by the wrist, and held me hard;
Then goes he to the length of all his arm;

* Head. † Sayings, sentences. ‡ Memorandum-book.
§ Hanging down like fetters.

And, with his other hand thus o'er his brow,
He falls to such perusal of my face,
As he would draw it. Long stay'd he so;
At last—a little shaking of mine arm,
And thrice his head thus waving up and down,—
He rais'd a sigh so piteous and profound,
As it did seem to shatter all his bulk *,
And end his being: That done, he lets me go:
And, with his head over his shoulder turn'd,
He seem'd to find his way without his eyes:
For out o' doors he went without their helps,
And, to the last, bended their light on me.

OLD AGE.

Beshrew my jealousy!
It seems it is as proper to our age
To cast beyond ourselves in our opinions,
As it is common for the younger sort
To lack discretion.

HAPPINESS CONSISTS IN OPINION.

Why, then 'tis none to you; for there is nothing either good or bad, but thinking makes it so: to me it is a prison.

REFLECTIONS ON MAN.

I have of late (but, wherefore, I know not), lost all my mirth, forgone all custom of exercises: and, indeed, it goes so heavily with my disposition, that this goodly frame, the earth, seems to me a steril promontory; this most excellent canopy, the air, look you, this brave o'erhanging firmament, this majestical-roof fretted with golden fire, why, it appears no other thing to me, than a foul and pestilent congregation of vapours. What a piece of work is a man! How noble in reason! how infinite in faculties! in form, and moving, how express and admirable! in action, how like an angel! in apprehension, how like a god! the beauty of the world! the paragon of

* Body.

animals! And yet, to me, what is this quintessence of dust? Man delights not me, nor woman neither; though, by your smiling, you seem to say so.

HAMLET'S REFLECTIONS ON THE PLAYER AND HIMSELF.

O, what a rogue and peasant slave am I!
Is it not monstrous, that this player here,
But in a fiction, in a dream of passion,
Could force his soul to his own conceit,
That from her working, all his visage wann'd;
Tears in his eyes, distraction in's aspect,
A broken voice, and his whole function suiting
With forms to his conceit? And all for nothing!
For Hecuba!
What's Hecuba to him, or he to Hecuba,
That he should weep for her? What would he do,
Had he the motive and the cue for passion
That I have? He would drown the stage with tears,
And cleave the general ear with horrid speech;
Make mad the guilty, and appal the free,
Confound the ignorant; and amaze, indeed,
The very faculties of eyes and ears.
Yet I,
A dull and muddy-mettled rascal, peak,
Like John a-dreams, unpregnant of my cause,
And can say nothing; no, not for a king,
Upon whose property, and most dear life,
A damn'd defeat* was made. Am I a coward?
Who calls me villain? breaks my pate across?
Plucks off my beard, and blows it in my face?
Tweaks me by the nose? gives me the lie i' the throat,
As deep as to the lungs?—Who does me this?
Ha!
Why, I should take it: for it cannot be,
But I am pigeon-liver'd, and lack gall
To make oppression bitter; or, ere this,
I should have fatted all the region kites
With this slave's offal: Bloody, bawdy† villain?

* Destruction. † Unnatural.

Remorseless, treacherous, lecherous, kindless * villain!
Why, what an ass am I? This is most brave;
That I, the son of a dear father murder'd,
Prompted to my revenge by heaven and hell,
Must, like a whore, unpack my heart with words,
And fall a cursing, like a very drab,
A scullion.
Fie upon't! foh! About my brains! Humph! I have heard,
That guilty creatures, sitting at a play,
Have by the very cunning of the scene
Been struck so to the soul, that presently
They have proclaim'd their malefactions;
For murder, though it have no tongue, will speak
With most miraculous organ. I'll have these players
Play something like the murder of my father,
Before mine uncle: I'll observe his looks;
I'll tent him † to the quick; if he do blench ‡,
I know my course. The spirit, that I have seen,
May be a devil: and the devil hath power
To assume a pleasing shape; yea, and, perhaps,
Out of my weakness, and my melancholy
(As he is very potent with such spirits),
Abuses me to damn me: I'll have grounds
More relative than this: The play's the thing,
Wherein I'll catch the conscience of the king.

ACT III.

HYPOCRISY.

We are oft to blame in this,—
'Tis too much prov'd §,—that, with devotion's visage,
And pious action, we do sugar o'er
The devil himself.

* Unnatural. † Search his wounds.
‡ Shrink, or start. § Too frequent.

King. O, 'tis too true! how smart
A lash that speech doth give my conscience!
The harlot's cheek, beautified with plastering art,
Is not more ugly to the thing that helps it,
Than is my deed to my most painted word.

SOLILOQUY ON LIFE AND DEATH.

To be, or not to be, that is the question :—
Whether 'tis nobler in the mind, to suffer
The slings and arrows of outrageous fortune;
Or to take arms against a sea of troubles,
And, by opposing, end them?—To die, to sleep,—
No more;—and, by a sleep, to say we end
The heart-ach, and the thousand natural shocks
That flesh is heir to,—'tis a consummation
Devoutly to be wish'd. To die;—to sleep;—
To sleep! perchance to dream;—ay, there's the rub;
For in that sleep of death what dreams may come,
When we have shuffled off this mortal coil *,
Must give us pause: there's the respect †,
That makes calamity of so long life:
For who would bear the whips and scorns of time,
The oppressor's wrong, the proud man's contumely ‡,
The pangs of déspised love, the law's delay,
The insolence of office, and the spurns
That patient merit of the unworthy takes,
When he himself might his quietus § make
With a bare bodkin ‖? who would fardels ¶ bear,
To grunt and sweat under a weary life;
But that the dread of something after death,—
The undiscover'd country, from whose bourn **
No traveller returns,—puzzles the will;
And makes us rather bear those ills we have,
Than fly to others that we know not of!
Thus conscience does make cowards of us all;
And thus the native hue of resolution
Is sicklied o'er with the pale cast of thought;

* Stir, bustle. † Consideration. ‡ Rudeness.
§ Acquittance. ‖ The ancient term for a small dagger.
¶ Pack, burden. ** Boundary, limits.

And enterprises of great pith and moment,
With this regard, their currents turn awry,
And lose the name of action.

CALUMNY.

Be thou as chaste as ice, as pure as snow, thou shalt not escape calumny.

A DISORDERED MIND.

O, what a noble mind is here o'erthrown!
The courtier's, soldier's, scholar's, eye, tongue, sword:
The expectancy and rose of the fair state,
The glass of fashion, and the mould * of form,
The observ'd of all observers! quite, quite down!
And I, of ladies most deject and wretched,
That suck'd the honey of his music vows,
Now see that noble and most sovereign reason,
Like sweet bells jangled, out of tune and harsh;
That unmatch'd form and feature of blown youth,
Blasted with ecstasy †.

HAMLET'S INSTRUCTIONS TO THE PLAYERS.

Speak the speech, I pray you, as I pronounced it to you, trippingly on the tongue: but if you mouth it, as many of our players do, I had as lief the town-crier spoke my lines. Nor do not saw the air too much with your hand, thus: but use all gently: for in the very torrent, tempest, and (as I may say) whirlwind of your passion, you must acquire and beget a temperance, that may give it smoothness. O, it offends me to the soul, to hear a robustious periwig-pated fellow tear a passion to tatters, to very rags, to split the ears of the groundlings ‡; who, for the most part, are capable of nothing but inexplicable dumb shows, and noise: I would have such a fellow whipped for out-doing Termagant; it out-herods Herod §. Pray you, avoid it.

* The model by whom all endeavoured to form themselves.
† Alienation of mind.
‡ The meaner people then seem to have sat in the pit.
§ Herod's character was always violent.

Play. I warrant your honour.

Ham. Be not too tame neither, but let your own discretion be your tutor: suit the action to the word, the word to the action; with this special observance, that you o'erstep not the modesty of nature: for any thing so overdone is from the purpose of playing, whose end, both at the first, and now, was, and is, to hold, as 'twere the mirror up to nature; to show virtue her own feature, scorn her own image, and the very age and body of the time his form and pressure*. Now this, overdone, or come tardy off, though it make the unskilful laugh, cannot but make the judicious grieve; the censure of which one, must, in your allowance †, overweigh a whole theatre of others. O, there be players, that I have seen play, and heard others praise, and that highly,—not to speak it profanely, that, neither having the accent of christians, nor the gait of christian, pagan, nor man, have so strutted, and bellowed, that I have thought some of nature's journeymen had made men, and not made them well, they imitated humanity so abominably.

Play. I hope, we have reformed that indifferently with us.

Ham. O, reform it altogether. And, let those that play your clowns, speak no more than is set down for them: for there be of them, that will themselves laugh, to set on some quantity of barren spectators to laugh too; though in the meantime, some necessary question ‡ of the play be then to be considered: that's villanous; and shows a most pitiful ambition in the fool that uses it.

ON FLATTERY, AND AN EVEN-MINDED MAN.

Nay, do not think I flatter:
For what advancement may I hope from thee,
That no revenue hast, but thy good spirits,

* Impression, resemblance. † Approbation.
‡ Conversation, discourse.

To feed and clothe thee? Why should the poor be flatter'd?
No, let the candied tongue lick absurd pomp;
And crook the pregnant* hinges of the knee,
Where thrift may follow fawning. Dost thou hear?
Since my dear soul was mistress of her choice,
And could of men distinguish her election,
She hath seal'd thee for herself: for thou hast been
As one, in suffering all, that suffers nothing;
A man that fortune's buffets and rewards
Hast ta'en with equal thanks: and bless'd are those,
Whose blood and judgment are so well comingled,
That they are not a pipe for fortune's finger
To sound what stop she please: Give me that man
That is not passion's slave, and I will wear him
In my heart's core, ay, in my heart of heart,
As I do thee.

MIDNIGHT.

'Tis now the very witching time of night;
When churchyards yawn, and hell itself breathes out
Contagion to this world: Now could I drink hot blood,
And do such business as the bitter day
Would quake to look on. Soft; now to my mother.—
O, heart, lose not thy nature; let not ever
The soul of Nero enter this firm bosom:
Let me be cruel, not unnatural:
I will speak daggers to her, but use none.

THE KING'S DESPAIRING SOLILOQUY, AND HAMLET'S REFLECTIONS ON HIM.

O, my offence is rank, it smells to heaven;
It hath the primal eldest curse upon't,
A brother's murder!—Pray can I not,
Though inclination be as sharp as will;
My stronger guilt defeats my strong intent;
And, like a man to double business bound,
I stand in pause where I shall first begin,

* Quick, ready.

And both neglect. What if this cursed hand
Were thicker than itself with brother's blood?
Is there not rain enough in the sweet heavens,
To wash it white as snow? Whereto serves mercy,
But to confront the visage of offence?
And what's in prayer, but this twofold force,—
To be forestalled ere we come to fall,
Or pardon'd, being down? Then I'll look up;
My fault is past. But, O, what form of prayer
Can serve my turn? Forgive me my foul murder!—
That cannot be; since I am still possess'd
Of those effects for which I did the murder,
My crown, mine own ambition, and my queen.
May one be pardon'd, and retain the offence?
In the corrupted currents of this world,
Offence's gilded hand may shove by justice;
And oft 'tis seen, the wicked prize itself
Buys out the law: But 'tis not so above·
There is no shuffling, there the action lies
In his true nature; and we ourselves compell'd,
Even to the teeth and forehead of our faults,
To give in evidence. What then? what rests?
Try what repentance can; What can it not?
Yet what can it, when one cannot repent!
O wretched state! O bosom black as death!
O limed * soul; that, struggling to be free,
Art more engag'd! Help, angels, make assay!
Bow, stubborn knees! and, heart with strings of steel;
Be soft as sinews of the new-born babe;
All may be well! [*Retires and kneels.*

Enter HAMLET.

Ham. Now might I do it, pat, now he is praying;
And now I'll do't; and so he goes to heaven:
And so am I reveng'd? That would be scann'd †:
A villain kills my father; and, for that,
I his sole ‡ son, do this same villain send

* Caught as with bird-lime. † Should be considered.
‡ Only.

To heaven.
Why, this is hire and salary *, not revenge.
He took my father grossly, full of bread;
With all his crimes broad blown, as flush as May;
And how his audit stands, who knows, save heaven?
But, in our circumstance and course of thought,
'Tis heavy with him: And am I then reveng'd,
To take him in the purging of his soul,
When he is fit and season'd for his passage?
No.
Up, sword; and know thou a more horrid hent †:
When he is drunk, asleep, or in his rage;
Or in the incestuous pleasures of his bed;
At gaming, swearing; or about some act
That has no relish of salvation in't:
Then trip him, that his heels may kick at heaven:
And that his soul may be as damn'd, and black,
As hell, whereto it goes.

HAMLET AND HIS MOTHER.

Queen. What have I done, that thou dar'st wag thy tongue
In noise so rude against me?
Ham. Such an act,
That blurs the grace and blush of modesty;
Calls virtue, hypocrite; takes off the rose
From the fair forehead of an innocent love,
And sets a blister there; makes marriage vows
As false as dicers' oaths: O, such a deed
As from the body of contraction ‡ plucks
The very soul; and sweet religion makes
A rhapsody of words: Heaven's face doth glow;
Yea, this solidity and compound mass,
With tristful § visage, as against the doom,
Is thought-sick at the act.
Queen. Ah me, what act,
That roars so loud, and thunders in the index ‖?

* Reward. † Seize him at a more horrid time.
‡ Marriage contract. § Sorrowful.
‖ Index of contents prefixed to a book.

Ham. Look here, upon this picture, and on this;
The counterfeit presentment of two brothers.
See, what a grace was seated on this brow:
Hyperion's* curls; the front of Jove himself;
An eye like Mars, to threaten and command;
A station † like the herald Mercury,
New-lighted on a heaven-kissing hill;
A combination, and a form, indeed,
Where every god did seem to set his seal,
To give the world assurance of a man:
This was your husband.—Look you now, what follows:
Here is your husband; like a mildew'd ear,
Blasting his wholesome brother. Have you eyes?
Could you on this fair mountain leave to feed,
And batten ‡ on this moor? Ha! have you eyes?
You cannot call it, love: for, at your age,
The hey-day in the blood is tame, it's humble,
And waits upon the judgment: And what judgment
Would step from this to this? Sense §, sure you have,
Else, could you not have motion: But, sure, that sense
Is apoplex'd; for madness would not err;
Nor sense to ecstasy ‖ was ne'er so thrall'd,
But it reserv'd some quantity of choice,
To serve in such a difference. What devil was't,
That thus hath cozen'd you at hoodman blind ¶?
Eyes without feeling, feeling without sight,
Ears without hands or eyes, smelling sans ** all,
Or but a sickly part of one true sense
Could not so mope ††.
O shame! where is thy blush? Rebellious hell,
If thou canst mutine in a matron's bones,
To flaming youth let virtue be as wax,
And melt in her own fire: Proclaim no shame,
When the compulsive ardour gives the charge;
Since frost itself as actively doth burn,
And reason panders will.
Queen. O Hamlet, speak no more:

* Apollo's. † The act of standing. ‡ To grow fat.
§ Sensation. ‖ Frenzy. ¶ Blindman's-buff.
** Without. †† Be so stupid.

Thou turn'st mine eyes into my very soul;
And there I see such black and grained spots,
As will not leave their tinct*.

Enter GHOST.

Ham. Save me, and hover o'er me with your wings,
You heavenly guards!—What would your gracious figure?

Queen. Alas, he's mad.

Ham. Do you not come your tardy son to chide,
That, laps'd in time and passion, lets go by
The important acting of your dread command?
O, say!

Ghost. Do not forget: This visitation
Is but to whet thy almost blunted purpose.
But, look! amazement on thy mother sits:
O, step between her and her fighting soul;
Conceit† in weakest bodies strongest works;
Speak to her, Hamlet.

Ham. How is it with you, lady?

Queen. Alas, how is't with you?
That you do bend your eye on vacancy,
And with the incorporal air do hold discourse?
Forth at your eyes your spirits wildly peep;
And, as the sleeping soldiers in the alarm,
Your bedded hair, like life in excrements‡,
Starts up, and stands on end. O gentle son,
Upon the heat and flame of thy distemper
Sprinkle cool patience. Whereon do you look?

Ham. On him! On him!—Look you, how pale he glares!
His form and cause conjoin'd, preaching to stones,
Would make them capable§.—Do not look upon me;
Lest, with this piteous action, you convert
My stern effects‖: then what I have to do

* Colour. † Imagination.

‡ The hair of animals is excrementitious, that is, without life or sensation.

§ Intelligent. ‖ Actions.

Will want true colour; tears, perchance *, for blood.
Queen. To whom do you speak this?
Ham. Do you see nothing there?
Queen. Nothing at all: yet all, that is, I see.
Ham. Nor did you nothing hear?
Queen. No, nothing, but ourselves.
Ham. Why, look you there! look, how it steals away!
My father, in his habit as he liv'd!
Look, where he goes, even now, out at the portal!
[*Exit* GHOST.
Queen. This is the very coinage of your brain:
This bodiless creation ecstasy †
Is very cunning in.
Ham. Ecstasy!
My pulse, as yours, doth temperately keep time,
And makes as healthful music: It is not madness,
That I have utter'd: bring me to the test,
And I the matter will re-word: which madness
Would gambol from. Mother, for love of grace,
Lay not that flattering unction to your soul,
That not your trespass, but my madness speaks:
It will but skin and film the ulcerous place;
Whiles rank corruption, mining all within,
Infects unseen. Confess yourself to heaven;
Repent what's past; avoid what is to come;
And do not spread the compost ‡ on the weeds,
To make them ranker. Forgive me this my virtue:
For in the fatness of these pursy times,
Virtue itself of vice must pardon beg;
Yea, curb § and woo, for leave to do him good.
Queen. O Hamlet! thou hast cleft my heart in twain.
Ham. O, throw away the worser part of it,
And live the purer with the other half.
Good night, but go not to my uncle's bed;
Assume a virtue if you have it not.
That monster, custom, who all sense doth eat
Of habit's devil, is angel yet in this;

* Perhaps. † Frenzy. ‡ Manure. § Bend.

That to the use of actions fair and good
He likewise gives a frock, or livery,
That aptly is put on: Refrain to-night;
And that shall lend a kind of easiness
To the next abstinence: the next more easy:
For use almost can change the stamp of nature,
And either curb the devil, or throw him out
With wondrous potency. Once more, good night!
And when you are desirous to be bless'd,
I'll blessing beg of you.—For this same lord,
[*Pointing to* POLONIUS.
I do repent: But heaven hath pleas'd it so,—
To punish me with this, and this with me,
That I must be their scourge and minister.
I will bestow him, and will answer well
The death I gave him. So, again, good night!
I must be cruel, only to be kind:
Thus bad begins, and worse remains behind.—
But one word more, good lady.

Queen. What shall I do?

Ham. Not this, by no means, that I bid you do:
Let the bloat king tempt you again to bed;
Pinch wanton on your cheek; call you his mouse *;
And let him, for a pair of reechy † kisses,
Or paddling in your neck with his damn'd fingers,
Make you to ravel all this matter out,
That I essentially am not in madness,
But mad in craft. 'Twere good, you let him know:
For who, that's but a queen, fair, sober, wise,
Would from a paddock ‡, from a bat, a gib §,
Such dear concernings hide? Who would do so?
No, in despite of sense and secrecy,
Unpeg the basket on the house's top,
Let the birds fly; and, like the famous ape,
To try conclusions ‖, in the basket creep,
And break your own neck down.

Queen. Be thou assur'd, if words be made of breath,

* A term of endearment. † Steaming with heat.
‡ Toad. § Cat. ‖ Experiments.

And breath of life, I have no life to breathe
What thou hast said to me.
Ham. I must to England: you know that?
Queen. Alack,
I had forgot; 'tis so concluded on.
Ham. There's letters seal'd: and my two school-fellows,—
Whom I will trust, as I will adders fang'd *,
They bear the mandate; they must sweep my way,
And marshal me to knavery: Let it work;
For 'tis the sport, to have the engineer
Hoist with his own petar †: and it shall go hard,
But I will delve one yard below their mines,
And blow them at the moon.

ACT IV.

HAMLET'S IRRESOLUTION.

How all occasions do inform against me,
And spur my dull revenge! What is a man,
If his chief good, and market ‡ of his time,
Be but to sleep, and feed? a beast, no more.
Sure, he, that made us with such large discourse §,
Looking before, and after, gave us not
That capability and godlike reason
To fust ‖ in us unus'd. Now, whether it be
Bestial oblivion, or some craven ¶ scruple
Of thinking too precisely on the event,—
A thought, which, quarter'd, hath but one part wisdom,
And, ever, three parts coward.—I do not know
Why yet I live to say, *This thing's to do;*
Sith ** I have cause, and will, and strength, and means,
To do't. Examples, gross as earth, exhort me:
Witness, this army of such mass, and charge,

* Having their teeth. † Blown up with his own bomb.
‡ Profit. § Power of comprehension.
‖ Grow mouldy. ¶ Cowardly. ** Since.

Led by a delicate and tender prince;
Whose spirit, with divine ambition puff'd,
Makes mouths at the invisible event;
Exposing what is mortal and unsure,
To all that fortune, death, and danger, dare,
Even for an egg-shell. Rightly to be great,
Is, not to stir without great argument;
But greatly to find quarrel in a straw,
When honour's at the stake. How stand I then,
That have a father kill'd, a mother stain'd,
Excitements of my reason, and my blood,
And let all sleep? while, to my shame, I see
The imminent death of twenty thousand men,
That, for a fantasy, and trick of fame,
Go to their graves like beds; fight for a plot
Whereon the numbers cannot try the cause,
Which is not tomb enough, and continent,
To hide the slain?—O, from this time forth,
My thoughts be bloody, or be nothing worth!

SORROWS RARELY SINGLE.

O Gertrude, Gertrude,
When sorrows come, they come not single spies,
But in battalions!

THE DIVINITY OF KINGS.

Let him go, Gertrude; do not fear our person;
There's such a divinity doth hedge a king,
That treason can but peep to what it would,
Acts little of his will.

DESCRIPTION OF OPHELIA'S DEATH.

Queen. There is a willow grows ascaunt the brook,
That shows his hoar leaves in the glassy stream;
Therewith fantastic garlands did she make
Of crow-flowers, nettles, daisies, and long purples*,
That liberal† shepherds give a grosser name,
But our cold maids do dead men's fingers call them:

* *Orchis morio mas.* † Licentious.

There on the pendent boughs her coronet weeds
Clambering to hang, an envious sliver broke;
When down her weedy trophies, and herself,
Fell in the weeping brook. Her clothes spread wide;
And, mermaidlike, a while they bore her up:
Which time, she chanted snatches of old tunes;
As one incapable * of her own distress,
Or, like a creature native and indu'd
Unto that element: but long it could not be,
Till that her garments, heavy with their drink,
Pull'd the poor wretch from her melodious lay
To muddy death.

ACT V.

HAMLET'S REFLECTIONS ON YORICK'S SCULL.

Grave-digger. A pestilence on him for a mad rogue! he poured a flagon of Rhenish on my head once. This same scull, sir, was Yorick's scull, the king's jester.

Ham. This? [*Takes the Scull.*

Grave-digger. E'en that.

Ham. Alas! poor Yorick!—I knew him, Horatio; a fellow of infinite jest; of most excellent fancy: he hath borne me on his back a thousand times; and now, how abhorred in my imagination it is! my gorge rises at it. Here hung those lips, that I have kissed I know not how oft. Where be your gibes now? your gambols? your songs? your flashes of merriment, that were wont to set the table on a roar? Not one now, to mock your own grinning? quite chap-fallen? Now get you to my lady's chamber, and tell her, let her paint an inch thick, to this favour † she must come; make her laugh at that.

OPHELIA'S INTERMENT.

Lay her i' the earth;—
And from her fair and unpolluted flesh,

* Insensible. † Countenance, complexion.

May violets spring!—I tell thee, churlish priest,
A ministering angel shall my sister be,
When thou liest howling.

MELANCHOLY.

This is mere madness:
And thus a while the fit will work on him:
Anon, as patient as the female dove,
When that her golden couplets are disclos'd*,
His silence will sit drooping.

PROVIDENCE DIRECTS OUR ACTIONS.

And that should teach us,
There's a divinity that shapes our ends,
Rough-hew them how we will.

A HEALTH.

Give me the cups;
And let the kettle to the trumpet speak,
The trumpet to the cannoneer without,
The cannons to the heavens, the heaven to earth,
Now the king drinks to Hamlet.

JULIUS CÆSAR.

ACT I.

PATRIOTISM.

WHAT is it that you would impart to me?
If it be aught toward the general good,
Set honour in one eye, and death i' the other,
And I will look on both indifferently:
For, let the gods so speed me, as I love
The name of honour more than I fear death.

* Hatched.

CONTEMPT OF CASSIUS FOR CÆSAR.

I was born free as Cæsar; so were you:
We both have fed as well; and we can both
Endure the winter's cold, as well as he.
For once, upon a raw and gusty* day,
The troubled Tyber chafing with her shores,
Cæsar said to me, *Dar'st thou*, Cassius, *now*
Leap in with me into this angry flood,
And swim to yonder point? Upon the word,
Accouter'd as I was, I plunged in,
And bade him follow; so, indeed, he did.
The torrent roar'd; and we did buffet it
With lusty sinews; throwing it aside
And stemming it with hearts of controversy.
But ere we could arrive the point propos'd,
Cæsar cry'd, *Help me*, Cassius, *or I sink.*
I, as Æneas, our great ancestor,
Did from the flames of Troy upon his shoulder
The old Anchises bear, so, from the waves of Tyber
Did I the tired Cæsar: And this man
Is now become a god; and Cassius is
A wretched creature, and must bend his body,
If Cæsar carelessly but nod on him.
He had a fever when he was in Spain,
And, when the fit was on him, I did mark
How he did shake; 'tis true, this god did shake:
His coward lips did from their colour fly;
And that same eye, whose bend doth awe the world,
Did lose his lustre: I did hear him groan:
Ay, and that tongue of his, that bade the Romans
Mark him, and write his speeches in their books,
Alas! it cried, *Give me some drink*, Titinius,
As a sick girl. Ye gods, it doth amaze me,
A man of such a feeble temper† should
So get the start of the majestic world,
And bear the palm alone. [*Shout. Flourish.*

Bru. Another general shout!

* Windy. † Temperament, constitution.

I do believe, that these applauses are
For some new honours that are heap'd on Cæsar.
Cas. Why, man, he doth bestride the narrow world,
Like a Colossus: and we petty men
Walk under his huge legs, and peep about
To find ourselves dishonourable graves.
Men at some time are masters of their fates:
The fault, dear Brutus, is not in our stars,
But in ourselves, that we are underlings.
Brutus, and Cæsar: What should be in that Cæsar?
Why should that name be sounded more than yours?
Write them together, yours is as fair a name;
Sound them, it doth become the mouth as well;
Weigh them, it is as heavy; conjure them,
Brutus will start a spirit as soon as Cæsar. [*Shout.*
Now in the name of all the gods at once,
Upon what meat doth this our Cæsar feed,
That he is grown so great? Age, thou art sham'd:
Rome, thou hast lost the breed of noble bloods!
When went there by an age, since the great flood,
But it was fam'd with more than with one man?
When could they say, till now, that talk'd of Rome,
That her wide walks encompass'd but one man?

CÆSAR'S DISLIKE OF CASSIUS.

'Would he were fatter:—But I fear him not:
Yet if my name were liable to fear,
I do not know the man I should avoid
So soon as that spare Cassius. He reads much;
He is a great observer, and he looks
Quite through the deeds of men: he loves no plays,
As thou dost, Antony; he hears no music:
Seldom he smiles; and smiles in such a sort,
As if he mock'd himself, and scorn'd his spirit
That could be mov'd to smile at any thing;
Such men as he be never at heart's ease,
Whiles they behold a greater than themselves;
And therefore are they very dangerous.
I rather tell thee what is to be fear'd,
Than what I fear, for always I am Cæsar.

SPIRIT OF LIBERTY.

I know where I will wear this dagger then;
Cassius from bondage will deliver Cassius:
Therein, ye gods, you make the weak most strong;
Therein, ye gods, you tyrants do defeat:
Nor stony tower, nor walls of beaten brass,
Nor airless dungeon, nor strong links of iron,
Can be retentive to the strength of spirit;
But life, being weary of these worldly bars,
Never lacks power to dismiss itself.
If I know this, know all the world besides,
That part of tyranny, that I do bear,
I can shake off at pleasure.

ACT II.

AMBITION CLOTHED IN SPECIOUS HUMILITY.

But 'tis a common proof*,
That lowliness is young ambition's ladder,
Whereto the climber-upward turns his face:
But when he once attains the upmost round,
He then unto the ladder turns his back,
Looks in the clouds, scorning the base degrees †
By which he did ascend.

CONSPIRACY DREADFUL TILL EXECUTED.

Between the acting of a dreadful thing
And the first motion, all the interim is
Like a phantasma ‡, or a hideous dream:
The genius, and the mortal instruments,
Are then in council; and the state of man,
Like to a little kingdom, suffers then
The nature of an insurrection.

* Experience. † Low steps. ‡ Visionary.

BRUTUS'S APOSTROPHE TO CONSPIRACY.

O conspiracy!
Sham'st thou to show thy dangerous brow by night,
When evils are most free! O, then, by day,
Where wilt thou find a cavern dark enough
To mask thy monstrous visage? Seek none, conspiracy;
Hide in it smiles and affability:
For if thou path thy native semblance * on,
Not Erebus † itself were dim enough
To hide thee from prevention.

AGAINST CRUELTY.

Gentle friends,
Let's kill him boldly, but not wrathfully;
Let's carve him as a dish fit for the gods,
Not hew him as a carcass fit for hounds:
And let our hearts, as subtle masters do,
Stir up their servants to an act of rage,
And after seem to chide them.

SLEEP.

Enjoy the honey-heavy dew of slumber:
Thou hast no figures ‡, nor no fantasies,
Which busy care draws in the brains of men;
Therefore thou sleep'st so sound.

PORTIA'S SPEECH TO BRUTUS.

You have ungently, Brutus,
Stole from my bed: And yesternight, at supper,
You suddenly arose, and walk'd about,
Musing, and sighing, with your arms across:
And when I ask'd you what the matter was,
You star'd upon me with ungentle looks:
I urg'd you further; then you scratch'd your head,
And too impatiently stamp'd with your foot:
Yet I insisted, yet you answer'd not;
But, with an angry wafture of your hand,

* Walk in thy true form. † Hell.
‡ Shapes created by imagination.

Gave sign for me to leave you: So I did;
Fearing to strengthen that impatience,
Which seem'd too much enkindled; and withal,
Hoping that it was but an effect of humour,
Which sometime hath his hour with every man.
It will not let you eat, nor talk, nor sleep:
And, could it work so much upon your shape,
As it hath much prevail'd on your condition*,
I should not know you, Brutus. Dear my lord,
Make me acquainted with your cause of grief.

CALPHURNIA'S ADDRESS TO CÆSAR ON THE PRODIGIES SEEN THE NIGHT BEFORE HIS DEATH.

Cal. Cæsar, I never stood on ceremonies †,
Yet now they fright me. There is one within,
Besides the things that we have heard and seen,
Recounts most horrid sights seen by the watch,
A lioness hath whelped in the streets;
And graves have yawn'd, and yielded up their dead:
Fierce fiery warriors fight upon the clouds,
In ranks, and squadrons, and right form of war,
Which drizzled blood upon the Capitol:
The noise of battle hurtled ‡ in the air,
Horses did neigh, and dying men did groan;
And ghosts did shriek, and squeal § about the streets.
O Cæsar! these things are beyond all use,
And I do fear them.
Cæs. What can be avoided,
Whose end is purpos'd by the mighty gods?
Yet Cæsar shall go forth: for these predictions
Are to the world in general, as to Cæsar.
Cal. When beggars die, there are no comets seen;
The heavens themselves blaze forth the death of princes.

AGAINST THE FEAR OF DEATH.

Cowards die many times before their deaths;
The valiant never taste of death but once.

* Temper. † Never paid a regard to prodigies or omens.
‡ Encountered. § Cry with pain.

Of all the wonders that I yet have heard,
It seems to me most strange that men should fear;
Seeing that death, a necessary end,
Will come when it will come.

DANGER.

Danger knows full well
That Cæsar is more dangerous than he.
We were two lions litter'd in one day,
And I the elder and more terrible.

ENVY.

My heart laments that virtue cannot live
Out of the teeth of emulation *.

ACT III.

ANTONY'S ADDRESS TO THE CORPSE OF CÆSAR.

O mighty Cæsar! Dost thou lie so low?
Are all thy conquests, glories, triumphs, spoils,
Shrunk to this little measure?—Fare thee well.

ANTONY'S SPEECH TO THE CONSPIRATORS.

I know not, gentlemen, what you intend,
Who else must be let blood, who else is rank †:
If I myself, there is no hour so fit
As Cæsar's death's hour; nor no instrument
Of half that worth, as those your swords, made rich
With the most noble blood of all this world.
I do beseech ye, if you bear me hard,
Now, whilst your purpled hands do reek and smoke,
Fulfil your pleasure. Live a thousand years,
I shall not find myself so apt to die:
No place will please me so, no mean of death,
As here by Cæsar, and by you cut off,
The choice and master spirits of this age.

* Envy. † Grown too high for the public safety.

REVENGE.

Cæsar's spirit, ranging for revenge,
With Até by his side, come hot from hell,
Shall in these confines, with a monarch's voice,
Cry *Havoc* *, and let slip † the dogs of war.

BRUTUS'S SPEECH TO THE PEOPLE.

If there be any in this assembly, any dear friend of Cæsar's, to him I say, that Brutus' love to Cæsar was no less than his. If then that friend demand, why Brutus rose against Cæsar, this is my answer, —Not that I loved Cæsar less, but that I loved Rome more. Had you rather Cæsar were living, and die all slaves; than that Cæsar were dead, to live all free men? As Cæsar loved me, I weep for him; as he was fortunate, I rejoice at it; as he was valiant, I honour him; but, as he was ambitious, I slew him. There is tears, for his love; joy, for his fortune; honour, for his valour; and death, for his ambition. Who is here so base, that would be a bondman? If any, speak; for him have I offended. Who is here so rude, that would not be a Roman? If any, speak; for him have I offended. Who is here so vile, that will not love his country? If any, speak; for him have I offended.

ANTONY'S FUNERAL ORATION.

Friends, Romans, countrymen, lend me your ears;
I come to bury Cæsar, not to praise him.
The evil, that men do, lives after them;
The good is oft interred with their bones;
So let it be with Cæsar. The noble Brutus
Hath told you, Cæsar was ambitious:
If it were so, it was a grievous fault;
And grievously hath Cæsar answer'd it.
Here, under leave of Brutus, and the rest,
(For Brutus is an honourable man;
So are they all, all honourable men;)
Come I to speak in Cæsar's funeral.

* The signal for giving no quarter. † To let slip a dog at a deer, &c. was the technical phrase of Shakspeare's time.

He was my friend, faithful and just to me:
But Brutus says he was ambitious;
And Brutus is an honourable man.
He hath brought many captives home to Rome,
Whose ransoms did the general coffers fill:
Did this in Cæsar seem ambitious?
When that the poor have cried, Cæsar hath wept:
Ambition should be made of sterner stuff:
Yet Brutus says, he was ambitious;
And Brutus is an honourable man.
You all did see, that on the Lupercal,
I thrice presented him a kingly crown,
Which he did thrice refuse. Was this ambition?
Yet Brutus says, he was ambitious;
And, sure, he is an honourable man.
I speak not to disprove what Brutus spoke,
But here I am to speak what I do know.
You all did love him once, not without cause;
What cause withholds you then to mourn for him?
O judgment, thou art fled to brutish beasts,
And men have lost their reason!—Bear with me;
My heart is in the coffin there with Cæsar,
And I must pause till it come back to me.

* * * * *

But yesterday, the word of Cæsar might
Have stood against the world: now lies he there,
And none so poor* to do him reverence.
O masters! if I were dispos'd to stir
Your hearts and minds to mutiny and rage,
I should do Brutus wrong, and Cassius wrong,
Who, you all know, are honourable men:
I will not do them wrong; I rather choose
To wrong the dead, to wrong myself, and you,
Than I will wrong such honourable men.
But here's a parchment, with the seal of Cæsar,
I found it in his closet, 'tis his will:
Let but the commons hear this testament
(Which, pardon me, I do not mean to read),
And they would go and kiss dead Cæsar's wounds,

* The meanest man is now too high to do reverence to Cæsar.

And dip their napkins * in his sacred blood;
Yea, beg a hair of him for memory,
And, dying, mention it within their wills,
Bequeathing it, as a rich legacy,
Unto their issue.

4 *Cit.* We'll hear the will: Read it, Mark Antony.

Cit. The will, the will; we will hear Cæsar's will.

Ant. Have patience, gentle friends, I must not read it;
It is not meet you know how Cæsar lov'd you.
You are not wood, you are not stones, but men;
And, being men, hearing the will of Cæsar,
It will inflame you, it will make you mad:
'Tis good you know not that you are his heirs;
For, if you should, O, what would come of it!

4 *Cit.* Read the will; we will hear it, Antony;
You shall read us the will: Cæsar's will.

Ant. Will you be patient! Will you stay a while?
I have o'ershot myself to tell you of it.
I fear, I wrong the honourable men,
Whose daggers have stabb'd Cæsar: I do fear it.

4 *Cit.* They were traitors: Honourable men!

Cit. The will! the testament!

2 *Cit.* They were villains, murderers: The will!
Read the will!

Ant. You will compel me then to read the will?
Then make a ring about the corpse of Cæsar,
And let me show you him that made the will.
Shall I descend? And will you give me leave?

Cit. Come down.

2 *Cit.* Descend. [*He comes down from the Pulpit.*

* * * * *

Ant. If you have tears, prepare to shed them now.
You all do know this mantle: I remember
The first time ever Cæsar put it on;
'Twas on a summer's evening, in his tent;
That day he overcame the Nervii:—
Look! in this place, ran Cassius' dagger through:

* Handkerchiefs.

See, what a rent the envious Casca made:
Through this, the well beloved Brutus stabb'd;
And, as he pluck'd his cursed steel away,
Mark how the blood of Cæsar follow'd it;
As rushing out of doors to be resolv'd
If Brutus so unkindly knock'd, or no;
For Brutus, as you know, was Cæsar's angel.
Judge, O you gods, how dearly Cæsar lov'd him!
This was the most unkindest cut of all:
For when the noble Cæsar saw him stab,
Ingratitude, more strong than traitors' arms,
Quite vanquish'd him: then burst his mighty heart;
And, in his mantle muffling up his face,
Even at the base of Pompey's statua *,
Which all the while ran blood, great Cæsar fell.
O, what a fall was there, my countrymen!
Then I, and you, and all of us fell down,
Whilst bloody treason flourish'd over us †.
O, now you weep; and, I perceive, you feel
The dint ‡ of pity: these are gracious drops.
Kind souls, what, weep you, when you but behold
Our Cæsar's vesture wounded? Look you here,
Here is himself, marr'd, as you see, with traitors.

1 *Cit.* O piteous spectacle!

* * * * *

2 *Cit.* We will be revenged: revenge; about,—seek,—burn,—fire,—kill,—slay!—let not a traitor live.

Ant. Good friends, sweet friends, let me not stir you up
To such a sudden flood of mutiny.
They, that have done this deed, are honourable;
What private griefs § they have, alas, I know not,
That made them do it; they are wise and honourable,
And will, no doubt, with reasons answer you.
I come not, friends, to steal away your hearts;
I am no orator, as Brutus is:

* Statua, for statue, is common among the old writers.
† Was successful. ‡ Impression. § Grievances.

But, as you know me all, a plain blunt man,
That love my friend; and that they know full well
That gave me public leave to speak of him.
For I have neither wit, nor words, nor worth,
Action nor utterance, nor the power of speech,
To stir men's blood: I only speak right on;
I tell you that, which you yourselves do know;
Show you sweet Cæsar's wounds, poor, poor dumb mouths,
And bid them speak for me: But were I Brutus,
And Brutus Antony, there were an Antony
Would ruffle up your spirits, and put a tongue
In every wound of Cæsar, that should move
The stones of Rome to rise and mutiny.

ACT IV.

CEREMONY INSINCERE.

Ever note, Lucilius,
When love begins to sicken and decay,
It useth an enforced ceremony.
There are no tricks in plain and simple faith:
But hollow men, like horses hot at hand,
Make gallant show and promise of their mettle:
But when they should endure the bloody spur,
They fall their crests, and, like deceitful jades,
Sink in the trial.

THE TENT SCENE BETWEEN BRUTUS AND CASSIUS.

Cas. That you have wrong'd me, doth appear in this:
You have condemn'd and noted Lucius Pella,
For taking bribes here of the Sardians;
Wherein my letters, praying on his side,
Because I knew the man, were slighted off.

Bru. You wrong'd yourself, to write in such a case.

Cas. In such a time as this, it is not meet
That every nice* offence should bear his comment.
Bru. Let me tell you, Cassius, you yourself
Are much condemn'd to have an itching palm;
To sell and mart your offices for gold,
To undeservers.
Cas. I an itching palm?
You know that you are Brutus that speak this,
Or, by the gods, this speech were else your last.
Bru. The name of Cassius honours this corruption,
And chastisement doth therefore hide his head.
Cas. Chastisement!
Bru. Remember March, the ides of March remember!
Did not great Julius bleed for justice' sake?
What villain touch'd his body, that did stab,
And not for justice? What, shall one of us,
That struck the foremost man of all this world,
But for supporting robbers; shall we now
Contaminate our fingers with base bribes?
And sell the mighty space of our large honours,
For so much trash, as may be grasped thus?—
I had rather be a dog, and bay† the moon,
Than such a Roman.
Cas. Brutus, bay not me,
I'll not endure it: you forget yourself,
To hedge me in‡; I am a soldier, I
Older in practice, abler than yourself
To make conditions§.
Bru. Go to; you're not, Cassius.
Cas. I am.
Bru. I say you are not.
Cas. Urge me no more, I shall forget myself;
Have mind upon your health, tempt me no further.
Bru. Away, slight man!
Cas. Is't possible?
Bru. Hear me, for I will speak.

* Trifling. † Bait, bark at. ‡ Limit my authority.
§ Terms, fit to confer the offices at my disposal.

Must I give way and room to your rash choler?
Shall I be frighted when a madman stares?

Cas. O ye gods! ye gods! Must I endure all this?

Bru. All this? ay, more: Fret, till your proud heart break;
Go, show your slaves how choleric you are,
And make your bondmen tremble. Must I budge?
Must I observe you? Must I stand and crouch
Under your testy humour? By the gods,
You shall digest the venom of your spleen,
Though it do split you: for, from this day forth,
I'll use you for my mirth, yea, for my laughter,
When you are waspish.

Cas. Is it come to this?

Bru. You say, you are a better soldier:
Let it appear so; make your vaunting true,
And it shall please me well: For mine own part,
I shall be glad to learn of noble men.

Cas. You wrong me every way, you wrong me, Brutus:
I said, an elder soldier, not a better:
Did I say, better?

Bru. If you did, I care not.

Cas. When Cæsar liv'd, he durst not thus have mov'd me.

Bru. Peace, peace; you durst not so have tempted him.

Cas. I durst not?

Bru. No.

Cas. What? durst not tempt him?

Bru. For your life you durst not.

Cas. Do not presume too much upon my love,
I may do that I shall be sorry for.

Bru. You have done that you should be sorry for.
There is no terror, Cassius, in your threats:
For I am arm'd so strong in honesty,
That they pass by me as the idle wind,
Which I respect not. I did send to you
For certain sums of gold, which you denied me;—
For I can raise no money by vile means:
By heaven I had rather coin my heart,

And drop my blood for drachmas*, than to wring
From the hard hands of peasants their vile trash,
By any indirection. I did send
To you for gold to pay my legions,
Which you denied me: Was that done like Cassius?
Should I have answer'd Caius Cassius so?
When Marcus Brutus grows so covetous,
To lock such rascal counters from his friends,
Be ready, gods, with all your thunderbolts,
Dash him to pieces!

Cas. I denied you not.

Bru. You did.

Cas. I did not:—he was but a fool,
That brought my answer back.—Brutus hath riv'd† my heart:
A friend should bear his friend's infirmities,
But Brutus makes mine greater than they are.

Bru. I do not, till you practise them on me.

Cas. You love me not.

Bru. I do not like your faults.

Cas. A friendly eye could never see such faults.

Bru. A flatterer's would not, though they do appear
As huge as high Olympus.

Cas. Come, Antony, and young Octavius, come,
Revenge yourselves alone on Cassius,
For Cassius is aweary of the world:
Hated by one he loves: brav'd by his brother:
Check'd like a bondman; all his faults observ'd,
Set in a note-book, learn'd, and conn'd by rote,
To cast into my teeth. O, I could weep
My spirit from mine eyes!—There is my dagger,
And here my naked breast; within, a heart
Dearer than Plutus' mine, richer than gold:
If that thou be'st a Roman, take it forth;
I, that denied thee gold, will give my heart:
Strike, as thou didst at Cæsar; for I know,
When thou didst hate him worst, thou lov'dst him better
Than ever thou lov'dst Cassius.

* Coin. † Split.

Bru. Sheath your dagger:
Be angry when you will, it shall have scope;
Do what you will, dishonour shall be humour.
O Cassius, you are yoked with a lamb
That carries anger as the flint bears fire;
Who, much enforced, shows a hasty spark,
And straight is cold again.
Cas. Hath Cassius liv'd
To be but mirth and laughter to his Brutus,
When grief, and blood ill temper'd, vexeth him?
Bru. When I spoke that, I was ill temper'd too.
Cas. Do you confess so much; Give me your hand.
Bru. And my heart too.
Cas. O Brutus!—
Bru. What's the matter?
Cas. Have you not love enough to bear with me,
When that rash humour, which my mother gave me,
Makes me forgetful?
Bru. Yes, Cassius; and henceforth,
When you are over-earnest with your Brutus,
He'll think your mother chides, and leave you so.

* * * * *

Bru. O Cassius, I am sick of many griefs.
Cas. Of your philosophy you make no use,
If you give place to accidental evils.
Bru. No man bears sorrow better:—Portia is dead.
Cas. Ha! Portia!
Bru. She is dead.
Cas. How scap'd I killing, when I cross'd you so?—
O insupportable and touching loss!—
Upon what sickness?
Bru. Impatient of my absence;
And grief, that young Octavius with Mark Antony
Have made themselves so strong;—for with her death
That tidings came.—With this she fell distract,
And, her attendants absent, swallow'd fire.
Cas. And died so?
Bru. Even so.
Cas. O ye immortal gods!

Enter LUCIUS *with Wine and Tapers.*

Bru. Speak no more of her.—Give me a bowl of wine:—
In this I'll bury all unkindness, Cassius. [*Drinks.*
Cas. My heart is thirsty for that noble pledge:
Fill, Lucius, till the wine o'erswell the cup;
I cannot drink too much of Brutus' love. [*Drinks.*

OPPORTUNITY TO BE SEIZED ON ALL OCCASIONS OF LIFE.

There is a tide in the affairs of men,
Which, taken at the flood, leads on to fortune;
Omitted, all the voyage of their life
Is bound in shallows, and in miseries.
On such a full sea are we now afloat;
And we must take the current when it serves,
Or lose our ventures.

ACT V.

THE PARTING OF BRUTUS AND CASSIUS.

Bru. No, Cassius, no: think not, thou noble Roman,
That ever Brutus will go bound to Rome;
He bears too great a mind. But this same day
Must end that work, the ides of March begun;
And whether we shall meet again, I know not.
Therefore our everlasting farewell take:
For ever, and for ever, farewell, Cassius!
If we do meet again, why we shall smile;
If not, why then this parting was well made.
Cas. For ever, and for ever, farewell, Brutus!
If we do meet again, we'll smile indeed;
If not, 'tis true, this parting was well made.
Bru. Why, then, lead on.—O, that a man might know
The end of this day's business, ere it come!

But it sufficeth, that the day will end,
And then the end is known.

MELANCHOLY, THE PARENT OF ERROR.

O hateful error, melancholy's child!
Why dost thou show to the apt thoughts of men
The things that are not! O error, soon conceiv'd,
Thou never com'st unto a happy birth,
But kill'st the mother that engender'd thee.

ANTONY'S CHARACTER OF BRUTUS.

This was the noblest Roman of them all:
All the conspirators, save only he,
Did that they did in envy of great Cæsar;
He, only, in a general honest thought,
And common good to all, made one of them.
His life was gentle; and the elements
So mix'd in him, that Nature might stand up,
And say to all the world, *This was a man!*

KING LEAR.

ACT I.

A FATHER'S ANGER.

Let it be so,—Thy truth then be thy dower:
For, by the sacred radiance of the sun;
The mysteries of Hecate, and the night;
By all the operations of the orbs,
From whence we do exist, and cease to be;
Here I disclaim all my paternal care,
Propinquity * and property of blood,
And as a stranger to my heart and me

* Kindred.

Hold thee from this*, for ever. The barbarous
Scythian,
Or he that makes his generation† messes
To gorge his appetite, shall to my bosom
Be as well neighbour'd, pitied, and reliev'd,
As thou my sometime daughter.

BASTARDY.

Thou, nature, art my goddess; to thy law
My services are bound: Wherefore should I
Stand in the plague‡ of custom; and permit
The curiosity§ of nations to deprive me,
For that I am some twelve or fourteen moonshines
Lag of a brother? Why bastard? wherefore base?
When my dimensions are as well compact,
My mind as generous, and my shape as true,
As honest madam's issue? Why brand they us
With base? with baseness? bastardy? base, base?
Who, in the lusty stealth of nature, take
More composition and fierce quality,
Than doth, within a dull, stale, tired bed,
Go to the creating a whole tribe of fops,
Got 'tween asleep and wake?

ASTROLOGY RIDICULED.

This is the excellent foppery of the world! that when we are sick in fortune (often the surfeit of our own behaviour), we make guilty of our disasters, the sun, the moon, and the stars: as if we were villains by necessity: fools by heavenly compulsion; knaves, thieves, and treachers‖, by spherical predominance; drunkards, liars, and adulterers, by an enforced obedience of planetary influence; and all that we are evil in, by a divine thrusting on: An admirable evasion of whoremaster man, to lay his goatish disposition to the charge of a star! My father compounded with my mother under the dragon's tail; and my nativity was under *ursa major*¶; so that it follows, I am rough and

* From this time. † His children. ‡ The injustice.
§ The nicety of civil institution. ‖ Traitors.
¶ Great Bear, the constellation so named.

lecherous.—Tut, I should have been that I am, had the maidenliest star in the firmament twinkled at my bastardizing.

FILIAL INGRATITUDE.

Ingratitude! thou marble-hearted fiend,
More hideous, when thou show'st thee in a child,
Than the seamonster!

A FATHER'S CURSE ON HIS CHILD.

Hear, nature, hear;
Dear goddess, hear! Suspend thy purpose, if
Thou didst intend to make this creature fruitful!
Into her womb convey sterility!
Dry up in her the organs of increase;
And from her derogate* body never spring
A babe to honour her! If she must teem,
Create her child of spleen; that it may live,
And be a thwart disnatur'd torment to her!
Let it stamp wrinkles on her brow of youth;
With cadent† tears fret channels in her cheeks;
Turn all her mother's pains, and benefits,
To laughter and contempt; that she may feel
How sharper than a serpent's tooth it is
To have a thankless child!

ACT II.

FLATTERING SYCOPHANTS.

That such a slave as this should wear a sword,
Who wears no honesty. Such smiling rogues as these,
Like rats, oft bite the holy cords atwain
Which are too intrinse‡ t'unloose! smooth every passion
That in the natures of their lords rebels;
Bring oil to fire, snow to their colder moods;

* Degraded. † Falling. ‡ Perplexed.

Renege *, affirm, and turn their halcyon † beaks
With every gale and vary of their masters,
As knowing nought, like dogs, but following.

PLAIN BLUNT MEN.

This is some fellow,
Who, having been prais'd for bluntness, doth affect
A saucy roughness, and constrains the garb,
Quite from his nature: He cannot flatter, he!—
An honest mind and plain, he must speak truth:
An they will take it, so; if not, he's plain.
These kind of knaves I know, which in this plainness
Harbour more craft, and more corrupter ends,
Than twenty silly ‡ ducking observants,
That stretch their duties nicely.

BEDLAM BEGGARS.

While I may scape,
I will preserve myself: and am bethought
To take the basest and most poorest shape,
That every penury, in contempt of man,
Brought near to beast: my face I'll grime with filth;
Blanket my loins; elf § all my hair in knots;
And with presented nakedness outface
The winds, and persecutions of the sky.
The country gives me proof and precedent
Of Bedlam beggars, who, with roaring voices,
Strike in their numb'd and mortified bare arms
Pins, wooden pricks ||, nails, sprigs of rosemary;
And with this horrible object, from low farms,
Poor pelting villages, sheep-cotes, and mills,
Sometime with lunatic bans ¶, sometime with prayers,
Enforce their charity.

* Disowned.

† The bird called the king-fisher, which, when dried and hung up by a thread, is supposed to turn his bill to the point from whence the wind blows. ‡ Simple or rustic.

§ Hair thus knotted was supposed to be the work of elves and fairies in the night. || Skewers. ¶ Curses.

THE FAULTS OF INFIRMITY PARDONABLE.

Fiery? the fiery duke?—Tell the hot duke, that—
No, but not yet:—may be, he is not well:
Infirmity doth still neglect all office,
Whereto our health is bound; we are not ourselves,
When nature, being oppress'd, commands the mind
To suffer with the body: I'll forbear:
And am fallen out with my more headier will,
To take the indispos'd and sickly fit
For the sound man.

UNKINDNESS.

Thy sister's naught: O, Regan, she hath tied
Sharp-tooth'd unkindness, like a vulture, here.
[*Points to his Heart.*

OFFENCES MISTAKEN.

All's not offence, that indiscretion finds,
And dotage terms so.

RISING PASSION.

I pr'ythee, daughter, do not make me mad;
I will not trouble thee, my child; farewell:
We'll no more meet, no more see one another:—
But yet thou art my flesh, my blood, my daughter;
Or, rather, a disease that's in my flesh,
Which I must needs call mine: thou art a boil,
A plague-sore, an embossed * carbuncle,
In my corrupted blood. But I'll not chide thee;
Let shame come when it will, I do not call it:
I do not bid the thunder-bearer shoot,
Nor tell tales of thee to high judging Jove.

THE NECESSARIES OF LIFE FEW.

O, reason not the need: our basest beggars
Are in the poorest thing superfluous:
Allow not nature more than nature needs,
Man's life is cheap as beast's.

* Swelling.

LEAR ON THE INGRATITUDE OF HIS DAUGHTERS.

You see me here, you gods, a poor old man,
As full of grief as age; wretched in both!
If it be you that stir these daughters' hearts
Against their father, fool me not so much
To bear it tamely; touch me with noble anger!
O, let not women's weapons, water-drops,
Stain my man's cheeks!—No, you unnatural hags,
I will have such revenges on you both,
That all the world shall—I will do such things,—
What they are, yet I know not; but they shall be
The terrors of the earth. You think, I'll weep;
No, I'll not weep:—
I have full cause of weeping; but this heart
Shall break into a hundred thousand flaws,
Or ere I'll weep:—O, fool, I shall go mad!

WILFUL MEN.

O, sir, to wilful men,
The injuries, that they themselves procure,
Must be their schoolmasters.

ACT III.

LEAR'S DISTRESS IN THE STORM.

Kent. Where's the king?
Gent. Contending with the fretful element:
Bids the wind blow the earth into the sea,
Or swell the curled waters 'bove the main,
That things might change, or cease: tears his white hair;
Which the impetuous blasts, with eyeless rage,
Catch in their fury, and make nothing of:
Strives in his little world of man to out-scorn
The to-and-fro-conflicting wind and rain.
This night, wherein the cub-drawn* bear would couch,

* Whose dugs are drawn dry by its young.

The lion and the belly-pinched wolf
Keep their fur dry, unbonneted he runs,
And bids what will take all.

LEAR'S EXCLAMATIONS IN THE TEMPEST.

Blow, wind, and crack your cheeks! rage! blow!
You cataracts, and hurricanoes, spout
Till you have drench'd our steeples, drown'd the cocks!
You sulphurous and thought-executing* fires,
Vaunt couriers† to oak-cleaving thunderbolts,
Singe my white head! And thou, all-shaking thunder,
Strike flat the thick rotundity o' the world!
Crack nature's moulds, all germens spill at once,
That make ingrateful man!

* * * * *

Rumble thy bellyfull! Spit, fire! spout, rain!
Nor rain, wind, thunder, fire, are my daughters:
I tax not you, you elements, with unkindness,
I never gave you kingdom, call'd you children,
You owe me no subscription‡; why then let fall
Your horrible pleasure; here I stand, your slave,
A poor, infirm, weak, and despis'd old man:—
But yet I call you servile ministers,
That have with two pernicious daughters join'd
Your high engender'd battles, 'gainst a head
So old and white as this. O! O! 'tis foul!

* * * * *

Kent. Alas, sir, are you here? things that love night,
Love not such nights as these; the wrathful skies
Gallow§ the very wanderers of the dark,
And make them keep their caves: Since I was man,
Such sheets of fire, such bursts of horrid thunder,
Such groans of roaring wind and rain, I never
Remember to have heard: man's nature cannot carry
The affliction, nor the fear.

* Quick as thought.
† *Avant couriers*, French
‡ Obedience.
§ Scare or frighten.

Lear. Let the great gods,
That keep this dreadful pother * o'er our heads,
Find out their enemies now. Tremble, thou wretch,
That hast within thee undivulged crimes,
Unwhipp'd of justice: Hide thee, thou bloody hand;
Thou perjur'd, and thou simular † man of virtue
That art incestuous: Caitiff, to pieces shake,
That under covert and convenient seeming ‡
Hast practis'd on man's life!—Close pent-up guilts,
Rive your concealing continents, and cry
These dreadful summoners grace §.—I am a man,
More sinn'd against, than sinning.

Kent. Alack, bareheaded!
Gracious my lord, hard by here is a hovel;
Some friendship will it lend you 'gainst the tempest.

* * * * *

Lear. Thou think'st 'tis much, that this contentious storm
Invades us to the skin: so 'tis to thee;
But where the greater malady is fix'd,
The lesser is scarce felt. Thou'dst shun a bear:
But if thy flight lay toward the raging sea,
Thou'dst meet the bear i' the mouth. When the mind's free,
The body's delicate: the tempest in my mind
Doth from my senses take all feeling else,
Save what beats there.—Filial ingratitude!
Is it not as this mouth should tear this hand,
For lifting food to't?—But I will punish home:—
No, I will weep no more.—In such a night
To shut me out!—Pour on; I will endure:—
In such a night as this! O Regan, Goneril!—
Your old kind father, whose frank heart gave all,—
O, that way madness lies; let me shun that;
No more of that,—

Kent. Good my lord, enter here.

Lear. Pr'ythee, go in thyself; seek thine own ease;

* Blustering noise. † Counterfeit.
‡ Appearance. § Favour.

This tempest will not give me leave to ponder
On things would hurt me more. But I'll go in:
In, boy; go first.—[*To the* Fool.] You houseless poverty,—
Nay, get thee in.—I'll pray, and then I'll sleep,—
[Fool *goes in.*
Poor naked wretches, wheresoe'er you are,
That bide the pelting of this pitiless storm,
How shall your houseless heads, and unfed sides,
Your loop'd and window'd raggedness, defend you
From seasons such as these? O, I have ta'en
Too little care of this! Take physic, pomp;
Expose thyself to feel what wretches feel;
That thou mayst shake the superflux to them,
And show the heavens more just.

* * * * *

Enter EDGAR, *disguised as a Madman.*

Edg. Away! the foul fiend follows me!—
Through the sharp hawthorn blows the cold wind.—
Humph! go to thy cold bed, and warm thee.
Lear. Hast thou given all to thy two daughters?
And art thou come to this?

* * * * *

Didst thou give them all?

* * * * *

Now, all the plagues that in the pendulous air
Hang fated o'er men's faults, light on thy daughters!
Kent. He hath no daughters, sir.
Lear. Death, traitor! nothing could have subdu'd nature
To such a lowness, but his unkind daughters.—
Is it the fashion, that discarded fathers
Should have thus little mercy on their flesh?
Judicious punishment! 'twas this flesh begot
Those pelican daughters.

ON MAN.

Is man no more than this? Consider him well: Thou owest the worm no silk, the beast no hide, the sheep no wool, the cat no perfume:—Ha! here's three of us are sophisticated!—Thou art the thing itself: unaccommodated man is no more but such a poor, bare, forked animal as thou art.—Off, off, you lendings.

ACT IV.

THE JUSTICE OF PROVIDENCE.

That I am wretched,
Makes thee the happier:—Heavens, deal so still!
Let the superfluous, and lust-dieted man,
That slaves your ordinance*, that will not see
Because he doth not feel, feel your power quickly;
So distribution should undo excess,
And each man have enough.

PATIENCE AND SORROW.

Patience and sorrow strove
Who should express her goodliest. You have seen
Sunshine and rain at once: her smiles and tears
Were like a better day: Those happy smiles
That play'd on her ripe lip, seem'd not to know
What guests were in her eyes; which parted thence,
As pearls from diamonds dropp'd.—In brief, sorrow
Would be a rarity most belov'd, if all
Could so become it.

LEAR'S DISTRACTION DESCRIBED.

Alack, 'tis he; why, he was met even now
As mad as the vex'd sea: singing aloud;
Crown'd with rank fumiter†, and furrow weeds,
With harlocks‡, hemlock, nettles, cuckoo-flowers,
Darnel, and all the idle weeds that grow
In our sustaining corn.

* *i. e.* To make it subject to us, instead of acting in obedience to it. † Fumitory. ‡ Charlocks.

DESCRIPTION OF DOVER CLIFF.

Come on, sir; here's the place;—stand still.—How
fearful
And dizzy 'tis, to cast one's eyes so low!
The crows, and choughs *, that wing the midway air,
Show scarce so gross as beetles: Half way down
Hangs one that gathers samphire †; dreadful trade!
Methinks he seems no bigger than his head:
The fishermen, that walk upon the beach,
Appear like mice; and yon' tall anchoring bark,
Diminish'd to her cock ‡; her cock, a buoy
Almost too small for sight: The murmuring surge,
That on the unnumber'd idle pebbles chafes,
Cannot be heard so high:—I'll look no more;
Lest my brain turn, and the deficient sight
Topple § down headlong.

GLOSTER'S FAREWELL TO THE WORLD.

O you mighty gods!
This world I do renounce; and, in your sights,
Shake patiently my great affliction off:
If I could bear it longer, and not fall
To quarrel with your great opposeless wills,
My snuff, and loathed part of nature, should
Burn itself out. If Edgar live, O, bless him!

LEAR ON HIS FLATTERERS.

They flatter'd me like a dog; and told me, I had white hairs in my beard, ere the black ones were there. To say *ay*, and *no*, to every thing I said!—Ay and no too was no good divinity. When the rain came to wet me once, and the wind to make me chatter; when the thunder would not peace at my bidding; there I found them, there I smelt them out. Go to, they are not men o' their words: they told me I was every thing; 'tis a lie; I am not ague-proof.

* Daws. † A vegetable gathered for pickling.
‡ Her cock-boat. § Tumble.

ON THE ABUSE OF POWER.

Thou rascal beadle, hold thy bloody hand:
Why dost thou lash that whore? Strip thine own back;
Thou hotly lust'st to use her in that kind
For which thou whipp'st her. The usurer hangs the cozener.
Through tatter'd clothes small vices do appear;
Robes, and furr'd gowns, hide all. Plate sin with gold,
And the strong lance of justice hurtless breaks;
Arm it in rags, a pigmy's straw doth pierce it.
None does offend, none, I say, none; I'll able 'em:
Take that of me, my friend, who have the power
To seal the accuser's lips. Get thee glass eyes;
And, like a scurvy politician, seem
To see the things thou dost not.

CORDELIA ON THE INGRATITUDE OF HER SISTERS.

O my dear father; Restoration, hang
Thy medicine on my lips; and let this kiss
Repair those violent harms, that my two sisters
Have in thy reverence made!

* * * * *

Had you not been their father, these white flakes
Had challeng'd pity of them. Was this a face
To be expos'd against the warring winds?
To stand against the deep dread-bolted thunder?
In the most terrible and nimble stroke
Of quick, cross lightning?

* * * * *

And wast thou fain, poor father,
To hovel thee with swine, and rogues forlorn,
In short and musty straw? Alack, alack!
'Tis wonder, that thy life and wits at once
Had not concluded all.

SCENE BETWEEN LEAR AND CORDELIA.

Cor. How does my royal lord? How fares your majesty?

Lear. You do me wrong, to take me out o' the grave:

Thou art a soul in bliss; but I am bound
Upon a wheel of fire, that mine own tears
Do scald like molten lead.

Cor. Sir, do you know me?

Lear. You are a spirit, I know: When did you die?

Cor. Still, still, far wide!

Phys. He's scarce awake; let him alone awhile.

Lear. Where have I been?—Where am I?—Fair day-light?—
I am mightily abus'd.—I should even die with pity,
To see another thus.—I know not what to say.—
I will not swear, these are my hands: let's see;
I feel this pin prick. 'Would I were assur'd
Of my condition.

Cor. O, look upon me, sir,
And hold your hands in benediction o'er me:—
No, sir, you must not kneel.

Lear. Pray, do not mock me:
I am a very foolish fond old man,
Fourscore and upward; and, to deal plainly,
I fear, I am not in my perfect mind.
Methinks I should know you, and know this man:
Yet I am doubtful: for I am mainly ignorant
What place this is; and all the skill I have
Remembers not these garments; nor I know not
Where I did lodge last night: Do not laugh at me;
For, as I am a man, I think this lady
To be my child Cordelia.

Cor. And so I am, I am.

Lear. Be your tears wet? Yes, 'faith. I pray, weep not:
If you have poison for me, I will drink it.
I know, you do not love me; for your sisters
Have, as I do remember, done me wrong:
You have some cause, they have not.

Cor. No cause, no cause.

Lear. Am I in France?

Kent. In your own kingdom, sir.

Lear. Do not abuse me.

Phys. Be comforted, good madam: the great rage,

You see, is cur'd in him: and yet it is danger
To make him even * o'er the time he has lost.
Desire him to go in; trouble him no more,
Till further settling.

Cor. Will't please your highness walk?

Lear. You must bear with me:
Pray now, forget and forgive: I am old, and foolish.

ACT V.

LEAR TO CORDELIA WHEN TAKEN PRISONERS.

No, no, no, no! Come, let's away to prison:
We two alone will sing like birds i' the cage:
When thou dost ask me blessing, I'll kneel down,
And ask of thee forgiveness: So we'll live,
And pray, and sing, and tell old tales, and laugh
At gilded butterflies, and hear poor rogues
Talk of court news; and we'll talk with them too,—
Who loses, and who wins; who's in, who's out;—
And take upon us the mystery of things,
As if we were God's spies: And we'll wear out,
In a wall'd prison, packs and sects of great ones,
That ebb and flow by the moon.

Edm. Take them away.

Lear. Upon such sacrifices, my Cordelia,
The gods themselves throw incense.

THE JUSTICE OF THE GODS.

The gods are just, and of our pleasant vices
Make instruments to scourge us.

EDGAR'S ACCOUNT OF HIS DISCOVERING HIMSELF TO HIS FATHER.

List † a brief tale;—
And, when 'tis told, O, that my heart would burst!—
The bloody proclamation to escape,

* To reconcile it to his apprehension. † Hear.

That follow'd me so near, (O our lives' sweetness!
That with the pain of death we'd hourly die,
Rather than die at once!) taught me to shift
Into a madman's rags; to assume a semblance
That very dogs disdain'd: and in this habit
Met I my father with his bleeding rings,
Their precious stones new lost; became his guide,
Led him, begg'd for him, sav'd him from despair;
Never (O fault!) reveal'd myself unto him,
Until some half hour past, when I was arm'd,
Not sure, though hoping, of this good success,
I ask'd his blessing, and from first to last
Told him my pilgrimage: But his flaw'd heart,
(Alack, too weak the conflict to support!)
'Twixt two extremes of passion, joy and grief,
Burst smilingly.
Edm. This speech of yours hath mov'd me,
And, shall, perchance, do good; but speak you on;
You look as you had something more to say.
Alb. If there be more, more woful, hold it in;
For I am almost ready to dissolve,
Hearing of this.
Edg. This would have seem'd a period
To such as love not sorrow; but another,
To amplify too much, would make much more,
And top extremity.
Whilst I was big in clamour, came there a man,
Who having seen me in my worst estate,
Shunn'd my abhorr'd society; but then, finding
Who 'twas that so endur'd, with his strong arms
He fasten'd on my neck, and bellow'd out
As he'd burst heaven; threw him on my father;
Told the most piteous tale of Lear and him,
That ever ear receiv'd: which in recounting
His grief grew puissant, and the strings of life
Began to crack: Twice then the trumpet sounded,
And there I left him tranc'd.

LEAR ON THE DEATH OF CORDELIA.

Howl, howl, howl, howl;—O, you are men of stones;
Had I your tongues and eyes, I'd use them so

That heaven's vault should crack:—O, she is gone for ever!—
I know when one is dead; and when one lives;
She's dead as earth:—Lend me a looking-glass;
If that her breath will mist or stain the stone,
Why, then she lives.

* * * * *

This feather stirs; she lives! if it be so,
It is a chance that does redeem all sorrows
That ever I have felt.

Kent. O my good master! [*Kneeling.*
Lear. Pr'ythee, away.

* * * * *

A plague upon you, murderers, traitors all!
I might have sav'd her; now she's gone for ever!—
Cordelia, Cordelia, stay a little. Ha!
What is't thou say'st?—Her voice was ever soft,
Gentle, and low.

LEAR DYING.

And my poor fool* is hang'd! No, no, no life:
Why should a dog, a horse, a rat, have life,
And thou no breath at all? O, thou wilt come no more,
Never, never, never, never, never!

MACBETH.

ACT I.

WITCHES DESCRIBED.

WHAT are these,
So wither'd, and so wild in their attire;
That look not like the inhabitants o' the earth,
And yet are on't? Live you? or are you aught

* *Poor fool*, in the time of Shakspeare, was an expression of endearment.

That man may question? You seem to understand me,
By each at once her choppy finger laying
Upon her skinny lips:—You should be women,
And yet your beards forbid me to interpret
That you are so.

MACBETH'S TEMPER.

Yet do I fear thy nature;
It is too full o' the milk of human kindness,
To catch the nearest way: Thou wouldst be great;
Art not without ambition; but without
The illness should attend it. What thou wouldst highly,
That wouldst thou holily; wouldst not play false,
And yet wouldst wrongly win.

LADY MACBETH'S SOLILOQUY ON THE NEWS OF DUNCAN'S APPROACH.

The raven himself is hoarse,
That croaks the fatal entrance of Duncan
Under my battlements. Come, come, you spirits
That tend on mortal * thoughts, unsex me here;
And fill me, from the crown to the toe, top-full
Of direst cruelty! make thick my blood,
Stop up the access and passage to remorse †;
That no compunctious visitings of nature
Shake my fell purpose, nor keep peace between
The effect and it! Come to my woman's breasts,
And take my milk for gall, you murd'ring ministers,
Wherever in your sightless substances
You wait on nature's mischief! Come, thick night,
And pall ‡ thee in the dunnest smoke of hell!
That my keen knife § see not the wound it makes;
Nor heaven peep through the blanket of the dark,
To cry, *Hold, Hold!*

MACBETH'S IRRESOLUTION.

If it were done, when 'tis done, then 'twere well
It were done quickly: If the assassination

* Murderous. † Pity. ‡ Wrap, as in a mantle.
§ Knife anciently meant a sword or dagger.

Could trammel upon the consequence, and catch,
With his surcease, success; that but this blow
Might be the be-all and the end-all here,
But here, upon this bank and shoal of time,—
We'd jump the life to come.—But, in these cases,
We still have judgment here; that we but teach
Bloody instructions, which, being taught, return
To plague the inventor: This even-handed justice
Commends the ingredients of our poison'd chalice
To our own lips. He's here in double trust:
First, as I am his kinsman and his subject,
Strong both against the deed; then, as his host,
Who should against his murderer shut the door,
Not bear the knife myself. Besides, this Duncan
Hath borne his faculties so meek, hath been
So clear in his great office, that his virtues
Will plead like angels, trumpet-tongued, against
The deep damnation of his taking-off:
And pity, like a naked new-born babe,
Striding the blast, or heaven's cherubin, hors'd
Upon the sightless couriers* of the air,
Shall blow the horrid deed in every eye,
That tears shall drown the wind.—I have no spur
To prick the sides of my intent, but only
Vaulting ambition, which o'erleaps itself,
And falls on the other.

TRUE FORTITUDE.

I dare do all that may become a man;
Who dares do more, is none.

ACT II.

THE MURDERING SCENE.

Is this a dagger, which I see before me,
The handle toward my hand? Come, let me clutch
thee:———

* Winds; sightless is invisible.

I have thee not, and yet I see thee still.
Art thou not, fatal vision, sensible
To feeling, as to sight? or art thou but
A dagger of the mind; a false creation,
Proceeding from the heat-oppressed brain?
I see thee yet, in form as palpable,
As this which now I draw.
Thou marshal'st me the way that I was going;
And such an instrument I was to use.
Mine eyes are made the fools o' the other senses,
Or else worth all the rest: I see thee still;
And on thy blade, and dudgeon*, gouts † of blood,
Which was not so before.—There's no such thing:
It is the bloody business, which informs
Thus to mine eyes.—Now o'er the one half world
Nature seems dead, and wicked dreams abuse
The curtain'd sleep; now witchcraft celebrates
Pale Hecate's offerings; and wither'd murder
Alarum'd by his sentinel, the wolf,
Whose howl's his watch, thus with his stealthy pace,
With Tarquin's ravishing strides, towards his design
Moves like a ghost.——Thou sure and firm-set earth,
Hear not my steps, which way they walk, for fear
Thy very stones prate of my where-about,
And take the present horror from the time,
Which now suits with it.—Whiles I threat, he lives;
Words to the heat of deeds too cold breath gives.
[*A Bell rings.*
I go, and it is done; the bell invites me.
Hear it not, Duncan; for it is a knell,
That summons thee to heaven, or to hell. [*Exit.*

Enter Lady MACBETH.

Lady M. That which hath made them drunk, hath made me bold:
What hath quench'd them, hath given me fire:—Hark! —Peace!
It was the owl that shriek'd, the fatal bellman,
Which gives the stern'st good night. He is about it:

* Haft. † Drops.

The doors are open; and the surfeited grooms
Do mock their charge with snores: I have drugg'd their possets,
That death and nature do contend about them,
Whether they live or die.

Macb. [*Within*] Who's there?—what, ho!

Lady M. Alack! I am afraid they have awak'd,
And 'tis not done:—The attempt, and not the deed,
Confounds us: Hark!—I laid their daggers ready,
He could not miss them.—Had he not resembled
My father as he slept, I had done't.—My husband!

Enter MACBETH.

Macb. I have done the deed:—Didst thou not hear a noise?

Lady M. I heard the owl scream, and the crickets cry.
Did not you speak?

Macb. When?

Lady M. Now.

Macb. As I descended?

Lady M. Ay.

Macb. Hark!—
Who lies i'the second chamber?

Lady M. Donalbain.

Macb. This is a sorry sight. [*Looking on his Hands.*

Lady M. A foolish thought, to say a sorry sight.

Macb. There's one did laugh in his sleep, and one cried, *murder!*
That they did wake each other; I stood and heard them:
But they did say their prayers, and address'd them
Again to sleep.

Lady M. There are two lodg'd together.

Macb. One cried, *God bless us!* and, *Amen*, the other;
As* they had seen me, with these hangman's hands.

* As if.

Listening their fear, I could not say, amen,
When they did say, God bless us.

Lady M. Consider it not so deeply.

Macb. But wherefore could not I pronounce, amen?
I had most need of blessing, and amen
Stuck in my throat.

Lady M. These deeds must not be thought
After these ways; so, it will make us mad.

Macb. Methought, I heard a voice cry, *Sleep no more!*
Macbeth does murder sleep, the innocent sleep;
Sleep, that knits up the ravell'd sleave * *of care,*
The death of each day's life, sore labour's bath,
Balm of hurt minds, great nature's second course,
Chief nourisher in life's feast;—

Lady M. What do you mean?

Macb. Still it cried, *Sleep no more!* to all the house:
Glamis hath murdered sleep; and therefore Cawdor
Shall sleep no more, Macbeth shall sleep no more!

Lady M. Who was it that thus cried? Why, worthy thane,
You do unbend your noble strength, to think
So brainsickly of things: Go, get some water,
And wash this filthy witness from your hand.—
Why did you bring these daggers from the place?
They must lie there: Go, carry them; and smear
The sleepy grooms with blood.

Macb. I'll go no more:
I am afraid to think what I have done;
Look on't again, I dare not.

Lady M. Infirm of purpose!
Give me the daggers: The sleeping, and the dead,
Are but as pictures: 'tis the eye of childhood,
That fears a painted devil. If he do bleed,
I'll gild the faces of the grooms withal,
For it must seem their guilt.

[*Exit. Knocking within.*

* Sleave, is unwrought silk.

Macb. Whence is that knocking?
How is't with me, when every noise appals me?
What hands are here? Ha! they pluck out mine eyes!
Will all great Neptune's ocean wash this blood
Clean from my hand? No; this my hand will rather
The multitudinous seas incarnardine *,
Making the green one red.

Re-enter Lady MACBETH.

Lady M. My hands are of your colour; but I shame
To wear a heart so white. [*Knock.*] I hear a knocking
At the south entry:—retire we to our chamber:
A little water clears us of this deed:
How easy is it then! Your constancy
Hath left you unattended.—[*Knocking.*] Hark! more knocking:
Get on your night-gown, lest occasion call us,
And show us to be watchers:—Be not lost
So poorly in your thoughts.
Macb. To know my deed,—'twere best not know myself. [*Knock.*
Wake Duncan with thy knocking! Ay, 'would thou couldst! [*Exeunt.*

ACT III.

MACBETH'S GUILTY CONSCIENCE, AND FEARS OF BANQUO.

Lady M. How now, my lord; why do you keep alone,
Of sorriest † fancies your companions making?
Using those thoughts, which should indeed have died
With them they think on? Things without remedy,
Should be without regard: what's done, is done.

* To incarnardine is to stain of a flesh colour.
† Most melancholy.

Macb. We have scotch'd the snake, not kill'd it;
She'll close, and be herself; whilst our poor malice
Remains in danger of her former tooth.
But let
The frame of things disjoint, both the worlds suffer,
Ere we will eat our meal in fear, and sleep
In the affliction of these terrible dreams,
That shake us nightly: Better be with the dead,
Whom we, to gain our place, have sent to peace,
Than on the torture of the mind to lie
In restless ecstasy*. Duncan is in his grave;
After life's fitful fever, he sleeps well;
Treason has done his worst: nor steel, nor poison,
Malice domestic, foreign levy, nothing
Can touch him further.

* * * * *

O, full of scorpions is my mind, dear wife!
Thou know'st that Banquo, and his Fleance, lives.
Lady M. But in them nature's copy's not eterne†.
Macb. There's comfort yet; they are assailable;
Then be thou jocund: Ere the bat hath flown
His cloister'd flight; ere, to black Hecate's summons,
The shard-borne beetle‡, with his drowsy hums,
Hath rung night's yawning peal, there shall be done
A deed of dreadful note.
Lady M. What's to be done?
Macb. Be innocent of the knowledge, dearest chuck§,
Till thou applaud the deed. Come, seeling‖ night,
Skarf up the tender eye of pitiful day;
And, with thy bloody and invisible hand,
Cancel, and tear to pieces, that great bond
Which keeps me pale!—Light thickens; and the crow
Makes wing to the rooky wood:
Good things of day begin to droop and drowse;
Whiles night's black agents to their prey do rouse.

* Agony.

† *i. e.* The copy, the lease, by which they hold their lives from nature, has its time of termination.

‡ The beetle borne in the air by its shards or scaly wings.

§ A term of endearment. ‖ Blinding.

THE BANQUET SCENE.

Lady M. My royal lord,
You do not give the cheer: the feast is sold,
That is not often vouch'd, while 'tis a making,
'Tis given with welcome: To feed, were best at home;
From thence, the sauce to meat is ceremony;
Meeting were bare without it.

Macb. Sweet remembrancer!—
Now, good digestion wait on appetite,
And health on both!

Len. May it please your highness sit?

[*The Ghost of* BANQUO *rises, and sits in* MACBETH's *place.*

Macb. Here had we now our country's honour roof'd,
Were the grac'd person of our Banquo present;
Whom I may rather challenge for unkindness,
Than pity for mischance!

Rosse. His absence, sir,
Lays blame upon his promise. Please it your highness
To grace us with your royal company?

Macb. The table's full.

Len. Here's a place reserv'd, sir.

Macb. Where?

Len. Here, my lord. What is't that moves your highness?

Macb. Which of you have done this?

Lords. What, my good lord!

Macb. Thou canst not say, I did it: never shake
Thy gory locks at me.

Rosse. Gentlemen, rise; his highness is not well.

Lady M. Sit, worthy friends:—my lord is often thus,
And hath been from his youth: 'pray you, keep seat;
The fit is momentary; upon a thought*
He will again be well: If much you note him,

* As quick as thought.

You shall offend him, and extend his passion *;
Feed, and regard him not.—Are you a man?
Macb. Ay, and a bold one, that dare look on that
Which might appal the devil.
Lady M. O proper stuff:
This is the very painting of your fear:
This is the air-drawn dagger, which, you said,
Led you to Duncan. O, these flaws †, and starts,
(Impostors to true fear) would well become
A woman's story, at a winter's fire,
Authoriz'd by her grandam. Shame itself!
Why do you make such faces? When all's done,
You look but on a stool.
Macb. Pr'ythee, see there! behold! look! lo! how say you?——
Why, what care I? If thou canst nod, speak too.—
If charnel-houses, and our graves, must send
Those that we bury back, our monuments
Shall be the maws of kites. [*Ghost disappears.*
Lady M. What! quite unmann'd in folly?
Macb. If I stand here, I saw him.
Lady M. Fie, for shame!
Macb. Blood hath been shed ere now, i' the olden time,
Ere human statute purg'd the gentle weal;
Ay, and since too, murders have been perform'd
Too terrible for the ear: the times have been,
That when the brains were out, the man would die,
And there an end: but now, they rise again,
With twenty mortal murders on their crowns,
And push us from our stools: This is more strange
Than such a murder is.
Lady M. My worthy lord,
Your noble friends do lack you.
Macb. I do forget:—
Do not muse ‡ at me, my most worthy friends;
I have a strange infirmity, which is nothing
To those that know me. Come, love and health to all;

* Prolong his suffering. † Sudden gusts. ‡ Wonder.

Then I'll sit down:——Give me some wine, fill full:—
I drink to the general joy of the whole table,

Ghost rises.

And to our dear friend Banquo, whom we miss;
Would he were here! to all, and him, we thirst,
And all to all*.

Lords. Our duties, and the pledge.

Macb. Avaunt! and quit my sight! Let the earth hide thee!
Thy bones are marrowless, thy blood is cold;
Thou hast no speculation in those eyes
Which thou dost glare with!

Lady M. Think of this, good peers,
But as a thing of custom: 'tis no other;
Only it spoils the pleasure of the time.

Macb. What man dare, I dare:
Approach thou like the rugged Russian bear,
The arm'd rhinoceros, or the Hyrcan tiger,
Take any shape but that, and my firm nerves
Shall never tremble: Or, be alive again,
And dare me to the desert with thy sword;
If trembling I inhibit† thee, protest me
The baby of a girl. Hence, horrible shadow!

[*Ghost disappears.*

Unreal mockery, hence!—Why, so; being gone,
I am a man again.—Pray you, sit still.

Lady M. You have displac'd the mirth, broke the good meeting,
With most admir'd disorder.

Macb. Can such things be,
And overcome‡ us like a summer's cloud,
Without our special wonder? You make me strange
Even to the disposition that I owe§,
When now I think you can behold such sights,
And keep the natural ruby of your cheeks,
When mine are blanch'd with fear.

* *i. e.* All good wishes to all. † Forbid.
‡ Pass over. § Possess.

Rosse. What sights, my lord?

Lady M. I pray you, speak not; he grows worse and worse;
Question enrages him: at once, good night:—
Stand not upon the order of your going,
But go at once.

Len. Good night, and better health
Attend his majesty!

Lady M. A kind good night to all!
[*Exeunt* Lords *and* Attendants.

Macb. It will have blood; they say, blood will have blood:
Stones have been known to move, and trees to speak;
Augurs, and understood relations, have
By magot-pies*, and choughs, and rooks, brought forth
The secret'st man of blood.

ACT IV.

THE POWER OF WITCHES.

I conjure you, by that which you profess,
(Howe'er you come to know it) answer me:
Though you untie the winds, and let them fight
Against the churches; though the yesty † waves
Confound and swallow navigation up;
Though bladed corn be lodg'd ‡, and trees blown down;
Though castles topple § on their warder's heads;
Though palaces, and pyramids, do slope
Their heads to their foundations; though the treasure
Of nature's germins || tumble all together,
Even till destruction sicken, answer me
To what I ask you.

* Magpies. † Frothy. ‡ Laid flat by wind or rain.
§ Tumble. || Seeds which have begun to sprout.

MALCOLM'S CHARACTER OF HIMSELF.

Mal. But I have none: The king-becoming graces,
As justice, verity, temperance, stableness,
Bounty, perseverance, mercy, lowliness,
Devotion, patience, courage, fortitude,
I have no relish of them; but abound
In the division of each several crime,
Acting it many ways. Nay, had I power, I should
Pour the sweet milk of concord into hell,
Uproar the universal peace, confound
All unity on earth.
Macd. O Scotland! Scotland!
Mal. If such a one be fit to govern, speak:
I am as I have spoken.
Macd. Fit to govern!
No, not to live.—O nation miserable,
With an untitled tyrant, bloody-sceptred,
When shalt thou see thy wholesome days again?
Since that the truest issue of thy throne
By his own interdiction stands accurs'd,
And does blaspheme his breed?—Thy royal father
Was a most sainted king; the queen, that bore thee,
Oftener upon her knees than on her feet,
Died every day she liv'd. Fare thee well!
These evils, thou repeat'st upon thyself,
Have banish'd me from Scotland.—O, my breast,
Thy hope ends here!
Mal. Macduff, this noble passion,
Child of integrity, hath from my soul
Wip'd the black scruples, reconcil'd my thoughts
To thy good truth and honour. Devilish Macbeth
By many of these trains hath sought to win me
Into his power; and modest wisdom plucks me
From overcredulous haste*: But God above
Deal between thee and me! for even now
I put myself to thy direction, and
Unspeak mine own detraction: here abjure
The taints and blames I laid upon myself,

* Overhasty credulity.

For strangers to my nature. I am yet
Unknown to woman; never was forsworn;
Scarcely have coveted what was mine own:
At no time broke my faith; would not betray
The devil to his fellow; and delight
No less in truth, than life: my first false speaking
Was this upon myself: What I am truly,
Is thine, and my poor country's, to command.

AN OPPRESSED COUNTRY.

Alas, poor country;
Almost afraid to know itself! It cannot
Be call'd our mother, but our grave; where nothing,
But who knows nothing, is once seen to smile;
Where sighs, and groans, and shrieks that rent the air,
Are made, not mark'd: where violent sorrow seems
A modern ecstasy*: the dead man's knell
Is there scarce ask'd, for who; and good men's lives
Expire before the flowers in their caps,
Dying, or ere they sicken.

MACDUFF'S BEHAVIOUR ON THE MURDER OF HIS WIFE AND CHILDREN.

Rosse. 'Would I could answer
This comfort with the like! But I have words
That would be howl'd out in the desert air,
Where hearing should not latch† them.
Macd. What concern they?
The general cause? or is it a fee-grief‡,
Due to some single breast?
Rosse. No mind, that's honest,
But in it shares some woe; though the main part
Pertains to you alone.
Macd. If it be mine,
Keep it not from me, quickly let me have it.
Rosse. Let not your ears despise my tongue for ever,

* Common distress of mind. † Catch.
‡ A grief that has a single owner.

Which shall possess them with the heaviest sound,
That ever yet they heard.

Macd. Humph! I guess at it.

Rosse. Your castle is surpris'd; your wife and babes,
Savagely slaughter'd: to relate the manner,
Were, on the quarry * of these murder'd deer,
To add the death of you.

Mal. Merciful heaven!—
What, man? ne'er pull your hat upon your brows;
Give sorrow words: the grief, that does not speak,
Whispers the o'er-fraught heart, and bids it break.

Macd. My children too?

Rosse. Wife, children, servants, all
That could be found.

Macd. And I must be from thence!
My wife kill'd too?

Rosse. I have said.

Mal. Be comforted:
Let's make us med'cines of our great revenge,
To cure this deadly grief.

Macd. He has no children.—All my pretty ones?
Did you say, all?—O, hell-kite!—All?
What, all my pretty chickens, and their dam,
At one fell swoop?

Mal. Dispute it like a man.

Macd. I shall do so;
But I must also feel it as a man:
I cannot but remember such things were,
That were most precious to me.—Did heaven look on,
And would not take their part? Sinful Macduff,
They were all struck for thee! naught that I am,
Not for their own demerits, but for mine,
Fell slaughter on their souls: Heaven rest them now!

Mal. Be this the whetstone of your sword: let grief
Convert to anger; blunt not the heart, enrage it.

Macd. O, I could play the woman with mine eyes,
And braggart with my tongue!——But, gentle heaven,

* The game after it is killed.

Cut short all intermission*; front to front,
Bring thou this fiend of Scotland, and myself;
Within my sword's length set him; if he scape,
Heaven forgive him too!

Mal. This tune goes manly.
Come, go we to the king; our power is ready;
Our lack is nothing but our leave: Macbeth
Is ripe for shaking, and the powers above
Put on their instruments. Receive what cheer you may;
The night is long that never finds the day.

ACT V.

SCENE. *Enter Lady* MACBETH, *with a Taper.*

Gent. Lo you, here she comes! This is her very guise; and, upon my life, fast asleep. Observe her; stand close.

Doct. How came she by that light?

Gent. Why, it stood by her: she has light by her continually; 'tis her command.

Doct. You see her eyes are open.

Gent. Ay, but their sense is shut.

Doct. What is it she does now? Look, how she rubs her hands.

Gent. It is an accustomed action with her, to seem thus washing her hands; I have known her continue in this a quarter of an hour.

Lady M. Yet here's a spot.

Doct. Hark, she speaks: I will set down what comes from her, to satisfy my remembrance the more strongly.

Lady M. Out, damned spot! out, I say!—One; Two; Why, then 'tis time to do't:——Hell is musky†!—Fie, my lord, fie! a soldier, and afear'd? What need we fear who knows it, when none can call our

* All pause. † Dark.

power to account?—Yet who would have thought the old man to have had so much blood in him?

Doct. Do you mark that?

Lady M. The thane of Fife had a wife; Where is she now?——What, will these hands ne'er be clean?—No more o' that, my lord, no more o' that: you mar all with this starting.

Doct. Go to, go to; you have known what you should not.

Gent. She has spoke what she should not, I am sure of that: Heaven knows what she has known.

Lady M. Here's the smell of the blood still: all the perfumes of Arabia will not sweeten this little hand. Oh! oh! oh!

Doct. What a sigh is there! The heart is sorely charged.

Gent. I would not have such a heart in my bosom, for the dignity of the whole body.

Doct. Well, well, well,—

Gent. 'Pray God, it be, sir.

Doct. This disease is beyond my practice: Yet I have known those which have walked in their sleep, who have died holily in their beds.

Lady M. Wash your hands, put on your night-gown; look not so pale:—I tell you yet again, Banquo's buried; he cannot come out of his grave.

Doct. Even so?

Lady M. To bed, to bed; there's knocking at the gate. Come, come, come, come, give me your hand; What's done, cannot be undone: To bed, to bed, to bed.

DESPISED OLD AGE.

I have liv'd long enough: my way of life
Is fall'n into the sear *, the yellow leaf:
And that which should accompany old age,
As honour, love, obedience, troops of friends,
I must not look to have; but, in their stead,

* Dry.

Curses, not loud, but deep, mouth-honour, breath,
Which the poor heart would fain deny, but dare not.

DISEASES OF THE MIND INCURABLE.

Canst thou not minister to a mind diseas'd;
Pluck from the memory a rooted sorrow;
Raze out the written troubles of the brain;
And, with some sweet oblivious antidote,
Cleanse the stuff'd bosom of that perilous stuff,
Which weighs upon the heart?

REFLECTIONS ON LIFE.

To-morrow, and to-morrow, and to-morrow,
Creeps in this petty pace from day to day,
To the last syllable of recorded time;
And all our yesterdays have lighted fools
The way to dusty death. Out, out, brief candle;
Life's but a walking shadow; a poor player,
That struts and frets his hour upon the stage,
And then is heard no more: it is a tale
Told by an idiot, full of sound and fury,
Signifying nothing.——

OTHELLO.

ACT I.

PREFERMENT.

'Tis the curse of service;
Preferment goes by letter, and affection,
Not by the old gradation, where each second
Stood heir to the first.

IAGO'S DISPRAISE OF HONESTY.

We cannot all be masters, nor all masters
Cannot be truly follow'd. You shall mark

Many a duteous and knee-crooking knave,
That, doting on his own obsequious bondage,
Wears out his time, much like his master's ass,
For nought but provender: and, when he's old, cashier'd:
Whip me such honest knaves: Others there are,
Who, trimm'd in forms and visages of duty,
Keep yet their hearts attending on themselves;
And, throwing but shows of service on their lords,
Do well thrive by them, and, when they have lin'd their coats,
Do themselves homage: these fellows have some soul;
And such a one do I profess myself.
For, sir,
It is as sure as you are Roderigo,
Were I the Moor, I would not be Iago:
In following him, I follow but myself;
Heaven is my judge, not I for love and duty,
But seeming so, for my peculiar end:
For when my outward action doth demonstrate
The native act and figure of my heart
In compliment extern*, 'tis not long after
But I will wear my heart upon my sleeve
For daws to peck at: I am not what I am.

LOVE, OTHELLO'S SOLE MOTIVE FOR MARRYING.

For know, Iago,
But that I love the gentle Desdemona,
I would not my unhoused † free condition
Put into circumscription and confine
For the sea's worth.

OTHELLO'S DESCRIPTION TO THE SENATE OF HIS WINNING THE AFFECTIONS OF DESDEMONA.

Most potent, grave, and reverend signiors,
My very noble and approv'd good masters,
That I have ta'en away this old man's daughter,
It is most true; true, I have married her;

* Outward show of civility. † Unsettled.

The very head and front of my offending
Hath this extent, no more. Rude am I in my speech,
And little bless'd with the set phrase of peace;
For since these arms of mine had seven years' pith,
Till now some nine moons wasted, they have us'd
Their dearest action * in the tented field;
And little of this great world can I speak,
More than pertains to feats of broil and battle;
And therefore little shall I grace my cause,
In speaking for myself: Yet, by your gracious patience,
I will a round unvarnish'd tale deliver
Of my whole course of love; what drugs, what charms,
What conjurations, and what mighty magic,
(For such proceeding I am charg'd withal)
I won his daughter with.

* * * *

Her father lov'd me; oft invited me;
Still question'd me the story of my life,
From year to year; the battles, sieges, fortunes,
That I have pass'd.
I ran it through, even from my boyish days,
To the very moment that he made me tell it.
Wherein I spoke of most disastrous chances,
Of moving accidents, by flood, and field;
Of hair-breadth scapes i' the imminent deadly breach;
Of being taken by the insolent foe,
And sold to slavery; of my redemption thence,
And portence † in my travel's history:

* * * *

These things to hear,
Would Desdemona seriously incline;
But still the house affairs would draw her thence;
Which ever as she could with haste dispatch,
She'd come again, and with a greedy ear
Devour up my discourse: Which I observing,
Took once a pliant hour; and found good means
To draw from her a prayer of earnest heart,

* Best exertion. † My behaviour.

That I would all my pilgrimage dilate,
Whereof by parcels* she had something heard,
But not intentively†: I did consent;
And often did beguile her of her tears,
When I did speak of some distressful stroke,
That my youth suffer'd. My story being done,
She gave me for my pains a world of sighs:
She swore,—In faith, 'twas strange, 'twas passing strange;
'Twas pitiful, 'twas wondrous pitiful:
She wish'd, she had not heard it; yet she wish'd
That heaven had made her such a man: she thank'd me;
And bade me, if I had a friend that lov'd her,
I should but teach him how to tell my story,
And that would woo her. Upon this hint, I spake:
She lov'd me for the dangers I had pass'd;
And I lov'd her, that she did pity them.

ACT II.

PERFECT CONTENT.

O my soul's joy!
If after every tempest come such calms,
May the winds blow till they have waken'd death!
And let the labouring bark climb hills of seas,
Olympus-high; and duck again as low
As hell's from heaven! If it were now to die,
'Twere now to be most happy; for, I fear,
My soul hath her content so absolute,
That not another comfort like to this
Succeeds in unknown fate.

* Parts.

† Intention and attention were once synonymous.

ACT III.

A LOVER'S EXCLAMATION.

Farewell, my Desdemona: I will come to thee straight.

* * * * *

[*Exit* DESDEMONA.

Excellent wretch! Perdition catch my soul,
But I do love thee, and when I love thee not,
Chaos is come again.

OTHELLO'S FIRST SUSPICION.

Oth. What dost thou think?
Iago. Think, my lord?
Oth. Think, my lord!
By heaven, he echoes me,
As if there were some monster in his thought
Too hideous to be shown.—Thou dost mean something:
I heard thee say but now,—Thou lik'dst not that,
When Cassio left my wife; What didst not like?
And, when I told thee—he was of my counsel
In my whole course of wooing, thou criest, *Indeed?*
And didst contract and purse thy brow together,
As if thou then hadst shut up in thy brain
Some horrible conceit: If thou dost love me,
Show me thy thought.
Iago. My lord, you know I love you.
Oth. I think, thou dost;
And, for I know thou art full of love and honesty,
And weigh'st thy words before thou giv'st them breath,—
Therefore these stops of thine fright me the more:
For such things, in a false disloyal knave,
Are tricks of custom; but in a man that's just,
They are close denotements, working from the heart,
That passion cannot rule.

REPUTATION.

Good name in man or woman, dear my lord,
Is the immediate jewel of their souls;
Who steals my purse, steals trash; 'tis something, nothing;
'Twas mine, 'tis his, and has been slave to thousands;
But he, that filches from me my good name,
Robs me of that, which not enriches him,
And makes me poor indeed.

OTHELLO'S JEALOUSY GAINING GROUND.

This fellow's of exceeding honesty,
And knows all qualities with a learned spirit,
Of human dealings: If I do prove her haggard *,
Though that her jesses † were my dear heart-strings,
I'd whistle her off, and let down the wind,
To prey at fortune. Haply, for I am black;
And have not those soft parts of conversation
That chamberers ‡ have:—Or, for I am declin'd
Into the vale of years;—yet that's not much;—
She's gone; I am abus'd; and my relief
Must be—to loathe her. O curse of marriage,
That we can call these delicate creatures ours,
And not their appetites! I had rather be a toad,
And live upon the vapour of a dungeon,
Than keep a corner in the thing I love,
For other's uses.

DEFINITION OF JEALOUSY.

Trifles, light as air,
Are, to the jealous, confirmations strong
As proofs of holy writ.

THE TORTURES OF JEALOUSY.

Iago. Look, where he comes! [*Enter* OTHELLO.]
Not poppy, nor mandragora §,

* A species of hawk, also a term of reproach applied to a wanton.

† Straps of leather by which a hawk is held on the fist.

‡ Men of intrigue.

§ The mandrake has a soporific quality.

Nor all the drowsy syrups of the world,
Shall ever medicine thee to that sweet sleep
Which thou ow'dst* yesterday.

Oth. Ha! ha! false to me?
To me?

Iago. Why, how now, general? no more of that.

Oth. Avaunt! be gone! thou hast set me on the rack:—
I swear, 'tis better to be much abus'd,
Than but to know't a little.

Iago. How now, my lord?

Oth. What sense had I of her stolen hours of lust?
I saw it not, thought it not, it harm'd not me:
I slept the next night well, was free and merry;
I found not Cassio's kisses on her lips:
He that is robb'd, not wanting what is stolen,
Let him not know it, and he's not robb'd at all.

Iago. I am sorry to hear this.

Oth. I had been happy, if the general camp,
Pioneers† and all, had tasted her sweet body,
So I had nothing known: O now, for ever,
Farewell the tranquil mind! farewell content!
Farewell the plumed troop, and the big wars,
That make ambition virtue! O, farewell!
Farewell the neighing steed, and the shrill trump,
The spirit-stirring drum, the ear-piercing fife,
The royal banner; and all quality,
Pride, pomp, and circumstance of glorious war!
And, O you mortal engines, whose rude throats
The immortal Jove's dread clamours counterfeit,
Farewell! Othello's occupation's gone!

Iago. Is it possible!—My lord,——

Oth. Villain, be sure thou prove my love a whore;
Be sure of it; give me the ocular proof;
[*Taking him by the Throat.*
Or, by the worth of mine eternal soul,
Thou hadst been better have been born a dog,
Than answer my wak'd wrath.

* Possessedst.

† The vilest of the camp. Pioneers were generally degraded soldiers.

Iago. Is it come to this?
Oth. Make me to see it; or (at the least) so prove it,
That the probation bear no hinge, nor loop,
To hang a doubt on; or, woe upon thy life!
Iago. My noble lord——
Oth. If thou dost slander her, and torture me,
Never pray more: abandon all remorse*;
On horror's head horrors accumulate:
Do deeds to make heaven weep, all earth amaz'd,
For nothing canst thou to damnation add,
Greater than that.
Iago. O grace! O heaven defend me!
Are you a man? have you a soul, or sense?—
God be wi' you; take mine office.—O wretched fool,
That liv'st to make thine honesty a vice!
O monstrous world! Take note, take note, O world,
To be direct and honest, is not safe.—
I thank you for this profit, and, from hence,
I'll love no friend, since love breeds such offence.
Oth. Nay, stay:—Thou shouldst be honest.
Iago. I should be wise; for honesty's a fool,
And loses that it works for.
Oth. By the world,
I think my wife be honest, and think she is not;
I think that thou art just, and think thou art not;
I'll have some proof: Her name, that was as fresh
As Dian's visage, is now begrim'd and black
As mine own face.—If there be cords, or knives,
Poison, or fire, or suffocating streams,
I'll not endure it.—'Would, I were satisfied!

OTHELLO'S STORY OF THE HANDKERCHIEF.

Oth. That handkerchief
Did an Egyptian to my mother give;
She was a charmer†, and could almost read
The thoughts of people: she told her, while she kept it,
'Twould make her amiable, and subdue my father

* All tenderness, all pity. † Enchantress.

Entirely to her love; but if she lost it,
Or made a gift of it, my father's eye
Should hold her loathly, and his spirits should hunt
After new fancies: She, dying, gave it me;
And bid me, when my fate would have me wive,
To give it her. I did so: and take heed of't,
Make it a darling like your precious eye;
To lose or give 't away, were such perdition,
As nothing else could match.

Des. Is it possible?

Oth. 'Tis true: there's magic in the web of it:
A sibyl that had number'd in the world
The sun to make two hundred compasses,
In her prophetic fury sew'd the work:
The worms were hallow'd, that did breed the silk;
And it was dyed in mummy, which the skilful
Conserv'd of maidens' hearts.

A LOVER'S COMPUTATION OF TIME.

What! keep a week away? seven days and nights?
Eight score eight hours? and lovers' absent hours,
More tedious than the dial eight score times?
O weary reckoning!

ACT IV.

OTHELLO'S DISTRACTION.

Oth. What hath he said?

Iago. 'Faith, that he did,—I know not what he did.

Oth. What, what?

Iago. Lie——

Oth. With her?

Iago. With her, on her; what you will.

Oth. Lie with her! lie on her!—We say, lie on her, when they belie her: Lie with her! that's fulsome.—Handkerchief,—confessions,—handkerchief. To confess, and be hanged for his labour*.—First to be hanged, and then to confess:—I tremble at it. Nature would not invest herself in such shadowing passion, without some instruction. It is not words, that shake me thus:—Pish!—Noses, ears, and lips:—Is it possible?—Confess!—Handkerchief!—O devil!—

[*Falls in a Trance.*

HIS FONDNESS.

A fine woman! a fair woman! a sweet woman!

Iago. Nay, you must forget that.

Oth. Ay, let her rot, and perish, and be damned to-night; for she shall not live: No, my heart is turned to stone: I strike it, and it hurts my hand. O, the world hath not a sweeter creature: she might lie by an emperor's side, and command him tasks.

Iago. Nay, that's not your way.

Oth. Hang her; I do but say what she is: So delicate with her needle!—An admirable musician! O, she will sing the savageness out of a bear!—Of so high and plenteous wit and invention!—

Iago. She's the worse for all this.

Oth. O, a thousand, a thousand times:—And then, of so gentle a condition†!

Iago. Ay, too gentle.

Oth. Nay, that's certain: But yet the pity of it, Iago!—O, Iago, the pity of it, Iago.

HIS CONFIRMED JEALOUSY.

Oth. Mistress,——

Des. My lord?

Oth. What would you with her, sir?

Lod. Who, I, my lord?

Oth. Ay; you did wish, that I would make her turn:
Sir, she can turn, and turn, and yet go on,
And turn again; and she can weep, sir, weep;
And she's obedient, as you say,—obedient,—

* A proverbial saying. † Of so sweet a disposition.

Very obedient;—Proceed you in your tears.—
Concerning this, sir,—O well painted passion!
I am commanded home;—Get you away;
I'll send for you anon.—Sir, I obey the mandate,
And will return to Venice;—Hence, avaunt!
[*Exit* DESDEMONA.
Cassio shall have my place. And,—sir, to-night,
I do entreat that we may sup together,
You are welcome, sir, to Cyprus.—Goats, and monkeys!
[*Exit.*

HIS PATHETIC UPBRAIDING OF DESDEMONA.

Des. Upon my knees, what doth your speech import?
I understand a fury in your words,
But not the words.
Oth. Why, what art thou?
Des. Your wife, my lord; your true
And loyal wife.
Oth. Come, swear it, damn thyself;
Lest, being like one of heaven, the devils themselves
Should fear to seize thee: therefore be double damn'd,
Swear—thou art honest.
Des. Heaven doth truly know it.
Oth. Heaven truly knows, that thou art false as hell.
Des. To whom, my lord? with whom? How am I false?
Oth. O Desdemona! away! away! away!
Des. Alas, the heavy day!—Why do you weep?
Am I the occasion of these tears, my lord?
If, haply, you my father do suspect,
An instrument of this your calling back,
Lay not your blame on me; if you have lost him,
Why, I have lost him too.
Oth. Had it pleas'd heaven
To try me with affliction; had he rain'd
All kinds of sores, and shames, on my bare head;
Steep'd me in poverty to the very lips;
Given to captivity me and my utmost hopes;
I should have found in some part of my soul
A drop of patience: but (alas!) to make me

A fixed figure, for the time of scorn
To point his slow unmoving finger at,—
O! O!
Yet could I bear that too; well, very well:
But there, where I have garner'd* up my heart;
Where either I must live, or bear no life;
The fountain from the which my current runs,
Or else dries up; to be discarded thence!
Or keep it as a cistern, for foul toads
To knot and gender in!—turn thy complexion there!
Patience, thou young and rose-lipp'd cherubim;
Ay, there, look grim as hell!

Des. I hope, my noble lord esteems me honest.

Oth. O, ay; as summer flies are in the shambles,
That quicken even with blowing. O thou weed,
Who art so lovely fair, and smell'st so sweet,
That the sense aches at thee.—'Would, thou hadst ne'er been born!

Des. Alas, what ignorant sin have I committed?

Oth. Was this fair paper, this most goodly book,
Made to write whore upon? What committed!
Committed!—O thou public commoner!
I should make very forges of my cheeks,
That would to cinders burn up modesty,
Did I but speak thy deeds.—What committed!
Heaven stops the nose at it, and the moon winks;
The bawdy wind, that kisses all it meets,
Is hush'd within the hollow mind of earth,
And will not hear it: What committed!—
Impudent strumpet!

Des. By heaven, you do me wrong.

Oth. Are not you a strumpet?

Des. No, as I am a christian:
If to preserve this vessel for my lord,
From any other foul unlawful touch,
Be—not to be a strumpet, I am none.

Oth. What, not a whore?

Des. No, as I shall be saved.

* Treasured up.

Oth. Is it possible?
Des. O, heaven forgive us!
Oth. I cry you mercy, then;
I took you for that cunning whore of Venice,
That married with Othello.

DESDEMONA'S FIDELITY.

O good Iago,
What shall I do to win my lord again?
Good friend, go to him: for, by this light of heaven,
I know not how I lost him. Here I kneel:—
If e'er my will did trespass 'gainst his love,
Either in discourse of thought, or actual deed;
Or that mine eyes, mine ears, or any sense,
Delighted them in any other form;
Or that I do not yet, and ever did,
And ever will—though he do shake me off
To beggarly divorcement,—love him dearly,
Comfort forswear me! Unkindness may do much;
And his unkindness may defeat my life,
But never taint my love.

ACT V.

OTHELLO'S IRRESOLUTION TO MURDER DESDEMONA.

SCENE. *A Bedchamber:* DESDEMONA *in Bed asleep. A Light burning.*

It is the cause, it is the cause, my soul,—
Let me not name it to you, you chaste stars!
It is the cause.—Yet I'll not shed her blood;
Nor scar that whiter skin of hers than snow,
And smooth as monumental alabaster.
[*Takes off his Sword.*
Yet she must die, else she'll betray more men.
Put out the light, and then put out the light*:

* *i. e.* The light of life.

If I quench thee, thou flaming minister,
I can again thy former light restore,
Should I repent me:—but once put out thine,
Thou cunning'st pattern of excelling nature,
I know not where is that Promethean heat,
That can thy light relume. When I have pluck'd thy rose,
I cannot give it vital growth again,
It needs must wither:—I'll smell it on the tree.— [*Kissing her.*
O balmy breath, that dost almost persuade
Justice to break her sword!—One more, one more.—
Be thus when thou art dead, and I will kill thee,
And love thee after:—One more, and this the last:
So sweet was ne'er so fatal. I must weep,
But they are cruel tears: This sorrow's heavenly;
It strikes, where it doth love.

HIS CONFUSION AFTER THE MURDER.

Yes;—'tis Emelia:—by and by. She's dead.
'Tis like she comes to speak of Cassio's death:
The noise was high.—Ha! no more moving?
Still as the grave. Shall she come in! Were't good?
I think, she stirs again:—No.—What's the best?
If she come in, she'll sure speak to my wife:
My wife! my wife! what wife?—I have no wife:
O, insupportable! O heavy hour!
Methinks it should be now a huge eclipse
Of sun and moon; and that the affrighted globe
Should yawn at alteration.

HIS LOVE.

Had she been true,
If heaven would make me such another world
Of one entire and perfect chrysolite*,
I'd not have sold her for it.

HIS REMORSE.

Behold! I have a weapon;
A better never did itself sustain

* A precious stone.

Upon a soldier's thigh: I have seen the day,
That, with this little arm, and this good sword,
I have made my way through more impediments
Than twenty times your stop:—But, O vain boast!
Who can control his fate? 'tis not so now.—
Be not afraid, though you do see me weapon'd;
Here is my journey's end, here is my butt,
And very sea-mark of my utmost sail.
Do you go back dismay'd? 'tis a lost fear;
Man but a rush against Othello's breast,
And he retires;—Where should Othello go?—
Now, how dost thou look now? O ill starr'd wench!
Pale as thy smock! when we shall meet at compt*
This look of thine will hurl my soul from heaven,
And fiends will snatch at it. Cold, cold, my girl?
Even like thy chastity.—
O cursed, cursed slave!—Whip me, ye devils,
From the possession of this heavenly sight!
Blow me about in winds, roast me in sulphur!—
Wash me in steep-down gulfs of liquid fire!—
O Desdemona! Desdemona! dead?
Dead? O! O! O!

HIS SPEECH BEFORE HIS DEATH.

Soft you; a word or two, before you go.
I have done the state some service, and they know it;
No more of that:—I pray you, in your letters,
When you shall these unlucky deeds relate,
Speak of me as I am; nothing extenuate,
Nor set down aught in malice: then must you speak
Of one, that lov'd not wisely, but too well;
Of one, not easily jealous, but, being wrought,
Perplex'd in the extreme; of one, whose hand,
Like the base Judean, threw a pearl away,
Richer than all his tribe; of one, whose subdu'd eyes,
Albeit unused to the melting mood,
Drop tears as fast as the Arabian trees

* Account.

Their medicipal gum:—Set you down this:
And say, besides,—that in Aleppo once,
Where a malignant and a turban'd Turk
Beat a Venetian, and traduc'd the state,
I took by the throat the circumcised dog,
And smote him—thus. [*Stabs himself.*

ROMEO AND JULIET.

ACT I.

LOVE.

Love is a smoke rais'd with the fume of sighs;
Being purg'd, a fire sparkling in lovers' eyes;
Being vex'd, a sea nourish'd with lovers' tears:
What is it else? a madness most discreet,
A choking gall, and a preserving sweet.

ON DREAMS.

O, then, I see, queen Mab hath been with you.
She is the fairies' midwife; and she comes
In shape no bigger than an agate-stone
On the fore-finger of an alderman,
Drawn with a team of little atomies *
Athwart men's noses as they lie asleep:
Her waggon-spokes made of long spinners' legs;
The cover, of the wings of grasshoppers;
The traces, of the smallest spider's web;
The collars, of the moonshine's wat'ry beams:
Her whip, of cricket's bone; the lash, of film:
Her waggoner, a small gray-coated gnat,
Not half so big as a round little worm
Prick'd from the lazy finger of a maid:
Her chariot is an empty hazel-nut,

* Atoms.

Made by the joiner squirrel, or old grub,
Time out of mind the fairies coach-makers.
And in this state she gallops night by night
Through lovers' brains, and then they dream of love:
On courtiers' knees, that dream on court'sies straight:
O'er lawyers' fingers, who straight dream on fees:
O'er ladies' lips, who straight on kisses dream;
Which oft the angry Mab with blisters plagues,
Because their breaths with sweetmeats tainted are.
Sometime she gallops o'er a courtier's nose,
And then dreams he of smelling out a suit*:
And sometimes comes she with a tithe-pig's tail,
Tickling a parson's nose as 'a lies asleep,
Then dreams he of another benefice:
Sometime she driveth o'er a soldier's neck,
And then dreams he of cutting foreign throats,
Of breaches, ambuscadoes, Spanish blades,
Of healths five fathom deep; and then anon
Drums in his ear; at which he starts, and wakes;
And, being thus frighted, swears a prayer or two,
And sleeps again. This is that very Mab,
That plats the manes of horses in the night;
And bakes the elf-locks† in foul sluttish hairs,
Which, once untangled, much misfortune bodes.
This is the hag, when maids lie on their backs,
That presses them, and learns them first to bear,
Making them women of good carriage.
This, this is she——

Rom. Peace, peace, Mercutio, peace;
Thou talk'st of nothing.

Mer. True, I talk of dreams;
Which are the children of an idle brain,
Begot of nothing but vain fantasy;
Which is as thin of substance as the air;
And more inconstant than the wind, who woos
Even now the frozen bosom of the north,
And, being anger'd, puffs away from thence,
Turning his face to the dew-dropping south.

* A place in court.

† *i. e.* Fairy locks, locks of hair clotted and tangled in the night.

DESCRIPTION OF A BEAUTY.

O, she doth teach the torches to burn bright?
Her beauty hangs upon the cheek of night
Like a rich jewel in an Ethiop's * ear:
Beauty too rich for use, for earth too dear!
So shows a snowy dove trooping with crows,
As yonder lady o'er her fellows shows.

ACT II.

THE GARDEN SCENE.

Enter Romeo.

Rom. He jests at scars, that never felt a wound.—
[Juliet *appears above, at a Window.*
But, soft! what light through yonder window breaks!
It is the east, and Juliet is the sun!
Arise, fair sun, and kill the envious moon,
Who is already sick and pale with grief,
That thou her maid art far more fair than she:
Be not her maid †, since she is envious;
Her vestal livery is but sick and green,
And none but fools do wear it; cast it off.—
It is my lady; O, it is my love:
O, that she knew she were!—
She speaks, yet she says nothing; What of that;
Her eye discourses, I will answer it.—
I am too bold, 'tis not to me she speaks:
Two of the fairest stars in all the heaven,
Having some business, do entreat her eyes
To twinkle in their spheres till they return.
What if her eyes were there, they in her head;
The brightness of her cheek would shame those stars,
As daylight doth a lamp; her eye in heaven

* An Ethiopian, a black.
† A votary to the moon, to Diana.

Would through the airy region stream so bright,
That birds would sing, and think it were not night.
See, how she leans her cheek upon her hand!
O, that I were a glove upon that hand,
That I might touch that cheek!

Jul. Ah, me!

Rom. She speaks:—
O, speak again, bright angel! for thou art
As glorious to this night, being o'er my head,
As is a winged messenger of heaven
Unto the white-upturned wond'ring eyes
Of mortals, that fall back to gaze on him,
When he bestrides the lazy-pacing clouds,
And sails upon the bosom of the air.

Jul. O Romeo, Romeo! wherefore art thou Romeo?
Deny thy father, and refuse thy name:
Or, if thou wilt not, be but sworn my love,
And I'll no longer be a Capulet.

Rom. Shall I hear more, or shall I speak at this? [*Aside.*

Jul. 'Tis but thy name, that is my enemy.

* * * * *

What's in a name? that which we call a rose,
By any other name would smell as sweet;
So Romeo would, were he not Romeo call'd,
Retain that dear perfection which he owes *,
Without that title:—Romeo, doff † thy name;
And for that name, which is no part of thee,
Take all myself.

Rom. I take thee at thy word:
Call me but love, and I'll be new baptiz'd;
Henceforth I never will be Romeo.

Jul. What man art thou, that, thus bescreen'd in night,
So stumblest on my counsel?

Rom. By a name
I know not how to tell thee who I am:
My name, dear saint, is hateful to myself,

* Owns, possesses. † Do off.

Because it is an enemy to thee;
Had I it written, I would tear the word.
Jul. My ears have not yet drunk a hundred words
Of that tongue's utterance, yet I know the sound;
Art thou not Romeo, and a Montague?
Rom. Neither, fair saint, if either thee dislike.
Jul. How cam'st thou hither, tell me? and wherefore?
The orchard walls are high, and hard to climb;
And the place death, considering who thou art,
If any of my kinsmen find thee here.
Rom. With love's light wings did I o'erperch these walls;
For stony limits cannot hold love out;
And what love can do, that dares love attempt,
Therefore thy kinsmen are no let* to me.
Jul. If they do see thee, they will murder thee.
Rom. Alack! there lies more peril in thine eye,
Than twenty of their swords; look thou but sweet,
And I am proof against their enmity.
Jul. I would not for the world, they saw thee here.
Rom. I have night's cloak to hide me from their sight;
And, but thou love me†, let them find me here:
My life were better ended by their hate,
Than death prorogued, wanting of thy love.
Jul. By whose direction found'st thou out this place?
Rom. By love, who first did prompt me to inquire;
He lent me counsel, and I lent him eyes.
I am no pilot; yet, wert thou as far
As that vast shore wash'd with the furthest sea,
I would adventure for such merchandise.
Jul. Thou know'st, the mask of night is on my face;
Else would a maiden blush bepaint my cheek,
For that which thou hast heard me speak to-night.
Fain would I dwell on form, fain, fain deny

* Hinderance. † Unless thou love me.

What I have spoke; But farewell compliment!
Dost thou love me? I know thou wilt say—Ay;
And I will take thy word: yet, if thou swear'st,
Thou mayst prove false; at lovers' perjuries,
They say, Jove laughs. O, gentle Romeo,
If thou dost love, pronounce it faithfully:
Or if thou think'st I am too quickly won,
I'll frown, and be perverse, and say thee nay,
So thou wilt woo; but, else, not for the world.
In truth, fair Montague, I am too fond;
And therefore thou mayst think my 'haviour * light:
But, trust me, gentleman, I'll prove more true
Than those that have more cunning to be strange †.
I should have been more strange, I must confess,
But that thou overheard'st, ere I was ware,
My true love's passion: therefore pardon me;
And not impute this yielding to light love,
Which the dark night hath so discovered.

Rom. Lady, by yonder blessed moon I swear,
That tips with silver all these fruit-tree tops—

Jul. O, swear not by the moon, the inconstant moon,
That monthly changes in her circled orb,
Lest that thy love prove likewise variable.

Rom. What shall I swear by?

Jul. Do not swear at all;
Or, if thou wilt, swear by thy gracious self,
Which is the god of my idolatry,
And I'll believe thee.

Rom. If my heart's dear love—

Jul. Well, do not swear: although I joy in thee,
I have no joy of this contract to-night:
It is too rash, too unadvis'd, too sudden:
Too like the lightning, which doth cease to be,
Ere one can say—It lightens. Sweet, good-night!
This bud of love, by summer's ripening breath,
May prove a beauteous flower when next we meet,
Good night, good night; as sweet repose and rest
Come to thy heart, as that within my breast!

* Behaviour. † Shy.

Rom. O, wilt thou leave me so unsatisfied?
Jul. What satisfaction canst thou have to-night?
Rom. The exchange of thy love's faithful vow for mine.
Jul. I gave thee mine before thou didst request it:
And yet I would it were to give again.
Rom. Wouldst thou withdraw it? for what purpose, love?
Jul. But to be frank*, and give it thee again.
And yet I wish but for the thing I have:
My bounty is as boundless as the sea,
My love as deep; the more I give to thee,
The more I have, for both are infinite.
[Nurse *calls within.*
I hear some noise within; Dear love, adieu!
Anon, good nurse!—Sweet Montague, be true.
Stay but a little, I will come again. [*Exit.*
Rom. O blessed, blessed night! I am afeard,
Being in night, all this is but a dream.
Too flattering-sweet to be substantial.

Re-enter JULIET, *above.*

Jul. Three words, dear Romeo, and good night, indeed.
If that thy bent† of love be honourable,
Thy purpose marriage, send me word to-morrow,
By one that I'll procure to come to thee,
Where, and what time, thou wilt perform the rite;
And all my fortunes at thy foot I'll lay,
And follow thee my lord throughout the world.
Nurse [*Within.*] Madam.
Jul. I come, anon:—But if thou mean'st not well,
I do beseech thee,—
Nurse. [*Within.*] Madam.
Jul. By and by, I come:—
To cease thy suit, and leave me to my grief:
To-morrow will I send.
Rom. So thrive my soul—
Jul. A thousand times good night! [*Exit.*

* Free. † Inclination.

Rom. A thousand times the worse, to want thy light.—
Love goes toward love, as schoolboys from their books;
But love from love, toward school with heavy looks.
[*Retiring slowly.*

Re-enter JULIET, *above.*

Jul. Hist! Romeo, hist!—O, for a falconer's voice,
To lure this tassel-gentle* back again!
Bondage is hoarse, and may not speak aloud;
Else would I tear the cave where echo lies,
And make her airy tongue more hoarse than mine
With repetition of my Romeo's name.
Rom. It is my soul, that calls upon my name:
How silver-sweet sound lovers' tongues by night,
Like softest music to attending ears!
Jul. Romeo!
Rom. My sweet!
Jul. At what o'clock to-morrow
Shall I send to thee?
Rom. At the hour of nine.
Jul. I will not fail; 'tis twenty years till then,
I have forgot why I did call thee back.
Rom. Let me stand here till thou remember it.
Jul. I shall forget, to have thee still stand there.
Rememb'ring how I love thy company.
Rom. And I'll still stay; to have thee still forget,
Forgetting any other home but this.
Jul. 'Tis almost morning, I would have thee gone:
And yet no further than a wanton's bird;
Who lets it hop a little from her hand,
Like a poor prisoner in his twisted gyves †,
And with a silk thread plucks it back again,
So loving-jealous of his liberty.
Rom. I would, I were thy bird.
Jul. Sweet, so would I:
Yet I should kill thee with much cherishing.

* The male of the goshawk. † Fetters.

Good night, good night! parting is such sweet sorrow,
That I shall say—good night, till it be morrow.

LOVE'S HERALDS.

Love's heralds should be thoughts,
Which ten times faster glide than the sun's beams,
Driving back shadows over low'ring hills:
Therefore do nimble-pinion'd doves draw love,
And therefore hath the wind-swift Cupid wings.

VIOLENT DELIGHTS NOT LASTING.

These violent delights have violent ends,
And in their triumph die; like fire and powder,
Which, as they kiss, consume.

LOVERS LIGHT OF FOOT.

O, so light a foot
Will ne'er wear out the everlasting flint:
A lover may bestride the gossomers*
That idle in the wanton summer air,
And yet not fall; so light is vanity.

ACT III.

A LOVER'S IMPATIENCE.

Gallop apace, you fiery-footed steeds,
Towards Phœbus' mansion; such a waggoner
As Phæton would whip you to the west,
And bring in cloudy night immediately.—
Spread thy close curtain, love performing night?
That run-away's eyes may wink; and Romeo
Leap to these arms, untalk'd of, and unseen!—
Lovers can see to do their amorous rites
By their own beauties: or, if love be blind,
It best agrees with night.

* The long white filament which flies in the air.

ROMEO ON HIS BANISHMENT.

SCENE. *Friar* Laurence's *Cell.*

Enter Friar LAURENCE *and* ROMEO.

Fri. A gentler judgment vanish'd from his lips,
Not body's death, but body's banishment.
Rom. Ha! banishment? be merciful, say—death:
For exile hath more terror in his look,
Much more than death: do not say—banishment.
Fri. Hence from Verona art thou banished:
Be patient: for the world is broad and wide.
Rom. There is no world without Verona walls,
But purgatory, torture, hell itself.
Hence banished, is banished from the world,
And world's exile is death:—then banishment
Is death misterm'd: calling death—banishment,
Thou cut'st my head off with a golden axe,
And smil'st upon the stroke that murders me.
Fri. O deadly sin! O rude unthankfulness!
Thy fault our law calls death; but the kind prince,
Taking thy part, hath rush'd aside the law,
And turn'd that black word death to banishment:
This is dear mercy, and thou seest is not.
Rom. 'Tis torture, and not mercy: heaven is here,
Where Juliet lives; and every cat, and dog,
And little mouse, every unworthy thing,
Live here in heaven, and may look on her,
But Romeo may not.—More validity *,
More honourable state, more courtship lives
In carrion flies, than Romeo: they may seize
On the white wonder of dear Juliet's hand,
And steal immortal blessing from her lips;
Who, even in pure and vestal modesty,
Still blush, as thinking their own kisses sin;
But Romeo may not; he is banished:
Flies may do this, when I from this must fly;
They are free men, but I am banished.

* Worth, value.

And say'st thou yet that exile is not death?
Hadst thou no poison mix'd, no sharp-ground knife,
No sudden mean of death, though ne'er so mean,
But—banished—to kill me; banished?
O friar, the damned use that word in hell;
Howlings attend it: how hast thou the heart,
Being a divine, a ghostly confessor,
A sin-absolver, and my friend profess'd,
To mangle me with that word—banishment?

Fri. Thou fond madman, hear me but speak a word.

Rom. O, thou wilt speak again of banishment.

Fri. I'll give thee armour to keep off that word;
Adversity's sweet milk, philosophy,
To comfort thee, though thou art banished.

Rom. Yet banished?—Hang up philosophy!
Unless philosophy can make a Juliet,
Displant a town, reverse a prince's doom;
It helps not, it prevails not, talk no more.

Fri. O, then I see that madmen have no ears.

Rom. How should they, when that wise men have no eyes?

Fri. Let me dispute with thee of thy estate.

Rom. Thou canst not speak of what thou dost not feel:
Wert thou as young as I, Juliet thy love,
An hour but married, Tybalt murdered,
Doting like me, and like me banished,
Then mightst thou speak, then mightst thou tear thy hair,
And fall upon the ground, as I do now,
Taking the measure of an unmade grave.

RELUCTANCE OF LOVERS TO PART.

SCENE. JULIET'S *Chamber.*

Jul. Wilt thou be gone? it is not yet near day:
It was the nightingle, and not the lark,
That pierc'd the fearful hollow of thine ear;
Nightly she sings on yon pomegranate tree:
Believe me, love, it was the nightingale.

Rom. It was the lark, the hérald of the morn,
No nightingale: look, love, what envious streaks
Do lace the severing clouds in yonder east:
Night's candles are burnt out, and jocund day
Stands tiptoe on the misty mountain tops;
I must be gone and live, or stay and die.
Jul. Yon light is not daylight, I know it, I:
It is some meteor that the sun exhales,
To be to thee this night a torch-bearer,
And light thee on thy way to Mantua:
Therefore stay yet, thou need'st not to be gone.
Rom. Let me be ta'en, let me be put to death;
I am content, so thou wilt have it so.
I'll say, yon gray is not the morning's eye,
'Tis but the pale reflex of Cynthia's brow *;
Nor that is not the lark, whose notes do beat
The vaulty heaven so high above our heads:
I have more care † to stay, than will to go;—
Come, death, and welcome! Juliet wills it so.—
How is't, my soul? let's talk, it is not day.

ACT IV.

JULIET'S RESOLUTION.

O, bid me leap, rather than marry Paris,
From off the battlements of yonder tower;
Or walk in thievish ways; or bid me lurk
Where serpents are; chain me with roaring bears;
Or shut me nightly in a charnel-house,
O'er cover'd quite with dead men's rattling bones,
With reeky shanks, and yellow chapless sculls;
Or bid me go into a new-made grave,
And hide me with a dead man in his shroud;
Things that, to hear them told, have made me tremble;

* Reflection of the moon. † Inclination.

And I will do it without fear or doubt,
To live an unstain'd wife to my sweet love.

JULIET'S SOLILOQUY ON DRINKING THE OPIATE.

Farewell!—God knows, when we shall meet again.
I have a faint cold fear thrills through my veins,
That almost freezes up the heat of life:
I'll call them back again to comfort me;—
Nurse!—What should she do here?
My dismal scene I needs must act alone.—
Come, phial.—
What if this mixture do not work at all?
Must I of force be married to the county?—
No, no;—this shall forbid it:—lie thou there.—
[*Laying down a Dagger.*
What if it be a poison, which the friar
Subtly hath minister'd to have me dead;
Lest in this marriage he should be dishonour'd,
Because he married me before to Romeo?
I fear, it is: and yet, methinks, it should not,
For he hath still been tried a holy man:
I will not entertain so bad a thought.—
How if, when I am laid into the tomb,
I wake before the time that Romeo
Come to redeem me? there's a fearful point!
Shall I not then be stifled in the vault,
To whose foul mouth no healthsome air breathes in,
And there die strangled ere my Romeo comes?
Or, if I live, is it not very like,
The horrible conceit of death and night,
Together with the terror of the place,—
As in a vault, an ancient receptacle,
Where, for these many hundred years, the bones
Of all my buried ancestors are pack'd;
Where bloody Tybalt, yet but green in earth,
Lies fest'ring in his shroud; where, as they say,
At some hours in the night spirits resort;
Alack, alack! is it not like, that I,
So early waking,—what with loathsome smells;
And shrieks like mandrakes torn out of the earth

That living mortals, hearing them, run mad * ;—
O! if I wake, shall I not be distraught †,
Environed with all these hideous fears?
And madly play with my forefathers' joints?
And pluck the mangled Tybalt from his shroud?
And, in this rage, with some great kinsman's bone,
As with a club, dash out my desperate brains?
O, look! methinks, I see my cousin's ghost
Seeking out Romeo, that did spit his body
Upon a rapier's point:—Stay, Tybalt, stay!
Romeo, I come! this do I drink to thee.
[*She throws herself on the Bed.*

JOY CHANGED TO SORROW.

All things, that we ordained festival,
Turn from their office to black funeral:
Our instruments to melancholy bells;
Our wedding cheer to a sad burial feast;
Our solemn hymns to sullen dirges change;
Our bridal flowers serve for a buried corse,
And all things change them to the contrary.

ACT V.

ROMEO'S DESCRIPTION OF AND DISCOURSE WITH THE APOTHECARY.

Well, Juliet, I will lie with thee to-night.
Let's see for means:—O, mischief, thou art swift
To enter in the thoughts of desperate men!
I do remember an apothecary,—
And hereabouts he dwells,—whom late I noted
In tatter'd weeds, with overwhelming brows,
Culling of simples ‡; meagre were his looks,
And in his needy shop a tortoise hung,

* The fabulous accounts of the plant called a *mandrake*, give it a degree of animal life, and when it is torn from the ground it groans, which is fatal to him that pulls it up.

† Distracted. ‡ Herbs.

Sharp misery had worn him to the bones:
An alligator stuff'd, and other skins
Of ill shap'd fishes; and about his shelves
A beggarly account of empty boxes,
Green earthen pots, bladders, and musty seeds,
Remnants of packthread, and old cakes of roses,
Were thinly scatter'd, to make up a show.
Noting this penury, to myself I said—
And if a man did need a poison now,
Whose sale is present death in Mantua,
Here lives a caitiff wretch would sell it him.
O, this same thought did but fore-run my need;
And this same needy man must sell it me.
As I remember, this should be the house:
Being holiday, the beggar's shop is shut.—
What, ho! apothecary!

Enter Apothecary.

Ap. Who calls so loud?
Rom. Come hither, man.—I see that thou art poor;
Hold, there is forty ducats: let me have
A dram of poison; such soon-speeding geer *
As will disperse itself through all the veins,
That the life-weary taker may fall dead;
And that the trunk may be discharg'd of breath
As violently, as hasty powder fir'd
Doth hurry from the fatal cannon's womb.
Ap. Such mortal drugs I have; but Mantua's law
Is death to any he that utters them.
Rom. Art thou so bare, and full of wretchedness,
And fear'st to die? famine is in thy cheeks,
Need and oppression starveth in thy eyes,
Upon thy back hangs ragged misery,
The world is not thy friend, nor the world's law:
The world affords no law to make thee rich;
Then be not poor, but break it, and take this.
Ap. My poverty, but not my will, consents.
Rom. I pay thy poverty, and not thy will.

* Stuff.

Ap. Put this in any liquid thing you will,
And drink it off; and if you had the strength
Of twenty men, it would despatch you straight.
Rom. There is thy gold, worse poison to men's souls,
Doing more murders in this loathsome world,
Than these poor compounds that thou mayst not sell:
I sell thee poison, thou hast sold me none.
Farewell; buy food, and get thyself in flesh.

THE CONTEST OF ROMEO AND PARIS.

Par. Stop thy unhallow'd toil, vile Montague;
Can vengeance be pursu'd further than death?
Condemned villain, I do apprehend thee:
Obey, and go with me; for thou must die.
Rom. I must, indeed, and therefore came I hither.—
Good gentle youth, tempt not a desperate man,
Fly hence and leave me;—think upon these gone;
Let them affright thee.—I beseech thee, youth,
Heap not another sin upon my head,
By urging me to fury—O, be gone!
By heaven, I love thee better than myself:
For I come hither arm'd against myself:
Stay not, begone;—live, and hereafter say—
A madman's mercy bade thee run away.
Par. I do defy thy conjurations*,
And do attach thee as a felon here.
Rom. Wilt thou provoke me? then have at thee, boy. [*They fight.*

* * * * *

Par. O, I am slain! [*Falls.*]—If thou be merciful,
Open the tomb, lay me with Juliet. [*Dies.*
Rom. In faith, I will:—Let me peruse this face;—
Mercutio's kinsman, noble county Paris:
What said my man, when my betossed soul
Did not attend him as we rode? I think,
He told me, Paris should have married Juliet:
Said he not so? or did I dream it so?
Or am I mad, hearing him talk of Juliet,

* I refuse to do as thou *conjurest* me to do; *i. e.* depart.

To think it was so?—O, give me thy hand,
One writ with me in sour misfortune's book!

ROMEO'S LAST SPEECH OVER JULIET IN THE TOMB.

O, my love! my wife!
Death that hath suck'd the honey of thy breath,
Hath had no power yet upon thy beauty:
Thou art not conquer'd; beauty's ensign yet
Is crimson in thy lips, and in thy cheeks,
And death's pale flag is not advanced there.—
Tybalt, liest thou there in thy bloody sheet?
O, what more favour can I do to thee,
Than with that hand that cut thy youth in twain,
To sunder his that was thine enemy?
Forgive me, cousin!—Ah, dear Juliet,
Why art thou yet so fair? Shall I believe
That unsubstantial death is amorous;
And that the lean abhorred monster keeps
Thee here in dark to be his paramour?
For fear of that, I will still stay with thee;
And never from this palace of dim night
Depart again; here, here, will I remain
With worms that are thy chambermaids; O, here
Will I set up my everlasting rest;
And shake the yoke of inauspicious stars
From this world-wearied flesh.—Eyes, look your last,
Arms, take your last embrace! and lips, O you
The doors of breath, seal with a righteous kiss
A dateless bargain to engrossing death!—
Come, bitter conduct*, come, unsavoury guide!
Thou desperate pilot, now at once run on
The dashing rocks thy seasick weary bark!
Here's to my love!—[*Drinks.*] O, true apothecary!
Thy drugs are quick.—Thus with a kiss I die. [*Dies.*

* Conductor.

TIMON OF ATHENS.

ACT I.

PAINTING.

The painting is almost the natural man;
For since dishonour traffics with man's nature,
He is but outside: These pencil'd figures are
Even such as they give out *.

THE PLEASURE OF DOING GOOD.

O, you gods, think I, what need we have any friends, if we should never have need of them? they were the most needless creatures living, should we ne'er have use for them: and would most resemble sweet instruments hung up in cases, that keep their sounds to themselves. Why, I have often wished myself poorer, that I might come nearer to you. We are born to do benefits: and what better or properer can we call our own, than the riches of our friends? O, what a precious comfort 'tis, to have so many, like brothers, commanding one another's fortunes!

ACT II.

A FAITHFUL STEWARD.

So the gods bless me,
When all our offices † have been oppress'd
With riotous feeders; when our vaults have wept

* Pictures have no hypocrisy; they are what they profess to be.

† The apartments allotted to culinary offices, &c.

With drunken spilth of wine; when every room
Hath blaz'd with lights, and bray'd with minstrelsy;
I have retir'd me to a wasteful cock *,
And set mine eyes at flow.

INGRATITUDE.

They answer, in a joint and corporate voice,
That now they are at fall †, want treasure, cannot
Do what they would; are sorry—you are honourable,—
But yet they could have wish'd—they know not—but
Something has been amiss—a noble nature
May catch a wrench—would all were well—'tis pity—
And so, intending ‡ other serious matters,
After distasteful looks, and these hard fractions §,
With certain half-caps ‖, and cold-moving nods,
They froze me into silence.

ACT III.

THE MISERABLE SHIFTS OF INGRATITUDE.

Ser. My honoured lord,— [*To* Lucius.

Luc. Servilius! you are kindly met, sir. Fare thee well:—Commend me to thy honourable virtuous lord, my very exquisite friend.

Ser. May it please your honour, my lord hath sent——

Luc. Ha! what has he sent? I am so much endeared to that lord; he's ever sending: How shall I thank him, thinkest thou? And what has he sent now?

Ser. He has only sent his present occasion now,

* A pipe with a turning stopple running to waste.
† i. e. At an ebb.
‡ Intending, had anciently the same meaning as attending.
§ Broken hints, abrupt remarks.
‖ A half cap is a cap slightly moved, not put off.

my lord; requesting your lordship to supply his instant use with so many talents.

Luc. I know, his lordship is but merry with me;
He cannot want fifty-five hundred talents.

Ser. But in the mean time he wants less, my lord.
If his occasion were not virtuous *,
I should not urge it half so faithfully.

Luc. Dost thou speak seriously, Servilius?

Ser. Upon my soul, 'tis true, sir.

Luc. What a wicked beast was I, to disfurnish myself against such a good time, when I might have shown myself honourable? how unluckily it happened, that I should purchase the day before for a little part, and undo a great deal of honour;—Servilius, now before the gods, I am not able to do't; the more beast, I say:—I was sending to use lord Timon myself, these gentleman can witness; but I would not, for the wealth of Athens, I had done it now. Commend me bountifully to his good lordship; and I hope, his honour will conceive the fairest of me, because I have no power to be kind: And tell him this from me, I count it one of my greatest afflictions, say, that I cannot pleasure such an honourable gentleman. Good Servilius, will you befriend me so far, as to use mine own words to him?

Ser. Yes, sir, I shall.

Luc. I will look you out a good turn, Servilius.—
[*Exit* SERVILIUS.
True, as you said, Timon is shrunk, indeed;
And he, that's once denied, will hardly speed. [*Exit.*

AGAINST DUELLING.

Your words have took such pains, as if they labour'd
To bring manslaughter into form, set quarrelling
Upon the head of valour; which, indeed,
Is valour misbegot, and came into the world
When sects and factions were but newly born:
He's truly valiant, that can wisely suffer

* "If he did not want it for a good use."

The worst that man can breathe; and make his wrongs
His outsides; wear them like his raiment, carelessly;
And ne'er prefer his injuries to his heart,
To bring it into danger.

ACT IV.

TIMON'S EXECRATION OF THE ATHENIANS.

SCENE. *Without the Walls of* Athens.

Let me look back upon thee, O thou wall,
That girdlest in those wolves! Dive in the earth,
And fence not Athens! Matrons, turn incontinent!
Obedience fail in children! slaves, and fools,
Pluck the grave wrinkled senate from the bench,
And minister in their steads! to general filths *
Convert o' the instant, green virginity!
Do't in your parent's eyes! bankrupts, hold fast;
Rather than render back, out with your knives,
And cut your trusters' throats! bound servants, steal!
Large handed robbers your grave masters are,
And pill by law! maid, to thy master's bed;
Thy mistress is o' the brothel! son of sixteen,
Pluck the lin'd crutch from the old limping sire,
With it beat out his brains! piety, and fear,
Religion to the gods, peace, justice, truth,
Domestic awe, night-rest, and neighbourhood,
Instruction, manners, mysteries, and trades,
Degrees, observances, customs, and laws,
Decline to your confounding contraries †,
And yet confusion live!—Plagues incident to men,
Your potent and infectious fevers heap
On Athens, ripe for stroke! thou cold sciatica,
Cripple our senators, that their limbs may halt
As lamely as their manners! lust and liberty ‡

* Common sewers.

† *i. e.* Contrarieties, whose nature it is to waste or destroy each other.

‡ For libertinism.

Creep in the minds and marrows of our youth;
That 'gainst the stream of virtue they may strive,
And drown themselves in riot? itches, blains,
Sow all the Athenian bosoms; and their crop
Be general leprosy! breath infect breath;
That their society, as their friendship, may
Be merely poison! Nothing I'll bear from thee,
But nakedness, thou detestable town!

A FRIEND FORSAKEN.

As we do turn our backs
From our companion, thrown into his grave:
So his familiars to his buried fortunes
Slink all away; leave their false vows with him,
Like empty purses pick'd: and his poor self,
A dedicated beggar to the air,
With his disease of all-shunn'd poverty,
Walks, like contempt, alone.

ON GOLD.

Earth, yield me roots! [*Digging.*
Who seeks for better of thee, sauce his palate
With thy most operant poison! What is here?
Gold? yellow, glittering, precious gold? No, gods,
I am no idle votarist *. Roots, you clear heavens!
Thus much of this, will make black, white; foul, fair;
Wrong, right; base, noble; old, young; coward, valiant.
Ha, you gods! why this? What this, you gods? Why this
Will lug your priests and servants from your sides;
Pluck stout men's pillows from below their heads:
This yellow slave
Will knit and break religions; bless the accurs'd;
Make the hoar leprosy ador'd; place thieves,
And give them title knee, and approbation,
With senators on the bench: this is it,
That makes the wappen'd † widow wed again;

* No insincere or inconstant supplicant. Gold will not serve me instead of roots.

† Sorrowful.

She, whom the spital-house, and ulcerous sores
Would cast the gorge at, this embalms and spices
To the April day again*. Come, damned earth,
Thou common whore of mankind, that put'st odds
Among the rout of nations, I will make thee
Do thy right nature.

TIMON TO ALCIBIADES.

Go on,—here's gold,—go on;
Be as a planetary plague, when Jove
Will o'er some high-vic'd city hang his poison
In the sick air: Let not thy sword skip one:
Pity not honour'd age for his white beard,
He's an usurer: Strike me the counterfeit matron;
It is her habit only that is honest,
Herself's a bawd: Let not the virgin's cheek
Make soft thy trenchant† sword; for those milk-paps,
That through the window-bars bore at men's eyes,
Are not within the leaf of pity writ,
Set them down horrible traitors: Spare not the babe,
Whose dimpled smiles from fools exhaust their mercy;
Think it a bastard‡, whom the oracle
Hath doubtfully pronounc'd thy throat shall cut,
And mince it sans remorse§: Swear against objects‖;
Put armour on thine ears, and on their eyes;
Whose proof nor yells of mothers, maids, nor babes,
Nor sight of priests in holy vestments bleeding,
Shall pierce a jot. There's gold to pay thy soldiers:
Make large confusion; and, thy fury spent,
Confounded be thyself! Speak not, begone.

TO THE COURTESANS.

Consumptions sow
In hollow bones of man; strike their sharp shins,
And mar men's spurring. Crack the lawyer's voice,
That he may never more false title plead,

* *i. e.* Gold restores her to all the sweetness and freshness of youth.

† Cutting.

‡ An allusion to the tale of Oedipus.

§ Without pity.

‖ *i. e.* Against objects of charity and compassion.

Nor sound his quillets* shrilly: hoar the flamen,
That scolds against the quality of flesh,
And not believes himself: down with the nose,
Down with it flat; take the bridge quite away
Of him, that his particular to foresee,
Smells from the general weal: make curl'd-pate ruffians bald;
And let the unscarr'd braggarts of the war
Derive some pain from you.

HIS REFLECTIONS ON THE EARTH.

That nature, being sick of man's unkindness,
Should yet be hungry!—Common mother, thou, [*Digging*.
Whose womb unmeasurable, and infinite breast†,
Teems, and feeds all; whose selfsame mettle,
Whereof thy proud child, arrogant man, is puff'd,
Engenders the black toad, and adder blue,
The gilded newt, and eyeless venom'd worm‡,
With all the abhorred births below crisp§ heaven
Whereon Hyperion's quickening fire doth shine;
Yield him, who all thy human sons doth hate,
From forth thy plenteous bosom one poor root!
Ensear thy fertile and conceptious womb,
Let it no more bring out ingrateful man!
Go great with tigers, dragons, wolves, and bears:
Teem with new monsters, whom thy upward face
Hath to the marbled mansion all above
Never presented!—O, a root,—Dear thanks!
Dry up thy marrows, vines, and plough-torn leas;
Whereof ingrateful man, with liquorish draughts,
And morsels unctuous, greases his pure mind,
That from it all consideration slips!

HIS DISCOURSE WITH APEMANTUS.

Apem. This is in thee a nature but affected;
A poor unmanly melancholy, sprung

* Subtilties. † Boundless surface.
‡ The serpent called the blind worm. § Bent.

From change of fortune. Why this spade? this place?
This slavelike habit? and these looks of care?
Thy flatterers yet wear silk, drink wine, lie soft;
Hug their diseas'd perfumes *, and have forgot
That ever Timon was. Shame not these woods,
By putting on the cunning of a carper †,
Be thou a flatterer now, and seek to thrive
By that which has undone thee: hinge thy knee,
And let his very breath, whom thou'lt observe,
Blow off thy cap; praise his most vicious strain,
And call it excellent: Thou wast told thus;
Thou gav'st thine ears, like tapsters, that bid welcome,
To knaves, and all approachers: 'Tis most just,
That thou turn rascal; hadst thou wealth again,
Rascals should hav't. Do not assume my likeness.

Tim. Were I like thee, I'd throw away myself.

Apem. Thou hast cast away thyself, being like thyself;
A madman so long, now a fool: What, think'st
That the bleak air, thy boisterous chamberlain,
Will put thy shirt on warm! Will these moss'd trees,
That have outliv'd the eagle, page thy heels,
And skip when thou point'st out. Will the cold brook,
Candied with ice, caudle thy morning taste,
To cure thy o'ernight's surfeit? call the creatures,—
Whose naked natures live in all the spite
Of wreakful heaven; whose bare unhoused trunks,
To the conflicting elements expos'd,
Answer mere nature,—bid them flatter thee;
O! thou shalt find——

* * * * *

Tim. Thou art a slave, whom Fortune's tender arm
With favour never clasp'd; but bred a dog.
Hadst thou, like us, from our first swath ‡, proceeded

* *i. e.* Their diseased perfumed mistresses.
† *i. e.* Shame not these woods by finding fault.
‡ From infancy.

The sweet degrees that this brief world affords
To such as may the passive drugs of it
Freely command, thou wouldst have plung'd thyself
In general riot; melted down thy youth
In different beds of lust; and never learn'd
The icy precepts of respect *, but follow'd
The sugar'd game before thee. But myself,
Who had the world as my confectionary;
The mouths, the tongues, the eyes, and hearts of men
At duty, more than I could frame employment;
That numberless upon me stuck, as leaves
Do on the oak, have with one winter's brush
Fell from their boughs, and left me open, bare
For every storm that blows;—I, to bear this,
That never knew but better, is some burden:
Thy nature did commence in sufferance, time
Hath made thee hard in't. Why shouldst thou hate
men?
They never flatter'd thee: What hast thou given?
If thou wilt curse,—thy father, that poor rag,
Must be thy subject; who, in spite, put stuff
To some she beggar, and compounded thee
Poor rogue hereditary. Hence! be gone!—
If thou hadst not been born the worst of men,
Thou hadst been a knave, and flatterer.

ON GOLD.

O, thou sweet king-killer, and dear divorce
[*Looking on the Gold.*
'Twixt natural son and sire; Thou bright defiler
Of Hymen's purest bed! thou valiant Mars!
Thou ever young, fresh, lov'd, and delicate wooer,
Whose blush doth thaw the consecrated snow
That lies on Dian's lap! thou visible god,
That solder'st close impossibilities,
And mak'st them kiss! that speak'st with every
tongue,
To every purpose; O, thou touch † of hearts!

* The cold admonitions of cautious prudence.
† For touchstone.

Think, thy slave man rebels; and by thy virtue
Set them into confounding odds, that beasts
May have the world in empire!

TIMON TO THE THIEVES.

Why should you want? Behold, the earth hath roots;
Within this mile break forth a hundred springs:
The oaks bear mast, the briars scarlet hips;
The bounteous housewife, nature, on each bush
Lays her full mess before you. Want? why want?
1 *Thief.* We cannot live on grass, on berries, water,
As beasts, and birds, and fishes.
Tim. Nor on the beasts themselves, the birds, and fishes;
You must eat men. Yet thanks I must you con,
That you are thieves profess'd; that you work not
In holier shapes: for there is boundless theft
In limited* professions. Rascal thieves,
Here's gold: Go, suck the subtle blood of the grape,
Till the high fever seeth your blood to froth,
And so 'scape hanging: trust not the physician;
His antidotes are poison, and he slays
More than you rob: take wealth and lives together;
Do, villany, do, since you profess to do't,
Like workmen. I'll example you with thievery:
The sun's a thief, and with his great attraction
Robs the vast sea: the moon's an arrant thief,
And her pale fire she snatches from the sun:
The sea's a thief, whose liquid surge resolves
The moon into soft tears: the earth's a thief,
That feeds and breeds by a composture† stolen
From general excrement: each thing's a thief;
The laws, your curb and whip, in their rough power
Have uncheck'd theft. Love not yourselves: away;
Rob one another. There's more gold: Cut throats;
All that you meet are thieves: To Athens, go,
Break open shops; nothing can you steal,
But thieves do lose it.

* For legal. † Compost, manure.

ON HIS HONEST STEWARD.

Forgive my general and exceptless rashness,
Perpetual sober gods! I do proclaim
One honest man,—mistake me not,—but one:
No more, I pray,—and he is a steward.—
How fain would I have hated all mankind,
And thou redeem'st thyself: But all, save thee,
I fell with curses.
Methinks thou art more honest now, than wise;
For, by oppressing and betraying me,
Thou mightst have sooner got another service:
For many so arrive at second masters,
Upon their first lord's neck.

ACT V.

PROMISING AND PERFORMANCE.

Promising is the very air o' the time: it opens the eyes of expectation: performance is ever the duller for his act; and, but in the plainer and simpler kind of people, the deed of saying* is quite out of use. To promise is most courtly and fashionable: performance is a kind of will or testament, which argues a great sickness in his judgment that makes it.

WRONG AND INSOLENCE.

Now breathless wrong
Shall sit and pant in your great chairs of ease;
And pursy insolence shall break his wind,
With fear and horrid flight.

* The doing of that we said we would do.

TITUS ANDRONICUS.

ACT I.

MERCY.

Wilt thou draw near the nature of the gods?
Draw near them then in being merciful:
Sweet mercy is nobility's true badge.

THANKS.

Thanks, to men
Of noble minds, is honourable meed.

ACT II.

INVITATION TO LOVE.

The birds chant melody on every bush;
The snake lies rolled in the cheerful sun;
The green leaves quiver with the cooling wind,
And make a chequer'd shadow on the ground:
Under their sweet shade, Aaron, let us sit,
And—whilst the babbling echo mocks the hounds,
Replying shrilly to the well tun'd horns,
As if a double hunt were heard at once,—
Let us sit down, and mark their yelling noise:
And, after conflict, such as was suppos'd
The wandering prince of Dido once enjoy'd,
When with a happy storm they were surpris'd,
And curtain'd with a counsel-keeping cave,—
We may, each wreathed in the other's arms,
Our pastimes done, possess a golden slumber;
Whiles hounds, and horns, and sweet melodious birds,
Be unto us, as is a nurse's song
Of lullaby, to bring her babe asleep.

DESCRIPTION OF A MELANCHOLY VALLEY.

A barren detested vale, you see, it is:
The trees, though summer, yet forlorn and lean,
O'ercome with moss, and baleful mistletoe.
Here never shines the sun; here nothing breeds,
Unless the nightly owl, or fatal raven.
And, when they show'd me this abhorred pit,
They told me, here, at dead time of the night,
A thousand fiends, a thousand hissing snakes,
Ten thousand swelling toads, as many urchins *,
Would make such fearful and confused cries,
As any mortal body, hearing it,
Should straight fall mad, or else die suddenly.

DESCRIPTION OF A RING.

Upon his bloody finger he doth wear
A precious ring, that lightens all the hole,
Which, like a taper in some monument,
Doth shine upon the dead man's earthy cheeks
And shows the ragged entrails of this pit.

LAVINIA AT HER LUTE.

Fair Philomela, she but lost her tongue,
And in a tedious sampler sew'd her mind:
But, lovely niece, that méan is cut from thee;
A craftier Tereus hast thou met withal,
And he hath cut those pretty fingers off,
That could have better sew'd than Philomel.
O, had the monster seen those lily hands
Tremble, like aspen leaves, upon a lute,
And make the silken strings delight to kiss them;
He would not then have touch'd them for his life:
Or, had he heard the heavenly harmony,
Which that sweet tongue hath made,
He would have dropp'd his knife, and fell asleep,
As Cerberus at the Thracian poet's † feet.

* Hedge-hogs. † Orpheus.

ACT III.

LAVINIA'S LOSS OF HER TONGUE DESCRIBED.

O, that delightful engine of her thoughts,
That blabb'd them with such pleasing eloquence,
Is torn from forth that pretty hollow cage:
Where, like a sweet melodious bird, it sung
Sweet varied notes, enchanting every ear!

DESPAIR.

For now I stand as one upon a rock,
Environ'd with a wilderness of sea;
Who marks the waxing tide grow wave by wave,
Expecting ever when some envious surge
Will, in his brinish bowels, swallow him.

TEARS.

When I did name her brothers, then fresh tears
Stood on her cheeks; as doth the honey dew
Upon a gather'd lily almost wither'd.

CRUELTY TO INSECTS.

Mar. Alas, my lord, I have but kill'd a fly.
Tit. But how, if that fly had a father and mother?
How would he hang his slender gilded wings,
And buz lamenting doings in the air?
Poor harmless fly!
That with his pretty buzzing melody,
Came here to make us merry; and thou hast kill'd him.

ACT V.

REVENGE.

Lo, by thy side where Rape and Murder stands;
Now give some 'surance that thou art Revenge,
Stab them, or tear them on thy chariot wheels;
And then I'll come, and be thy waggoner,

And whirl along with thee about the globes.
Provide thee proper palfries, black as jet,
To hale thy vengeful waggon swift away,
And find out murderers in their guilty caves:
And, when thy car is loaden with their heads,
I will dismount, and by the waggon wheel
Trot, like a servile footman, all day long;
Even from Hyperion's rising in the east,
Until his very downfal in the sea.

TROILUS AND CRESSIDA.

ACT I.

LOVE IN A BRAVE YOUNG SOLDIER.

CALL here my varlet *, I'll unarm again:
Why should I war without the walls of Troy,
That find such cruel battle here within?
Each Trojan, that is master of his heart,
Let him to field; Troilus, alas! hath none.

* * * * *

The Greeks are strong, and skilful to their strength,
Fierce to their skill, and to their fierceness valiant;
But I am weaker than a woman's tear,
Tamer than sleep, fonder † than ignorance;
Less valiant than the virgin in the night,
And skill-less as unpractis'd infancy.

* * * * *

O Pandarus! I tell thee, Pandarus,—
When I do tell thee, There my hopes lie drown'd,
Reply not in how many fathoms deep
They lie indrench'd. I tell thee, I am mad
In Cressid's love: Thou answer'st, She is fair;

* A servant to a knight. † Weaker.

Pour'st in the open ulcer of my heart
Her eyes, her hair, her cheek, her gait, her voice;
Handlest in thy discourse, O, that her hand,
In whose comparison all whites are ink,
Writing their own reproach; to whose soft seisure
The cygnet's down is harsh, and spirit of sense
Hard as the palm of ploughmen! This thou tell'st me,
As true thou tell'st me, when I say—I love her;
But, saying thus, instead of oil and balm,
Thou lay'st in every gash that love hath given me
The knife that made it.

SUCCESS NOT EQUAL TO OUR HOPES.

The ample proposition, that hope makes
In all designs begun on earth below,
Fails in the promis'd largeness: checks and disasters
Grow in the veins of actions highest rear'd:
As knots, by the conflux of meeting sap,
Infect the sound pine, and divert his grain
Tortive and errant* from his course of growth.

ADVERSITY THE TRIAL OF MAN.

Why then, you princes,
Do you with cheeks abash'd behold our works;
And think them shames, which are, indeed, nought else,
But the protractive trials of great Jove,
To find persistive constancy in men?
The fineness of which metal is not found
In fortune's love: for, the bold and coward,
The wise and fool, the artist and unread,
The hard and soft, seem all affin'd† and kin:
But, in the wind and tempest of her frown,
Distinction, with a broad and powerful fan,
Puffing at all, winnows the light away;
And what hath mass, or matter, by itself
Lies, rich in virtue, and unmingled.

* Twisted and rambling. † Joined by affinity.

ON DEGREE.

Take but degree away, untune that string,
And, hark, what discord follows! each thing meets
In mere* oppugnancy: The bounded waters
Should lift their bosoms higher than the shores,
And make a sop of all this solid globe:
Strength should be lord of imbecility,
And the rude son should strike his father dead:
Force should be right; or, rather, right and wrong,
(Between whose endless jar justice resides)
Should lose their names, and so should justice too
Then every thing includes itself in power,
Power into will, will into appetite;
And appetite, an universal wolf,
So doubly seconded with will and power,
Must make perforce an universal prey,
And, last, eat up himself.

ACHILLES DESCRIBED BY ULYSSES.

The great Achilles,—whom opinion crowns
The sinew and the forehand of our host,—
Having his ear full of his airy fame,
Grows dainty of his worth, and in his tent
Lies mocking our designs: With him, Patroclus,
Upon a lazy bed the livelong day
Breaks scurril jests;
And with ridiculous and awkward action
(Which, slanderer, he imitation calls,)
He pageants† us. Sometime, great Agamemnon,
Thy topless‡ deputation he puts on;
And, like a strutting player,—whose conceit
Lies in his hamstring, and doth think it rich
To hear the wooden dialogue and sound
'Twixt his stretch'd footing and the scaffoldage§,—
Such to-be-pitied and o'er-wrested|| seeming
He acts thy greatness in: and when he speaks,

* Absolute. † In modern language, *takes us off*.
‡ Supreme. § The galleries of the theatre.
|| Beyond the truth.

'Tis like a chime a mending; with terms unsquar'd *,
Which, from the tongue of roaring Typhon dropp'd,
Would seem Hyperboles. At this fusty stuff,
The large Achilles, on his press'd bed lolling,
From his deep chest laughs out a loud applause;
Cries—*Excellent!—'tis* Agamemnon *just.—*
Now play me Nestor;—*hem, and stroke thy beard,*
As he, being drest to some oration.
That's done;—as near as the extremest ends
Of parallels; as like as Vulcan and his wife:
Yet good Achilles still cries, *Excellent!*
'Tis Nestor *right! Now play him me,* Patroclus,
Arming to answer in a night alarm.
And then, forsooth, the faint defects of age
Must be the scene of mirth; to cough, and spit,
And with a palsy-fumbling on his gorget,
Shake in and out the rivet:—and at this sport,
Sir Valour dies; cries, *O!—enough*, Patroclus,
Or give me ribs of steel! I shall split all
In pleasure of my spleen. And in this fashion,
All our abilities, gifts, natures, shapes,
Severals and generals of grace exact,
Achievements, plots, orders, preventions,
Excitements to the field, or speech for truce,
Success, or loss, what is, or is not, serves
As stuff for these two to make paradoxes.

CONDUCT IN WAR SUPERIOR TO ACTION.

The still and mental parts,—
That do contrive how many hands shall strike,
When fitness calls them on; and know, by measure,
Of their observant toil, the enemies' weight,—
Why, this hath not a finger's dignity:
They call this—bed-work, mappery, closet-war:
So that the ram, that batters down the wall,
For the great swing and rudeness of his poise,
They place before his hand that made the engine;
Or those, that with the fineness of their souls
By reason guide his execution.

* Unadapted.

RESPECT.

I ask, that I might waken reverence,
And bid the cheek be ready with a blush
Modest as morning when she coldly eyes
The youthful Phœbus.

ACT II.

DOUBT.

The wound of peace is surety,
Surety secure; but modest doubt is call'd
The beacon of the wise, the tent that searches
To the bottom of the worst.

PLEASURE AND REVENGE.

For pleasure, and revenge,
Have ears more deaf than adders to the voice
Of any true decision.

THE SUBTILTY OF ULYSSES, AND STUPIDITY OF AJAX.

Ajax. I do hate a proud man, as I hate the engendering of toads.

Nest. And yet he loves himself: Is it not strange? [*Aside.*

Ulyss. Achilles will not to the field to-morrow.
Agam. What's his excuse?
Ulyss. He doth rely on none;
But carries on the stream of his dispose,
Without observance or respect of any,
In will peculiar and in self-admission.
Agam. Why will he not, upon our fair request,
Untent his person, and share the air with us?
Ulyss. Things small as nothing, for request's sake only,
He makes important: Possess'd he is with greatness;
And speaks not to himself, but with a pride
That quarrels at self-breath: imagin'd worth

Holds in his blood such swoln and hot discourse,
That, 'twixt his mental and his active parts,
Kingdom'd Achilles in commotion rages,
And batters down himself: What should I say?
He is so plaguy proud, that the death tokens of it
Cry—*No recovery.*

Agam. Let Ajax go to him.—
Dear lord, go you and greet him in his tent:
'Tis said, he holds you well; and will be led,
At your request, a little from himself.

Ulyss. O Agamemnon, let it not be so!
We'll consecrate the steps that Ajax makes
When they go from Achilles: Shall the proud lord,
That bastes his arrogance with his own seam *,
And never suffers matter of the world
Enter his thoughts,—save such as do revolve
And ruminate himself,—shall he be worship'd
Of that we hold an idol more than he?
No, this thrice worthy and right valiant lord
Must not so stale his palm, nobly acquir'd;
Nor, by my will, assubjugate his merit,
As amply titled as Achilles is,
By going to Achilles:
That were to enlard his fat-already pride;
And add more coals to Cancer † when it burns
With entertaining great Hyperion †.
This lord go to him! Jupiter forbid;
And say in thunder—*Achilles, go to him.*

Nest. O, this is well; he rubs the vein of him. [*Aside.*

Dio. And how his silence drinks up this applause! [*Aside.*

Ajax. If I go to him, with my arm'd fist I'll pash ‡ him
Over the face.

Agam. O, no, you shall not go.

* Fat.

† The sign in the zodiac into which the sun enters June 21
"And Cancer reddens with the solar blaze."
Thomson.

‡ Strike.

Ajax. An he be proud with me, I'll pheeze * his pride:
Let me go to him.

Ulyss. Not for the worth that hangs upon our quarrel.

Ajax. A paltry insolent fellow,——

Nest. How he describes
Himself! [*Aside.*

Ajax. Can he not be sociable?

Ulyss. The raven
Chides blackness. [*Aside.*

Ajax. I will let his humours blood.

Agam. He'll be physician, that should be the patient. [*Aside.*

Ajax. An all men
Were o' my mind,——

Ulyss. Wit would be out of fashion. [*Aside.*

Ajax. He should not bear it so,
He should eat swords first: Shall pride carry it?

Nest. An 'twould, you'd carry half. [*Aside.*

Ulyss. He'd have ten shares. [*Aside.*

Ajax. I'll knead him, I will make him supple:——

Nest. He's not yet thorough warm: force † him with praises:
Pour in, pour in; his ambition is dry. [*Aside.*

Ulyss. My lord, you feed too much on this dislike. [*To* AGAMEMNON.

Nest. O noble general, do not do so.

Dio. You must prepare to fight without Achilles.

Ulyss. Why, 'tis this naming of him does him harm.
Here is a man—But 'tis before his face;
I will be silent.

Nest. Wherefore should you so?
He is not emulous ‡, as Achilles is.

Ulyss. Know the whole world, he is as valiant.

* Comb, or currey. † Stuff. ‡ Envious.

Ajax. A whoreson dog, that shall palter* thus with us!
I would, he were a Trojan.
Nest. What a vice
Were it in Ajax now——
Ulyss. If he were proud?
Dio. Or covetous of praise?
Ulyss. Ay, or surly borne?
Dio. Or strange, or self-affected?
Ulyss. Thank the heavens, lord, thou art of sweet composure;
Praise him that got thee, she that gave thee suck:
Fam'd be thy tutor, and thy parts of nature
Thrice fam'd, beyond all erudition:
But he that disciplin'd thy arms to fight,
Let Mars divide eternity in twain,
And give him half; and, for thy vigour,
Bull-bearing Milo his addition † yield
To sinewy Ajax. I will not praise thy wisdom
Which, like a bourn ‡, a pale, a shore, confines
Thy spacious and dilated parts: Here's Nestor,—
Instructed by the antiquary times.
He must, he is, he cannot but be wise;—
But pardon, father Nestor, were your days
As green as Ajax', and your brain so temper'd,
You should not have the eminence of him,
But be as Ajax.
Ajax. Shall I call you father?
Nest. Ay, my good son.
Dio. Be rul'd by him, lord Ajax.
Ulyss. There is no tarrying here; the hart Achilles
Keeps thicket. Please it our great general
To call together all his state of war;
Fresh kings are come to Troy; To-morrow,
We must with all our main of power stand fast:
And here's a lord—come knights from east to west,
And cull their flower, Ajax shall cope the best.
Agam. Go we to council. Let Achilles sleep:
Light boats sail swift, though greater hulks draw deep.

* Trifle. † Titles. ‡ Stream, rivulet.

ACT III.

AN EXPECTING LOVER.

No, Pandarus: I stalk about her door,
Like a strange soul upon the Stygian banks,
Staying for waftage. O, be thou my Charon,
And give me swift transportance to those fields,
Where I may wallow in the lily beds
Propos'd for the deserver! O gentle Pandarus,
From Cupid's shoulder pluck his painted wings,
And fly with me to Cressid!

* * * * *

I am giddy; expectation whirls me round.
The imaginary relish is so sweet
That it enchants my sense: What will it be,
When that the wat'ry palate tastes indeed
Love's thrice-reputed nectar? death, I fear me;
Swooning destruction; or some joy too fine,
Too subtle-potent, tun'd too sharp in sweetness,
For the capacity of my ruder powers:
I fear it much; and I do fear besides,
That I shall lose distinction in my joys;
As doth a battle, when they charge on heaps
The enemy flying.

* * * * *

Even such a passion doth embrace my bosom:
My heart beats thicker than a feverous pulse;
And all my powers do their bestowing lose,
Like vassalage at unawares encount'ring
The eye of majesty.

CONSTANCY IN LOVE PROTESTED.

Tro. True swains in love shall, in the world to come,
Approve their truths by Troilus: when their rhymes,
Full of protest, of oath, and big compare *,

* Comparison.

Want similes, truth tir'd with iteration,—
As true as steel, as plantage to the moon,
As sun to day, as turtle to her mate,
As iron to adamant, as earth to the centre,—
Yet, after all comparisons of truth,
As truth's authentic author to be cited,
As true as Troilus shall crown up * the verse,
And sanctify the numbers.

Cres. Prophet may you be!
If I be false, or swerve a hair from truth,
When time is old and hath forgot itself,
When waterdrops have worn the stones of Troy,
And blind oblivion swallow'd cities up,
And mighty states characterless are grated
To dusty nothing; yet let memory,
From false to false, among false maids in love,
Upbraid my falsehood! when they have said—as false
As air, as water, wind, or sandy earth,
As fox to lamb, as wolf to heifer's calf,
Pard to the hind, or stepdame to her son;
Yea, let them say, to stick the heart of falsehood,
As false as Cressid.

PRIDE CURES PRIDE.

Pride hath no other glass
To show itself, but pride; for supple knees
Feed arrogance, and are the proud man's fees.

GREATNESS CONTEMPTIBLE WHEN ON THE DECLINE.

'Tis certain, greatness, once fallen out with fortune,
Must fall out with men too: What the declin'd is,
He shall as soon read in the eyes of others,
As feel in his own fall: for men, like butterflies,
Show not their mealy wings, but to the summer;
And not a man, for being simply man,
Hath any honour; but honour for those honours
That are without him, as place, riches, favour,
Prizes of accident as oft as merit:

* Conclude it.

Which when they fall, as being slippery standers,
The love that lean'd on them as slippery too,
Do one pluck down another, and together
Die in the fall.

HONOUR MUST BE ACTIVE TO PRESERVE ITS LUSTRE.

Time hath, my lord, a wallet at his back,
Wherein he puts alms for oblivion,
A great-sized monster of ingratitudes:
Those scraps are good deeds past: which are devoured
As fast as they are made, forgot as soon
As done: Perseverance, dear my lord,
Keeps honour bright: To have done, is to hang
Quite out of fashion, like a rusty mail
In monumental mockery. Take the instant way,
For honour travels in a strait so narrow,
Where one but goes abreast: keep then the path;
For emulation hath a thousand sons,
That one by one pursue: If you give way,
Or hedge aside from the direct forthright,
Like to an enter'd tide, they all rush by,
And leave you hindmost:—
Or, like a gallant horse fallen in first rank,
Lie there for pavement to the abject rear,
O'errun and trampled on: Then what they do in present,
Though less than yours in past, must o'ertop yours:
For time is like a fashionable host,
That slightly shakes his parting guest by the hand;
And with his arms out-stretch'd, as he would fly,
Grasps-in the comer: Welcome ever smiles,
And farewell goes out sighing. O, let not virtue seek
Remuneration for the thing it was;
For beauty, wit,
High birth, vigour of bone, desert in service,
Love, friendship, charity, are subjects all
To envious and calumniating time.
One touch of nature makes the whole world kin,—

That all, with one consent, praise new-born gawds *,
Though they are made and moulded of things past;
And give to dust, that is a little gilt,
More laud than gilt o'er-dusted.
The present eye praises the present object.

LOVE SHOOK OFF BY A SOLDIER.

Sweet, rouse yourself; and the weak wanton Cupid
Shall from your neck unloose his amorous fold,
And, like a dew-drop from the lion's mane,
Be shook to air.

THERSITES MIMICKING AJAX.

Ther. A wonder!

Achil. What?

Ther. Ajax goes up and down the field, asking for himself.

Achil. How so?

Ther. He must fight singly to-morrow with Hector: and is so prophetically proud of an heroical cudgelling, that he raves in saying nothing.

Achil. How can that be?

Ther. Why, he stalks up and down like a peacock, a stride, and a stand: ruminates, like an hostess, that hath no arithmetic but her brain to set down her reckoning: bites his lip with a politic regard, as who should say—there were wit in this head, an 'twould out; and so there is; but it lies as coldly in him as fire in a flint, which will not show without knocking. The man's undone for ever; for if Hector break not his neck i' the combat he'll break it himself in vain-glory. He knows not me; I said, *Good morrow*, Ajax; and he replies, *Thanks*, Agamemnon. What think you of this man, that takes me for the general? He is grown a very land-fish, languageless, a monster. A plague of opinion! a man may wear it on both sides, like a leather jerkin.

Achil. Thou must be my ambassador to him, Thersites.

* New-fashioned toys.

Ther. Who, I? why, he'll answer nobody; he professes not answering; speaking is for beggars; he wears his tongue in his arms. I will put on his presence; let Patroclus make demands to me, you shall see the pageant of Ajax.

Achil. To him, Patroclus: Tell him,—I humbly desire the valiant Ajax, to invite the most valorous Hector to come unarmed to my tent; and to procure safe conduct for his person, of the magnanimous, and most illustrious, six-or-seven-times-honoured captain general of the Grecian army, Agamemnon. Do this.

Patr. Jove bless great Ajax.

Ther. Humph!

Patr. I come from the worthy Achilles,——

Ther. Ha!

Patr. Who most humbly desires you to invite Hector to his tent!——

Ther. Humph!

Patr. And to procure safe conduct from Agamemnon.

Ther. Agamemnon?

Patr. Ay, my lord.

Ther. Ha!

Patr. What say you to't?

Ther. God be wi' you, with all my heart.

Patr. Your answer, sir.

Ther. If to-morrow be a fair day, by eleven o'clock it will go one way or other; howsoever, he shall pay for me ere he has me.

Patr. Your answer, sir.

Ther. Fare you well, with all my heart.

Achil. Why, but he is not in this tune, is he?

Ther. No, but he's out o' tune thus. What music will be in him when Hector has knocked out his brains, I know not: But I am sure, none; unless the fiddler Apollo get his sinews to make catlings* on.

Achil. Come, thou shalt bear a letter to him straight.

* Lute-strings made of catgut.

Ther. Let me bear another to his horse; for that's the more capable * creature.

Achil. My mind is troubled, like a fountain stirr'd;
And I myself see not the bottom of it.
[*Exeunt* ACHILLES *and* PATROCLUS.

Ther. Would the fountain of your mind were clear again, that I might water an ass at it! I had rather be a tick in a sheep, than such a valiant ignorance.

ACT IV.

LOVERS' PARTING IN THE MORNING.

Tro. O Cressida! but that the busy day,
Wak'd by the lark, hath rous'd the ribald † crows,
And dreaming night will hide our joys no longer,
I would not from thee.
Cres. Night hath been too brief.
Tro. Beshrew the witch! with venomous wights she stays,
As tediously as hell; but flies the grasps of love,
With wings more momentary swift than thought.

A LOVER'S FAREWELL.

Injurious time now, with a robber's haste,
Crams his rich thievery up, he knows not how:
As many farewells as be stars in heaven,
With distinct breath, and consign'd ‡ kisses to them,
He fumbles up into a loose adieu;
And scants us with a single famish'd kiss,
Distasted with the salt of broken § tears.

* Intelligent. † Lewd, noisy.
‡ Sealed. § Interrupted.

TROILUS'S CHARACTER OF THE GRECIAN YOUTHS.

The Grecian youths are full of quality *;
They're loving, well compos'd, with gifts of nature flowing,
And swelling o'er with arts and exercise;
How novelty may move, and parts with person,
Alas, a kind of godly jealousy
(Which I beseech you, call a virtuous sin),
Makes me afeard.

A TRUMPETER.

Now crack thy lungs, and split thy brazen pipe:
Blow, villain, till thy sphered bias cheek
Out-swell the colic of puff'd Aquilon:
Come, stretch thy chest, and let thy eyes spout blood;
Thou blow'st for Hector.

DIOMEDES' MANNER OF WALKING.

'Tis he, I ken the manner of his gait;
He rises on the toe: that spirit of his
In aspiration lifts him from the earth.

DESCRIPTION OF CRESSIDA.

There's language in her eye, her cheek, her lip,
Nay, her foot speaks; her wanton spirits look out
At every joint and motive † of her body.
O, these encounterers, so glib of tongue,
That give a coasting welcome ere it comes,
And wide unclasp the tables of their thoughts
To every ticklish reader! set them down
For sluttish spoils of opportunity,
And daughters of the game.

CHARACTER OF TROILUS.

The youngest son of Priam, a true knight;
Not yet mature, yet matchless; firm of word;
Speaking in deeds, and deedless ‡ in his tongue;
Not soon provok'd, nor, being provok'd, soon calm'd:

* Highly accomplished. † Motion. ‡ No boaster.

His heart and hand both open, and both free;
For what he has, he gives, what thinks, he shows;
Yet gives he not till judgment guide his bounty,
Nor dignifies an impair * thought with breath:
Manly as Hector, but more dangerous;
For Hector, in his blaze of wrath, subscribes †
To tender objects; but he, in heat of action,
Is more vindicative than jealous love.

HECTOR IN BATTLE.

I have, thou gallant Trojan, seen thee oft,
Labouring for destiny, make cruel way,
Through ranks of Greekish youth: and I have seen thee,
As hot as Perseus, spur thy Phrygian steed,
Despising many forfeits and subduements,
When thou hast hung thy advanced sword i' the air,
Not letting it decline on the declin'd ‡;
That I have said to some my standers-by,
Lo, Jupiter is yonder, dealing life!
And I have seen thee pause, and take thy breath,
When that a ring of Greeks have hemm'd thee in,
Like an Olympian wrestling.

ACHILLES SURVEYING HECTOR.

Tell me, you heavens, in which part of his body
Shall I destroy him? whether there, there, or there?
That I may give the local wound a name;
And make distinct the very breach whereout
Hector's great spirit flew: Answer me, heavens!

ACT V.

RASH VOWS.

The gods are deaf to hot and peevish § vows,
They are polluted offerings, more abhorr'd
Than spotted livers in the sacrifice.

* Unsuitable to his character.
† Yields, gives way.
‡ Fallen.
§ Foolish.

HONOUR MORE DEAR THAN LIFE.

Mine honour keeps the weather of my fate:
Life every man holds dear; but the dear man
Holds honour far more precious-dear * than life.

PITY TO BE DISCARDED IN WAR.

For the love of all the gods,
Let's leave the hermit pity with our mother;
And when we have our armours buckled on,
The venom'd vengeance ride upon our swords.

* Valuable.

THE END.

INDEX

TO THE

BEAUTIES OF SHAKSPEARE.

INDEX.

INDEX.

INDEX.

INDEX.

C. Whittingham, College House, Chiswick.

POPULAR WORKS.

ENFIELD'S NATURAL THEOLOGY;

OR, A

Demonstration of the Being and Attributes of God,

FROM HIS WORKS OF CREATION.

18mo. Price 2*s.* 6*d.* in extra boards.

"The object of this work is to impress the youthful mind with a deep and abiding sense of the existence and attributes of God, and awaken them to a veneration of that Being who hath called them into existence."—*Gentlemen's Magazine.*

THE BOOK OF NATURE LAID OPEN,

In a Popular Survey of the Phenomena and Constitution of the Universe, and the Appearances of Nature during each month of the year.

BY THE REV. W. HUTTON, M.A.

Price 3*s.* 6*d.* in extra boards.

A GUIDE TO ETERNAL HAPPINESS,

Being a Treasure of Religious Wisdom, adapted to the practical use of Christians; designed, with the blessing of God, to make him who peruses it, and follows its precepts, wise unto salvation.

BY JER. TAYLOR, D.D.

CHAPLAIN IN ORDINARY TO KING CHARLES I.

Price, in boards, 3*s.* 6*d.*

THE SPIRIT OF ENGLISH WIT;

OR,

Post Chaise Companion.

Price 6*s.* boards.

THE SPIRIT OF IRISH WIT.

Price 6*s.* boards.

www.ingramcontent.com/pod-product-compliance
Lightning Source LLC
Chambersburg PA
CBHW030418310726
48979CB00007B/1097

* 9 7 8 1 6 0 8 8 8 1 2 2 2 *